Caribbean Certificate History

Emancipation to Emigration

Book 2

R. Greenwood
S. Hamber

 MACMILLAN
CARIBBEAN

First published 1980
Reprinted 1982

Published by
Macmillan Education Limited
London and Basingstoke
Companies and representatives throughout the world

ISBN 0 333 28148 9

Printed in Hong Kong

Contents

Acknowledgements

The authors and publishers wish to acknowlege the following photographic sources:

Anne Bolt   pp 103,113,116,118,122,124,136
The Fotomas Index   p 9
Mary Evans Picture Library   pp 12,14,26 bottom, 33,34,54,89,92,98,99,102,107,108,109,119 right, 127,128 top
Institute of Jamaica   pp 16,42
The Mansell Collection   pp 5,17,20,26 top,29,31, 37,40,43,49,62,71,75,78,80,86,87,96,104,115,128, bottom, 131
National Maritime Museum   p 1
Peter Newark's Western Americana   pp 30,74,82,
Popperfoto   pp 101,130
Radio Times Hulton Picture Library   pp 3,10,13, 23,25,57,58,63,64,65,68,69,93,97,119 left
Royal Commonwealth Society   pp 35,67,133
Royal Geographical Society   pp 135,137
West India Committee   p 61 and cover
The Trustees of the Wedgwood Museum   p 55
William Wilberforce Museum   p 38

The publishers have made every effort to trace the copyright holders but if they have inadvertently overlooked any, they will be pleased to make the necessary arrangements at the first opportunity.

Introduction

This book is the second of three aimed at covering the Caribbean Examination Council's new syllabus in Caribbean History and it, therefore, follows their thematic approach fairly closely. It deals with seven themes in the syllabus, namely: European Rivalry; the Haitian Revolution and its Effects; Resistance and Revolt; Movement towards Emancipation; Adjustments to the Labour Problems of Emancipation; Alternatives to Sugar; Social Welfare, 1838-1914. It also covers these topics in the Cambridge and London 'O' level syllabi.

In attempting to meet the needs of both the old and new syllabi, we have given fuller treatment here to such topics as: the origins of the buccaneers; English and French buccaneers in the seventeenth century; why the West Indies became the 'cockpit of Europe' in the eighteenth century; the effects of the eighteenth century wars on the West Indies; the Haitian Revolution in all its aspects; attitudes to slavery inside and outside the West Indies; the law and the slave in the English, French and Spanish islands; the treatment of slaves in the different islands; the slaves' response to slavery; Maroons and Bush Negroes; slave revolts; the stirring of European consciences against slavery; the abolition movement in Britain; Nonconformist missionary activity before emancipation; amelioration and its failure; the difficulties caused by emancipation; the apprenticeship system and dissatisfaction with it; the free village movement; freed slaves and estate labour; immigrant labour, especially East Indian; the effects of immigrant labour; the difficulties of the sugar industry in the British islands; competition from Cuba, Brazil, Louisiana and European beet sugar; the relative backwardness of British sugar production; alternative crops to sugar; development of mineral resources; attempts to put new life into the sugar industry; emigration from the British islands, especially to Panama; education in the British islands; public health and public works under Crown Colony Government. Most of the book concentrates on taking a close look at the nineteenth century as a transitional period in West Indian History, thus preparing the ground for Book III which deals with twentieth century developments, especially the constitutional ones.

Remembering the Cambridge History Syllabus's advice that 'factual answers are required', and the need for 'in depth' study required by the new CXC syllabus, we have concentrated on a factual approach whenever possible. We have tried to treat all topics at the level required by the examining boards both in factual content and comprehension. Special attention has been given to the reading level of 'O' level age students.

The revision questions at the end of each book concentrate on essay questions and questions based on some of the many illustrations in the book. The essay questions tend to focus on the new areas of the syllabus with which both students and teachers will be less familiar. We realise that the new syllabus will use objective questioning techniques. These have not been included here, but we would refer teachers and students to Robert Greenwood's *Multiple Choice and Objective Questions* (Macmillan).

In the further reading list, we have suggested the standard general texts for Caribbean history. In addition, we have also listed a few more specialised texts which could reasonably be expected to be available in school libraries in the West Indies.

The new syllabus is due to be launched in June 1979. The minds of the examiners will be then more clearly revealed and we hope that this book anticipates their expectations.

Acknowledgements
I wish to thank my wife, Margaret, for her encouragement and understanding during the writing of this book.

Robert Greenwood.

1

European Rivalry in the Caribbean

Sir Henry Morgan

Spain's claim to control the Caribbean

After the Treaty of Tordesillas in 1494, Spain adopted a policy of *Mare Clausum* (sea closed to others). All foreign ships were excluded from the Caribbean and from trade with Spanish colonies. After the Reformation, European countries might have accepted Spain's claim to lands she already occupied, but not to lands which were unoccupied or inhabited by pagan natives, such as the Lesser Antilles, the Wild Coast and Florida. Their view was that there was plenty of land for all in the Americas and Spain's claim was unreasonable.

Spain's monopoly was challenged by various European powers. France, the traditional enemy of Spain, was at war with her from 1515 to 1559, with minor interruptions like the Peace of Cambrai in 1529 and the Treaty of Créspy in 1544. Spain insisted on her monopoly of the Caribbean, and France on her right to send ships there. Spain could not keep foreign ships out of the Caribbean especially after Piet Heyn's success in 1628, but she tried to stop other European countries establishing colonies there. This was not possible, because of Dutch domination of the sea and because, strategically, Spain's colonies were badly sited to stop the settlement of the islands to the windward.

'No peace beyond the line'

At the Treaty of Câteau-Cambrésis in 1559, France and Spain made peace in Europe and

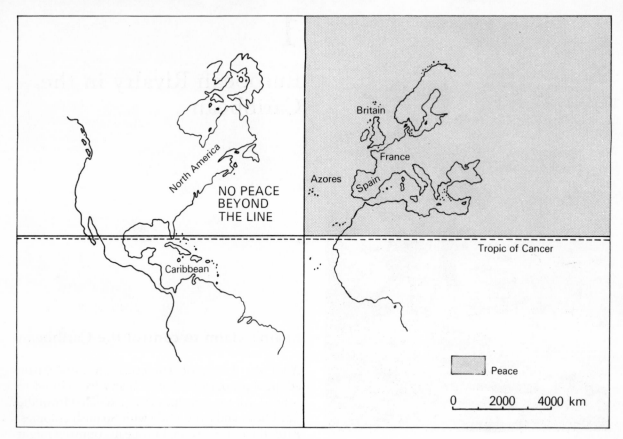

Map 1   Lines of Amity

excluded the Caribbean by establishing a formula of 'No peace beyond the line'. A new line was drawn across the Atlantic, and only north-east of this line would peace apply. Spain did not want this but France, England and the Netherlands insisted on it. Acts of violence and aggression beyond the line were not acts of war, or causes of war, whereas if they had happened in Europe they would have been.

This formula was recognised in the Treaty of Vervins between France and Spain in 1598, and in the Treaty of London between England and Spain in 1604. It was maintained for the first half of the seventeenth century until it was brought to an end in separate treaties with Spain. In the Treaty of Munster, 1648, Spain recognised the right of the Dutch to navigate and hold colonies in the Caribbean. In the Treaty of Madrid, 1670, Spain recognised England's claim to colonies in the Caribbean, in return for the promise to stop buccaneering.

Peace between France and Spain was harder to achieve as they were such implacable enemies, and the French claim to the western end of Hispaniola was a particularly strong obstacle. However, in return for Spain's recognition of St Domingue, Louis XIV promised to end buccaneering at the Truce of Ratisbon, 1685. Thereafter, if two countries were at war in Europe, they were also at war in the West Indies, and vice-versa.

The buccaneers

The word 'buccaneer' comes from the French word, *boucanier*. The British turned *boucanier* into 'buccaneer'. However, the French preferred to use *filibustiers* for these sea raiders, and the Dutch used *vrij-bueters* or 'freebooter' in English.

Who were the buccaneers?

Hispaniola was the original home of the buccaneers. There were large tracts of uninhabited land in the north-west and neither the Spanish nor the mulatto hunters from around Santo Domingo had penetrated the area. There were many wild pigs and cattle and the original buccaneers hunted them and supplied the passing ships with barbecued meat.

The buccaneers were essentially West Indian. Their homes and attachments were in the West Indies, even if they had been born in a European country. Others were already second generation West Indian and knew no other home. They bore European names, like 'Morgan', 'L'Ollonais' and 'van Horn', but to say that they were British, French and Dutch would be misleading. Nationality meant little to them except that they were anti-Spanish. Religion was more important than nationality in that they were generally Protestant which contributed to their anti-Spanish feeling. Their loyalty was to their own special way of life and their band of brothers.

Anyone could become a buccaneer by joining one of the colonies at Providence Island, Tortuga or Port Royal. In the early seventeenth century, buccaneers tended to come from certain groups of West Indian settlers. Firstly, there were those who had been driven out of St Kitts and Nevis in the Spanish attack of 1629. They wanted revenge on the Spaniards and, by their eviction, had been given a taste of 'the sweet trade' - the life of freedom and profit from raiding the Spaniards.

Secondly, there were indentured servants running away to break their contracts. They had to keep away from the masters to whom they were bound and so took refuge in the buccaneer bases out of the reach of the law. Frequently such men came from Barbados where conditions for indentured servants were particularly harsh.

Thirdly, there were the indentured servants who were the losers when the sugar revolution came. These were the small landowners, the holders of two to twelve hectares, who were dispossessed of their land in the sugar revolution. Again many came from Barbados, which moved from having 12,000 landowners to under 800 in twenty years.

Fourthly, some of the soldiers from Cromwell's army of 1655 became buccaneers at Port Royal. Cromwell wanted them to settle Jamaica and become farmers, but they wanted adventure and plunder instead of working hard on the land.

Finally, there were those who were pure adventurers, attracted by freedom from the law and the expectation of profit. In other times they would have been known as pirates but, in this period, they were buccaneers.

François L'Ollonais

Their new way of life soon made them tough. They dressed in shirt and baggy trousers with shoes made of hide, and no socks. Their clothes were frequently red with the blood of the cattle they killed. Armed with knives and long muskets, they hunted in pairs in Western Hispaniola and shared everything.

The Spaniards, considering their monopoly infringed, tried to drive them out by exterminating the cattle on which they lived. This caused the buccaneers' hatred of the Spaniards, and their practice of ruthlessly raiding Spanish ships and settlements. In Hispaniola, they could not raid Santo Domingo because it was too strong, so they began to raid passing ships. The cow-hunters changed to 'the sweet trade' gradually, by first going out in a rowing boat or canoe to a small Spanish ship and overpowering it. With this small ship they would capture a larger one. When a few Spanish ships had been captured, they were in a position to undertake bigger raids against villages and even small towns.

The buccaneers quickly developed a fierce loyalty to their new community. The French buccaneers called themselves *frères de la côte*, 'brethren of the coast'. They had rules which were very strictly applied, known as *les coutumes de la côte*, 'the customs of the coast'.

The buccaneers were fierce, skilled fighters who were both ruthless and cruel. Unnecessary violence and murder were part of their lives and, even by the standards of the seventeenth century, their cruelty was shocking. Buccaneering communities were masculine societies and it was uncommon for buccaneers to be married. Buccaneers had women, but not in permanent alliances. Drunkenness was also a common characteristic, and many of them lost their loot or squandered it in wild parties of celebration in places such as Port Royal.

'Militia of the sea'

European governments, especially England, unable to back up their attacks because of lack of ships and forces, saw in the buccaneers a means of destroying Spanish power. The buccaneers were expert seamen and fearsome fighters and their lawlessness and past crimes could be forgotten temporarily. A mercenary system was used, but with a special system of pay. It was the system of letters of marque or reprisal. 'Marque' refers to the crossing of frontiers to obtain redress, and 'reprisal' refers to the taking of compensation. Payment was made by reprisal so the system was often called a 'commission of reprisal'.

The buccaneer was recruited by such a letter to fight the King's enemies and was allowed to keep a percentage of what he captured. In practice, he usually kept it all. Letters of marque gave respectability to bucceneering and they made an important distinction between the pirates of the sixteenth century and the buccaneers of the seventeenth. Most letters of marque were issued against the Spanish and were very popular.

Buccaneer bases

An early base was Providence Island (Santa Catalina), off the coast of Nicaragua, which was well placed on the route of the treasure galleons making for the Yucatan Strait, on their way to Havana, after loading at Porto Bello. Although a Puritan foundation in 1629, Providence quickly degenerated into a haven for buccaneers and among the first of these was Anthony Hilton from Nevis. In 1634 the Spanish destroyed the pirates' base. It was re-established and became even more dangerous to the Spanish who could not tolerate a buccaneer base in the middle of one of their most important treasure routes and they destroyed it in 1641.

Tortuga began as a refuge for the cow-killers of Western Hispaniola in 1629. They were joined by the English refugees from Nevis and St Kitts with Anthony Hilton as governor. In 1640, de Poincy, the Governor-General of all the French islands, sent Le Vasseur, to be Governor of Tortuga, and its importance as a buccaneer base dates from this time. It remained the centre of French buccaneering for over fifty years.

Port Royal in Jamaica was founded by the English buccaneers who left Tortuga after the various Spanish attacks. Their numbers increased in 1659 when Tortuga was recognised as French. By 1660 Port Royal was already famous as a market for goods taken from the Spaniards, and as a port where ships could be fitted out for attacks on them. Spanish Town was still the capital of Jamaica, but Port Royal quickly surpassed it in size and importance.

The English buccaneers of Port Royal

Governor Modyford

The restoration of Charles II in England brought peace with Spain in Europe, but not beyond the line. The buccaneers at Port Royal had already been given letters of marque against the Spaniards and Charles allowed these operations to continue.

In 1662 an English force from Jamaica captured and destroyed Santiago de Cuba, taking £1,000,000 in prizes. This encouraged the buccaneers as Santiago had previously been thought impregnable. After Modyford, the Governor appointed by Charles II in 1664, had changed his initial policy of trying to suppress them, he easily recruited 1,500 buccaneers for the war against the Dutch and the French. They did not like fighting the Dutch and after capturing Tobago, St Eustatius and Saba, joined in the raids against the Spaniards which had been going on successfully from Port Royal for some time; for example, São Thomé, at the mouth of the Orinoco, had been captured by Captain Barnard in 1663; Lewis Scot captured Campeche in Mexico in the same year; and in 1664 John Davis looted Granada in Nicaragua.

Edward Mansfield (his Dutch name was 'Mansvelt') was recruited by Modyford in 1664 and this led to the capture of Sancti Spiritus in Cuba, the sacking of Granada in Nicaragua and the recapturing of Providence Island, in 1665. On

Mansfield's death at the end of 1666, Morgan took over and was first commissioned by Modyford in 1668.

Henry Morgan

Morgan's first expeditions were against Puerto del Principe in Cuba (Camaguey) which he looted, and Puerto Bello on the Isthmus where he showed great ruthlessness and cruelty. The brutality and bestiality of Morgan's buccaneers was shown in the torture and drunkenness which lasted for several days. Over 300,000 pieces of eight were taken and another 100,000 obtained as ransom money.

In 1669 Morgan led an expedition to the Gulf of Maracaibo. He captured Maracaibo and Gibraltar very easily, but found little of value because it had already been looted by L'Ollonais in 1668. He was nearly caught by three Spanish ships at the entrance to the Gulf, but he tricked them into believing that his men had landed for an attack on the fort and drifted his ships past them in the darkness.

After Morgan's raids, the Spaniards decided to take revenge and raided Jamaica several times.

Morgan and Modyford suspected that the Spaniards were planning a full-scale attack from Cuba, so Morgan attacked them in 1670. He captured Providence Island, sacked Rio de la Hacha and took the castle of San Lorenzo. Then he made a forced march across the Isthmus against Spanish resistance, until he arrived at the walls of Panama. His men were outnumbered, but they fought so fiercely that they captured the city which they burnt to the ground. They tortured and killed all the inhabitants. The buccaneers got away with vast amounts of treasure which Morgan divided evenly. This is interesting, as one of the criticisms of Morgan was that he deceived his men in the sharing out of spoils after raids.

While Morgan was in Panama, England and Spain had made the Treaty of Madrid and, to appease the Spaniards, the English government was forced to make a show of disapproval of the buccaneers' exploits, especially the part played by Governor Modyford. Modyford was replaced as Governor of Jamaica, recalled to England and put in the Tower of London for a short time. However, he was soon released and returned to Jamaica where he was a hero, and a rich man from his share

The sacking of Panama

of the loot. His successor, Sir Thomas Lynch, was powerless to carry out the terms of the Treaty of Madrid and stop buccaneering.

The buccaneers themselves received no official condemnation. In fact the English Parliament praised them, and the Jamaican Council gave Morgan a vote of thanks for his raid on Panama. In 1674 Morgan was knighted and became Lieutenant-Governor of Jamaica under Lord Vaughan. Morgan's responsiblity was to act against the buccaneers, but in practice he remained in league with them. Eventually he was removed from office in 1683 for drunkenness.

Sir Thomas Lynch, who was prepared to deal severely with the buccaneers, was reappointed as Governor. He realised that the Spanish were no longer any danger to the English in the Caribbean and that the buccaneers were the only obstacle to peace. But his efforts met with little success and he died in 1684.

He was succeeded by Colonel Molesworth who held similar views. However, buccaneering was profitable and there was still strong anti-Spanish feeling in Jamaica and England, due mainly to religion. In 1685 a determined effort was made to stop buccaneering and a squadron was sent out from England to catch the buccaneers. They were brought back to Kingston harbour, hanged and 'sun-dried' on Execution Dock as examples to all of what would happen if buccaneering did not stop. So buccaneering was finally suppressed. Even Port Royal came to an end when it was submerged by an earthquake in 1692.

The importance of the English buccaneers

The English buccaneers undoubtedly helped towards breaking the Spanish monopoly of the Caribbean. They disrupted Spanish trade over a long period and completed the eclipse of Spanish naval supremacy. Later, however, they became an embarrassment to the English government and to Jamaica. Their suppression was slow, and embittered relations between the English and the Spanish when peace would have benefited both sides by allowing trade to develop.

The French buccaneers

In the 1650s, French buccaneers from Tortuga had begun to make settlements at Port Margot and Port de Paix on Hispaniola which were the original settlements of the great colony of St Domingue. Thereafter Tortuga and St Domingue complemented each other. Tortuga was the buccaneer base and St Domingue the plantation settlement. When Tortuga was threatened by the Spaniards, the buccaneers could take refuge in St Domingue and hide themselves amongst the peaceful planters. When the danger had passed, they would return and resume their activities in Tortuga. At the same time, some of the peaceful planters of St Domingue could indulge in a little unsuspected buccaneering. Many of the gains from buccaneering won by Tortuga helped to develop the rising settlement of St Domingue. This was the main cause of friction between French and Spanish in the Caribbean.

Le Vasseur, Governor of Tortuga between 1640 and 1652, had set the pattern of combining his official duties with illegal activities as a buccaneer. This was carried on even more successfully by Bertrand d'Ogeron, appointed Governor in 1665. He brought out women from France to marry the buccaneers and make St Domingue into an ordered plantation colony. He encouraged cultivation of subsistence crops and fostered the planting of sugar. The new town of Leogane was founded.

The great age of the French buccaneers 1678-1685

Louis XIV of France, having failed to secure Spanish recognition of his claim to St Domingue in the Peace of Nijmegen in 1678, issued letters of marque to the Tortuga buccaneers to attack Spanish possessions in the Caribbean. Most of the famous French buccaneering raids took place in this period. In 1678 de Grammont raided the Gulf of Maracaibo. In 1679 de Maintenon plundered the pearl fisheries of Margarita and even raided Trinidad. De Maintenon was a French marquis who became the largest plantation owner in Martinique from his buccaneering profits.

The greatest buccaneering raid of all was carried out in 1683 by three buccaneers, de Graaf, de Grammont and van Horn, against Vera Cruz. The loot was considerable. De Graaf and van Horn quarrelled over it, and van Horn was killed. This raid was the culmination of Franco-Spanish hostility in the Caribbean, though de Grammont did make a raid on Campeche in Mexico in 1685.

In the truce of Ratisbon, 1685, the French

promised to stop buccaneering in return for Spanish recognition of St Domingue. By now the buccaneers were an embarrassment to Louis. The first Governor in St Domingue to try to stop buccaneering, de Cussy, was not successful, but his successor du Casse, appointed in 1691, managed to end buccaneering from Tortuga. The buccaneers respected du Casse and he had a policy which offered them an attractive alternative. In the War of the League of Augsburg, France was fighting an alliance which included England. Du Casse led the French buccaneers against Jamaica and Cartagena. When peace was made in the Treaty of Ryswick in 1697, du Casse was able to persuade the buccaneers to settle down to a peaceful life as planters in St Domingue. The era of buccaneering was at an end.

The buccaneers - conclusion

Spanish naval power in the Caribbean had first been broken by the Dutch. The activities of the English and French buccaneers in the second half of the seventeenth century showed how weak Spain had become. A few organised pirates operating from only two bases had the Spanish islands at their mercy. The French were the strongest power from 1670-1697, having wrested supremacy from the Dutch. But although they broke Spanish naval power, the buccaneers were counter-productive towards the end of the century. They impeded the development of Jamaica and St Domingue as plantation colonies. Moreover, the English and French sugar trade was becoming too important for the authorities to tolerate large-scale disruption of trade and they were forced to end buccaneering. It was incompatible with the peaceful economic development of the West Indies.

The Dutch Wars and the West Indies, 1652-1678

Commercial rivalry was the major cause of the Dutch Wars. Cromwell fought the First Dutch War to break the Dutch domination of trade and force them to accept the Navigation Acts. The fighting took place in European waters between 1652 and 1654. The Dutch were successful at first, but the victory of the English admirals, Blake and Monk, in 1653 made the Dutch agree to accept English commercial regulations in the Treaty of Westminster, 1654. However, in practice, the Dutch still continued to trade with the English islands.

The Second Dutch War from 1665 to 1667 cut the supply of slaves to the English islands because the Dutch admiral, de Ruyter, attacked the slaving stations of the Royal Adventurers in West Africa. Naval blockade of the Dutch and their French allies in the Eastern Caribbean disrupted the export of sugar to England; even Barbados, far to far to the east, could not get her sugar away.

The West Indian islands, especially the Leewards, were heavily involved in the fighting. After failing to capture Barbados in April 1665, de Ruyter turned against the Leewards and captured sixteen English ships. The French harassed the English and the Caribs of Dominica took advantage of English difficulties to launch many attacks on the Leewards. The French captured St Kitts, Antigua and Montserrat, but Nevis stayed in English hands. Admiral Berry won back Antigua and Montserrat, but the French kept St Kitts. Even when they were required to hand back the English half of St Kitts by the Treaty of Breda they made excuses not to, for example, offering to exchange it for Grenada. Eventually the English fully recovered their half in July, 1671.

Both Barbados and Jamaica felt threatened. To forestall an expected Dutch invasion of Jamaica, Modyford sent the Port Royal buccaneers to capture Tobago, St Eustatius and Saba in 1666. The Dutch recaptured these islands in 1667 and retaliated further by capturing Surinam which was a prosperous sugar colony.

In the Treaty of Breda, 1667, which ended the war, the English, Dutch and French handed back each others' colonies, except for Surinam which remained Dutch in exchange for New York which became English.

In the Third Dutch War, 1672 to 1678, the French changed sides and allied themselves with the English. The English again had their supply of slaves cut and the Royal Africa Company suffered losses. However, the English realised that the Dutch were no longer their main rivals and they concluded a separate peace in 1674. They gave back Tobago which they had captured in 1672, but at the request of the Dutch held on to St Eustatius, Saba and Tortola to protect them from the French

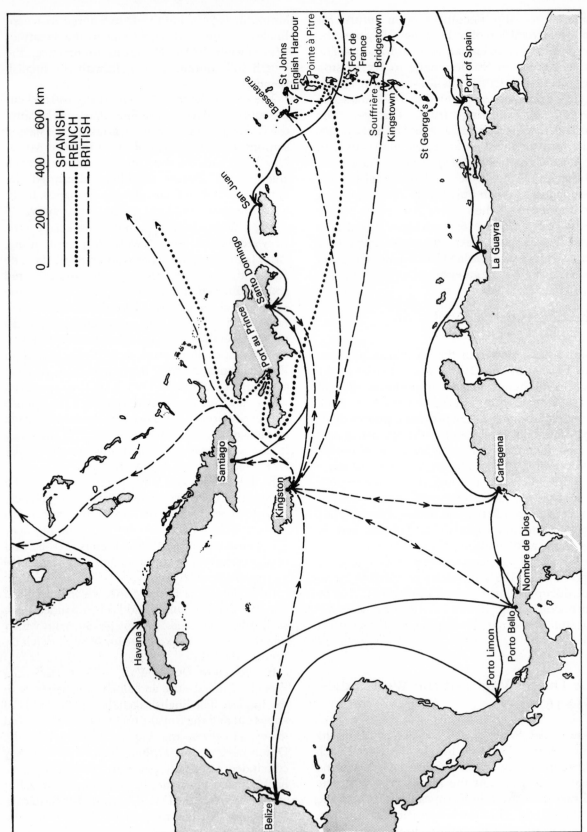

Map 2 Shipping routes and chief ports in the Caribbean

8

The French proved too strong for the Dutch and they captured Cayenne and devastated Tobago. The French navy forced the Dutch into a minor role in the Caribbean by 1674 and ended the Dutch domination of trade. The Peace of Nijmegen, 1678, marked the end of the Dutch wars and the beginning of the English and French struggle for supremacy in the eighteenth century.

Relative positions of the European powers in the Caribbean

At the beginning of the century France and England were the chief rivals in the Caribbean. In territorial possessions they were evenly balanced. In the Greater Antilles, England had Jamaica, and France had St Domingue. In the Lesser Antilles, England was the leading power in the Leewards with Anguilla, St Kitts, Montserrat, Nevis, Antigua and Barbuda, while France held the pre-dominance in the Windwards with Guadeloupe, Marie Galante, Martinique and Grenada. England had Barbados. Dominica, St Vincent and St Lucia were still in dispute between the English, French and Caribs, although there were more French settlers on them than English.

By the beginning of the century, the English had made their colonies more productive and thus they were more valuable and their population was higher. But the French islands were potentially more valuable as they had more acreage and more virgin soil. The total area of the English islands, excluding the Bahamas, was about 13,000 square kilometres, while that of the French was about 32,000 square kilometres. In St Domingue, the French had potentially the richest sugar island in the Caribbean

Naval power

England had the advantage here because she possessed two naval bases in the Caribbean, English Harbour, Antigua, and Port Royal in Jamaica. Thus the English could keep fleets permanently in the Caribbean by provisioning and refitting them there. English sailors serving in the Caribbean had a chance to become acclimatised because they were sometimes in the tropics for more than two years.

The French did not have a naval base in the Caribbean until 1784 and they had all the disadvantages of having to send their fleets from Europe every year. This limited their operating season, as they could only sail out in April when the European winter had passed and they had to return by August before the hurricane season in the Caribbean.

English Harbour, Antigua

Economic aims of the powers

In a mercantilist age the West Indies were very important. The sugar trade was something that everyone thought was worth fighting for. But, by the end of the century, mercantilism had become mixed with imperialism and England and France both wanted to enlarge their empires at the expense of the other, so the islands themselves became worth fighting for. The West Indies suffered the fate of other colonies in having no say in the policies which involved them in war, hardship and sometimes ruin.

The effects of the eighteenth century wars on the West Indies

There were five major wars in the Caribbean in the eighteenth century and they occupied thirty-four years of fighting. This excludes the Revolutionary Wars which began in 1793, but which carried on into the Napoleonic Wars and so belong to the next century.

1 The War of Spanish Succession, 1702 to 1713. This was a European war arising from Louis XIV's claim to the Spanish throne. England resisted his claim, and England and France became involved in a colonial war. One West Indian issue for which they were fighting was the *Asiento* which Louis had claimed in 1702.

Most of the fighting was in the Leewards. Christopher Codrington captured the French part of St Kitts in 1702. In 1706 the French counterattacked in the Leewards and, thereafter, dominated the naval war there. The Leewards, of course, felt the main effects of the war. Nevis, raided in 1706, and Montserrat, raided in 1712, never fully recovered. Their planters were killed and their slaves carried off. The English Leewards were not able to export any sugar until after the war. Slaves suffered because they were regarded as booty and carried off after a raid and, when peace returned, there was no labour to start up the plantations again.

Admiral Benbow saved Jamaica from attack at the beginning of the war and thereafter she was untroubled, except by pirates. Jamaica maintained

Walpole and Captain Jenkin's ear

her exports of sugar to England and imported 11,000 slaves.

In the Peace of Utrecht, 1713, St Kitts became completely English and has remained so ever since. England was given the *Asiento*, but on terms which led to another major war in the Caribbean.

2 The War of Jenkins' Ear, 1739 This was a purely Caribbean war. The *Asiento* of 1713 allowed Britain to supply 4,800 slaves per year for thirty years to the Spanish colonies. No other trade could be carried on, apart from one ship of general cargo per year to the Porto Bello Fair. A quarter of this cargo was to belong to the King of Spain together with five per cent of the net profit from the slave trading. The Spanish emphasised that the British must not engage in 'unlawful trade'.

Spanish *guardacostas* claimed that the *Asiento* gave them the right to search British ships and they confiscated all the goods they could. Jamaica's trade with Spanish possessions suffered especially. The British retaliated against the searches and they fought minor wars with the Spanish in 1718 and 1727 in which the metropolitan governments did not become involved. Then, in 1738, Captain Jenkins claimed before Parliament that the Spanish had cut off his ear. Robert Walpole, the Prime Minister, tried to settle grievances in the Convention of El Pardo, 1739, and the British claimed damages of £95,000 for losses suffered in 1718 and 1727. The Spanish agreed to pay the damages subject to the South Sea Company paying what it owed under the *Asiento,* but this was not done. Therefore the Spanish suspended the *Asiento* and this, together with the conduct of the *guardacostas,* was thought sufficient cause for war. Other minor causes were the Spanish dislike of the British Baymen cutting logwood in Honduras, and the dispute over the boundary between the English colony of Georgia and the Spanish colony of Florida in North America. War against Spain meant war against France as the rulers of the two countries were both members of the same family, the Bourbons. This alliance became known as 'The Family Compact'.

Britain defeated Spain very easily in the western Caribbean. Porto Bello, Cartagena and Santiago de Cuba were raided and Spanish trade was so badly affected that only one treasure fleet reached home in ten years. British trade, on the other hand, flourished. In the eastern Caribbean, Britain and France aimed at destroying each other's com- petitiveness in the sugar trade and, as Britain had command of the sea, she was successful. Only one French fleet, under D'Antin in 1740, was sent to the Caribbean and it returned after a few months without fighting.

3 The War of Austrian Succession, 1740 to 1748 This was a continuation of the War of Jenkins' Ear. The fighting was on a small scale and was carried out mainly by privateers. The British dominated the sea to such an extent that goods could not reach the French islands and prices rose dramatically.

At the Peace of Aix-la-Chapelle, 1748, which settled both wars, the Spanish agreed to pay compensation of £100,000 for having suspended the *Asiento* four years early. In Honduras, the British removed their settlers from Roatan, but left those on the Belize River and Moskito Coast in spite of Spanish protest. Britain and France re- stored each other's islands and Dominica, St Vincent, St Lucia and Tobago were declared 'Neutral Islands'. British and French settlers were to evacuate them and leave them for the Caribs.

The most important effects of the wars were in the sugar market. The British enjoyed a sugar boom between 1748 and 1756 because supplies had been restricted and French exports cut com- pletely. Prices rose to new levels on the British market, from about 16 shillings per cwt before the wars to about 33 shillings in the 1750s. Jamaica profited by this, because she was in a position to increase her supply without increasing her costs by bringing new land under sugar.

The Spanish took over supplying slaves to their own possessions, and the British, without the cover of the *Asiento,* could be detected smuggling more easily. Unfortunately British and French settlers did not leave the Neutral Islands and the Caribs were pushed into the less fertile parts of the islands, killed or deported.

4 The Seven Years' War, 1756 to 1763 This was the greatest colonial war in history. It was most famous for what happened in India and Canada, but it was also a very important war in West Indian history. William Pitt, the British Prime Minister, believed that Britain's future strength lay in com- merce and empire and he wanted to win as many French colonies as he could. If this led to a surplus of sugar on the British market, he hoped to re- export this to a new market on the continent of Europe.

Pitt saw the war as a global struggle and did not want to commit too many ships to the Caribbean.

Lord Rodney

The British islands saw the war from the Caribbean viewpoint and they felt seriously threatened. In view of the danger, local militias were easily recruited, but they were hardly used as most of the fighting was at sea. Pitt held that he was defending the West Indies by blockading the French ports in Europe, but the British Islands would have felt more comfortable had they been able to see British warships in their own waters.

After an initial setback, when the French captured Minorca in 1756 and French ships were able to escape from the Mediterranean and reach the Caribbean, the British were clearly winning the colonial war by 1758. Pitt was ready to start capturing the French sugar islands. First he took Gorée, the great French slave trading station in West Africa, and cut off the French supply of slaves.

In 1759 the British tried to capture Martinique but found it too strong, so they turned against Guadeloupe which surrendered in May, 1759. Then Marie Galante, Désirade, Les Saintes and Petite Terre all surrendered. The treatment of Guadeloupe caused much dissatisfaction among the British planters. She was allowed to keep French laws and the Catholic religion. She could go on producing sugar which she had to sell on the British market, thus reducing the price of sugar. Guadeloupe could import food from North America and, in the four years of the war remaining, the British imported 40,000 slaves into Guadeloupe, thus enabling her to become a major sugar competitor. Barbados and Antigua were particularly affected by the drop in sugar prices.

By 1759 the British were in command of the Caribbean. In 1761 Dominica was captured and in 1762 Admiral Rodney took Martinique. St Lucia and Grenada were also captured in 1761. Because of the Family Compact, Spain entered the war in 1762. The British sent a large expedition to Cuba. Troops were landed and Havana was besieged for two months. The surrender of Havana marked the end of the Seven Years' War in the West Indies.

Before the Peace of Paris, 1763, which concluded the war, William Pitt fell from office and was succeeded by the Earl of Bute. He feared that Britain's greatly enlarged empire would excite the jealousy of the other powers, so he gave back much of what had been won in the war. Martinique and Guadeloupe with its neighbouring islands were restored to France. Of the Neutral Islands, France was given St Lucia, while Britain kept Dominica, St Vincent and Tobago. England also kept Grenada. In the treaty with Spain, Britain gave back Cuba, but kept Florida, and insisted on the right to keep logwood cutters in Honduras, promising that there would be no fortifications.

The effects of the war on the sugar market were felt as early as 1759. The future looked bleak for the British islands. Sugar prices were falling as French production, especially in Guadeloupe and St Domingue, increased. Some British planters moved from the islands to Guiana where costs were lower. The British government took little notice of the planters' pleas to restrict French sugar on the British market, and to enforce the Molasses Act. The supply of slaves had dropped because many had been diverted to Guadeloupe and Cuba during the war, and there was a new demand from the ex-Neutral Islands where sugar planting was beginning. Consequently the price of slaves in the old islands were much higher; planters were having to pay £40 for a good Gold Coast slave after the war.

For the French islands, a sugar boom was beginning. Gorée had been restored so they regained their supply of slaves. For the first time the French islands overtook the British islands in quantity of sugar produced. French production in 1767 was

British expedition against Havana in 1762

78,000 tonnes and British was 73,000 tonnes. French sugar was cheaper because virgin land meant lower production costs. It was also of better quality because much of it was semi-refined. Finally, the French islands were winning a larger share of the North American market in spite of the Molasses Act.

In the British islands, the future was bleakest for Barbados and the Leewards which were facing problems of soil exhaustion. Their production costs were high because the land needed much fertilisation, and they also had to pay the 4½ per cent export duty which Jamaica and the former Neutral Islands did not have to pay.

The attitude of the British government and British manufacturers to the West Indies was changing, in spite of the West Indian interest being fifty strong in Parliament. The Sugar Act of 1764 lowered the duties by half, but all the islands had to pay and the duties were carefully collected. Moreover the government did little to stop the illegal trade between the French islands and the North American colonies.

English sugar refiners did not like having to pay such high prices for sugar, although they were not yet calling for free trade. However, they did not expect the government to show favour to the British islands as they had done before the war.

5   *The War of American Independence, 1776 to 1783*
This involved the West Indies because France supported the North American colonies in their revolt and turned a civil war into another colonial struggle between Britain and France, to avenge her losses in the Seven Years' War. After that war, Choiseul, the French Foreign Minister, had strengthened the French navy and urged Spain to strengthen hers. France joined the war in 1778, Spain in 1779 and the Dutch in 1780. Britain thus found herself fighting her North American colonies and the three other major colonial powers.

The sympathies of the British islands lay with the North American colonies. They shared the same grievances against England, such as trade restrictions, taxation and legislation imposed on them from England. In 1775 the Jamaican Assembly sent a petition to Parliament saying that the colonies had a right to legislate for themselves. This view was supported by Barbados and the other islands. However, only Bermuda openly sided with the rebel colonies. The British West Indian colonies did not rebel because they needed the protection of the navy.

Before the French entered the war, there were attacks by American privateers on British ships in

13

Admiral Hood

The battle of the Saints between Rodney and De Grasse in April, 1782, was the only full-scale naval engagement in the Caribbean in the century. A British victory saved Jamaica, and deterred the French and the Spanish from making any further attacks. Thus it brought an end to the war in the West Indies. The British had lost their North American colonies, but had salvaged a little pride from Rodney's great victory and they were thus able to obtain better terms at the Peace of Versailles, 1783. All the colonies were restored to their former owners, with the exception of Tobago which was retained by the French.

The effects of the War of American Independence on the West Indies were more profound than those of any of the previous wars. Every British island except Barbados, Antigua and Jamaica had been captured. For the first time, Barbados and Jamaica were in grave danger of being captured and they maintained their militias under constant call for five years, even though the British government refused their call for financial help. Unlike the British treatment of Guadeloupe and Martinique in the previous war, the French treated their captured islands very harshly. They were garrisoned by French soldiers and subjected to strict laws. Planters were evacuated and their plantations pillaged. The slaves were carried off to the French islands.

The economic effects of the war were grave. Cutting the trade with the North American colonies had deprived the West Indies of timber, saltfish, meat, grain and rice. The slaves suffered starvation and death. In Jamaica 14,000 slave deaths were attributed to famine or disease contracted due to malnutrition. In the Leeward Islands, 3,000 slaves died. Again Barbados suffered most because she could not produce her own food to alleviate the shortages and 15,000 slaves died there. Even after the war, the fear of famine remained until trade with the north was resumed. Antigua spoke of famine in 1785.

The British islands wanted a resumption of trade with the newly-independent United States, but Canada was anxious to supply the islands. The United States was now a foreign country, although some concessions were allowed in trade with the West Indies. Sugar, molasses, rum, coffee and pimento could be exported to the United States, and timber, beef-cattle, grain and flour imported from them, provided that all the trade was carried in British ships.

the West Indies, and they even carried off slaves from as far south as the Grenadines. The French and Dutch allowed these privateers to use their harbours in the West Indies.

Due to Choiseul's policy, the French were much stronger at sea and, for the first time in the century, they were superior to the British at the start of the war. By 1780 the French had captured Dominica, St Vincent and Grenada, while the British had captured only St Lucia. However, when Admiral Hood joined Rodney in Barbados, the British navy was approaching the strength of the French. Rodney turned against the Dutch. His capture of St Eustatius caused much controversy because he stayed there to distribute the prizes from 180 ships instead of proceeding to North America to relieve Cornwallis. The latter had to surrender and this allowed de Grasse, the French admiral, to sail to the Caribbean. The other Dutch possessions, Saba, St Martin, St Bartholomew, Demerara, Berbice and Essequibo all surrendered to Rodney but were recaptured when he left.

De Grasse attacked the Leewards in 1781, capturing St Kitts, Nevis and Montserrat. This was the peak of French success.

The omission of meat, fish and maize from the list of permitted imports was particularly serious for the islands' slave economies. These had now to come from Canada and prices were 30-40 per cent higher on average than before the war. Maize could be 400 per cent higher! Canada was not yet in a position to fulfil the needs of the West Indies in the same way that the North American colonies had done.

Other costs for the planters went up. Insurance charges rose throughout the war. Sugar duties went up progressively from 6/3d per cwt in 1776 to 15/- in 1791 in an attempt to make the colonies pay for the war. Many planters were forced to mortgage their estates, or sell up.

The War of American Independence taught the British islands many lessons which were however largely unheeded. Firstly, it showed their vulnerability once the British navy lost command of the sea; the islands could be captured by the enemy and trade could be easily stopped. They had been exporting about 80,000 tonnes of sugar per year to Britain at the beginning of the war. By 1778 this had been cut by half and the naval war against France had not yet properly started.

Another valuable lesson was the danger of not being self-sufficient in food in time of war. Every resource had been given over to plantation agriculture and food was imported. When food supplies were cut, they starved. They talked of turning to food crops, but little was done.

Finally, they should have detected a change in attitude on the part of the British government who felt that too many favours had been shown to the sugar interests. Duties had been raised almost 300 per cent. Favourable trade terms were not given after the peace, and, more seriously, people in Britain – not only the economists, but also the merchants and manufacturers – were talking about 'free trade'.

Conclusion

For about forty years of the eighteenth century, European powers were engaged in major wars and, because of their colonial interests in the Caribbean, there was fighting in the West Indies for many of these years. On balance this had brought difficulties to the islands as sugar producers, though there had been boom years. The Revolutionary and Napoleonic Wars at the end of the century benefited the sugar producers in the British islands.

However, it was a false promise, as in the new century the planters had to face the problems of abolition, emancipation, free trade and increased foreign competition which made earlier economic difficulties seem only minor.

2

The Haitian Revolution

Toussaint L'Ouverture

There would probably have been a revolution in St Domingue sooner or later because of the terrible slave conditions, class divisions and racial hatred. However, the revolution in France triggered off a chain of events which resulted in St Domingue becoming the independent country of Haiti between 1791 and 1803.

The French Revolution

In August, 1789, the National Assembly in Paris issued the 'Declaration of the Rights of Man'. This document insisted on the freedom and equality of man and gave the French Revolution its slogan of 'Liberty, Equality and Fraternity'. In France this meant the ending of privilege and feudalism, and equality between peasant and noble. In the French empire it led to demands for equal political rights and social equality by the mulattoes. Logically it should have meant the ending of slavery, but this step was not officially taken by the Revolutionary Government until 1794. However, once the slaves in the French islands in the West Indies had heard the slogan, they did not wait for the decree, but seized their own freedom.

The effect of the Revolution in the French empire

The news of the French Revolution spread slowly through the empire. Most people did not know whether to remain loyal to the King or join the revolutionary cause. Those with property and power were reluctant to support the Revolution because they were not sure of the strength of the movement and thought that if the King regained power they would be in trouble. Others with nothing to lose were inclined to join the Revolution at its outset.

Generally the planters remained loyal to the King and were known as 'royalists'. Freedom and equality were dangerous to their position and they felt that they had to resist the movement from the beginning. The mulattoes wanted equality with the whites politically and socially. The slaves just wanted their freedom.

Each class selfishly pursued its own ends and resisted gains by the other classes. White and mulatto tended to combine to resist freedom for slaves. In the colonies nobody wanted to help the blacks. Help for the blacks came from a group in France known as the *'Amis des Noirs'*. Whites and mulattoes combined with the blacks only when they thought that the added strength of the blacks would save them.

The dilemma of the whites was well illustrated in Martinique, where the planters outside St Pierre were royalist while the whites from the city were revolutionaries. There was fighting between the two white groups in 1789. However, the whites united as soon as the slaves revolted and stayed united in 1790 to put down a rising of mulattoes who were demanding equal political rights.

In both France and the empire, revolutionaries refused to accept orders from officers who had been appointed by the King. This led to mutinies in the French islands; for example, French soldiers in Tobago mutinied in 1790 and in St Lucia in 1792 the revolutionaries expelled the Governor. There was anarchy and revolt in the empire due more to the local population taking advantage of the lack of control from France than to any belief on their part in the Revolution.

The effect of the Revolution in St Domingue

In 1789 the population of St Domingue consisted of about 35,000 whites, 25,000 mulattoes and 450,000 slaves. There were rigid legal distinctions

Opening of the States-General at Versailles, May 1789

between these groups based on colour, and there was a mutual distrust and hatred which was far deeper than in the other French islands.

The whites were not a united group. At the top were the very rich planters, the 'seigneurs', far superior in status to the planters of Martinique and Guadeloupe. Grouped with them socially were the leading civil and military officers. All together they were known as the *grands blancs*. Some of them had aristocratic origins in France and when the Revolution came they joined the royalists. Earlier, when the *grands blancs* heard of the calling of the States-General, they drew up lists of planters and elected deputies to send to the meeting in an attempt to keep political power in their hands. This action caused their relations with the other classes in St Domingue to deteriorate.

The merchants and the professional men were cut off socially from the *grands blancs*. In Martinique and Guadeloupe, the planters were frequently in debt to the merchants, but this was not the case in St Domingue where the *grands blancs,* free of any obligation, despised them. In the Revolution some of the merchants were royalist and some republican. They all hoped for political and social equality with the *grands blancs*, but did not want equality extended to the mulattoes.

The third class of whites was the *petits blancs.* They were the poor whites; the overseers, artisans and small shopkeepers. They often had affinities through marriage with the mulattoes, and were republican in the Revolution until they themselves were in mortal danger from the blacks. On top of all these divisions, all Creole whites (those born in the West Indies) were despised by those born in France.

The mulattoes, or free coloureds, were known as *affranchis* in St Domingue. They were unique among the mulatto populations of the West Indies in that, not only were they very numerous, but some were also very rich. Some of them had been educated in France and some even chose to live there.

The *Code Noir* had allowed the mulattoes the rights of free men, but the restrictive laws which came later, especially those of 1766, had taken away much of their freedom. They could not hold public office or any legal position, nor could they be officers in the militia. They were not allowed to carry firearms and they had to wear different clothes from the whites. However, they were free to own property, including land and slaves, and

they had made the most of this freedom. In 1789 one-third of all fertile land in St Domingue belonged to mulattoes and many of them owned very large estates. Property put them on the side of the whites when it came to the question of freedom for slaves.

On the other hand their legal and social disabilities made them closer to the slaves. They were forced to serve in the militia for longer periods than whites and they were conscripted into gangs for labour on the roads. Moreover, because they were of mixed race, they could never aspire to equality with the whites. They were in a dilemma between the whites and the blacks, not liking either. On balance, the desire to keep slavery put them on the side of the whites at first. Later, after emancipation, they felt more affinity with the blacks.

The vast number of slaves in St Domingue was due to the rapid expansion of the economy, especially the sugar industry. In 1789 St Domingue was producing nearly 80,000 tonnes of sugar per year from 800 plantations. This was nearly as much as the combined production of all the British islands. St Domingue's economy was also more diversified than that of the other West Indian islands, due to its fertile soil. Coffee, cotton and indigo plantations employed thousands of slaves.

During the eighteenth century the French colonies in the New World imported about one million slaves from Africa. In the early years of the century only a small proportion went to St Domingue. As the century progressed, the proportion grew larger until, in the last decade before the Revolution, three out of four slaves ended up in St Domingue either directly from West Africa, or as Creole slaves from other French colonies.

St Domingue flourished because of her trade with the newly-independent United States and because she supplied Europe, outside Britain, with half its tropical products. To maintain the production which made these exports possible, 30,000 slaves per year entered St Domingue. Of the 450,000 slaves there, most were African born which was unusual in the West Indies. It is sometimes held that Creole slaves led revolts and that African slaves were more servile.

In the Haitian Revolution we have examples of leaders from both these groups. Toussaint was a Creole, while Dessalines was African. Dessalines was the second most prominent leader after Toussaint, and he was definitely the most ruthless. However, the other black leaders, including Boukman (Jamaica) and Christophe (St Kitts) were Creoles.

The condition and treatment of slaves in St Domingue was worse than in any other West Indian island, including Jamaica. It had become the extreme example of a slave economy. In the boom, planters were making much bigger profits than elsewhere, to the detriment of the slaves. They were worked excessively hard and were poorly fed. The death-rate of slaves in St Domingue in the 1780s was the highest in the West Indies. On some estates, the whole labour force had to be renewed every five years.

The terrible life of the slaves was accentuated by the luxurious life of the planters, both white and mulatto. Consequently the hatred felt by slaves towards their masters was correspondingly great. When the Revolution broke out and anarchy prevailed, the slaves were determined to exterminate the whites.

The French Revolution had a greater impact on St Domingue because of the structure of its society and the great divisions between classes. The whites had been demanding political representation in their own assembly before the Revolution began. Without waiting for authority from the National Assembly, they set up Provincal Assemblies and denied mulattoes representation in them. At first the whites managed to pacify the mulattoes by allowing them equality with whites in the militia but, in January, 1790, the King sent orders that a single Colonial Assembly should be set up in St Domingue. Again the whites denied the mulattoes representation in spite of a decree from France in March, 1790, giving the vote to all free persons over twenty-five years old possessing a certain income.

In October, 1790, James Ogé arrived in St Domingue to lead the mulattoes in revolt. Ogé had been educated in Paris and, on his return to St Domingue, he became the spokesman for the mulattoes. He went back to France to collect arms and ammunition for the rising and returned via Britain and the United States. Then with another mulatto, Chavanne, he led a rising which was doomed to failure. Ogé wanted to keep slavery so he refused to lead the blacks and his forces were easily put down. He fled into the Spanish part of Hispaniola, but the Spaniards handed him over and he was broken on the wheel. An important result of this mulatto rising and Ogé's execution was to turn public opinion in France against the whites.

The slave rising around Cap Français in 1791

In May 1791, the National Assembly decreed that all persons, of whatever colour, born of free parents, should be equal and have equal political rights in the Colonial Assembly. The white Assembly of St Marc in St Domingue refused this decree,

Map 3 St Domingue

saying that the laws of the National Assembly had to be ratified by the Assembly of St Marc. The Governor also refused to enforce the decree. Apart from the action of the whites, the mulattoes were annoyed with the decree itself because it insisted that both parents had to be free, and most mulattoes had slave mothers. In fact only 400 mulattoes would have been eligible for political rights under this law. In August, 1791, the mulattoes revolted again and this time included the slaves in the revolt. In the slave rising, the blacks were led by Boukman from Jamaica who claimed that he was a high priest of voudun. Around Cap Français 2,000 whites, men, women and children, were massacred and 180 sugar estates and 900 coffee and indigo plantations were laid waste. In an attempt to suppress this uprising, 10,000 slaves and mulattoes were killed or executed but the revolt quickly spread over the whole North Plain.

Matters became worse in September. The whites and mulattoes united against the slaves. The whites agreed to allow free-born mulattoes into the Assembly. However, the National Assembly in Paris reversed its decree of May and disqualified mulattoes. The mulattoes considered that they had been betrayed and they joined the slaves in a war to exterminate the whites. The white planters appealed to Jamaica for help and a British squadron was sent to Cap Français to defend the town and evacuate the French women and children.

The Jacobin Commission, 1792

In France the *Société des Amis des Noirs* (1787), who supported equality for mulattoes and the emancipation of slaves, put pressure on the Jacobins in the National Assembly to pass laws giving equality to the mulattoes as a first step. To make sure that these laws were enforced in St Domingue, three Commissioners, Sonthonax, Polverel and Ailhaud, were sent with 6,000 republican soldiers. The Commissioners were extreme Jacobins. In August 1792, Sonthonax promised the slaves freedom in order to win their support, as he was meeting resistance from the whites. No doubt emancipation was coming legally from France, but Sonthonax anticipated the Revolutionary government's wishes and produced a 'black terror' in St Domingue. He promised the blacks plunder, and heavy fighting and bloodshed followed. The evacuation of whites began from all parts of the colony. They settled in the United States, Jamaica, Cuba, Puerto Rico and Trinidad. The settlement of Mayagüez in Puerto Rico took on a characteristically French appearance from this time.

Légér Félicité Sonthonax behaved like a dictator in St Domingue. He murdered the new Governor, Galbaud, and his supporters when they arrived in Cap Français in 1793 and anarchy prevailed. Cap Français and some fortified camps in the western mountains were in white hands, but the rest of the north was terrorised by bands of armed blacks. In the west the situation was more confused. The slaves were in revolt and the whites and mulattoes were fighting each other. The mulattoes under their very good general, André Rigaud, were winning. In the south Port-au-Prince was in the hands of the *petits blancs*. Outside the city the planters had armed their loyal slaves against the mulattoes. Sonthonax made matters worse in the north by entering Cap Français and freeing the rest of the slaves, leaving them to terrorise the area.

Louis XVI

The Revolutionary Wars

British intervention in St Domingue

The execution of Louis XVI was regarded by Britain as a cause for war, which began on 1 February, 1793. St Domingue was easily the most important island in the West Indies and Prime Minister Pitt, the son of William Pitt the Elder, realised the strategic importance of its central position in the Caribbean. It could link the scattered British possessions in the east and west and, in alliance with Spain, provide a base for Britain's defence of the West Indies against France and the United States.

Britain was invited to take over St Domingue by the royalist planters, who thought she would guarantee monarchy, white domination and slavery. In return they wanted the right to continue their trade with the United States. Jamaica also urged Britain to take action in St Domingue, because she was frightened of the Revolution spreading. Finally, Britain saw a chance of revenge against France for assisting the North American colonies in 1778 in their revolt against Britain, and so decided to intervene.

Early British successes in St Domingue

After the capture of Tobago in April, 1793, and an abandoned attack on Martinique in May, Colonel Whitelocke with a force of 900 men was sent to St Domingue. They landed unopposed at Jérémie and raised the British flag, warmly welcomed by the French planters. The British then occupied Mole St Nicolas in the north. Léogane surrendered, and in January 1794 Tiburón was captured. Other towns also fell to the British; some surrendered willingly, while others had to be fought for. But in the south, the mulatto army of General Rigaud, fighting for the French, was in control. British losses were heavy, caused mostly by disease; 40 officers and 600 men had died. Luckily for the British, General Rigaud's army was suffering from the same yellow fever epidemic. When reinforcements arrived from Britain, Port-au-Prince was captured in June 1794 and the British appointed General Williamson as Governor.

However, in spite of all the reinforcements they had sent, the British were not really in control. French and mulatto forces still held towns in the south. General Rigaud recaptured Tiburón in December 1794, and the French held Jacmel and Les Cayes, two towns on the south coast from which privateers could operate against Jamaica.

A further setback was the Second Maroon War in Jamaica in 1795. Because of this, the British were unwilling to release more troops from Jamaica. In the north of St Domingue in 1794-5 a new figure had appeared. He was Pierre-Dominique Toussaint 'L'Ouverture'.

Pierre-Dominique Toussaint 'L'Ouverture'

Toussaint's rise to power

Toussaint was the son of a coachman on the plantation of a Monsieur Bréda in the north of St Domingue. Monsieur Bréda was a kind master who permitted Toussaint's father to marry and raise a family in which Toussaint was the eldest of eight children. His father held a responsible position for a slave and he managed to have his son, Toussaint, educated in French, Latin and Mathematics by his godfather. His father's occupation enabled Toussaint to become such an expert horseman that he was later nicknamed 'the centaur of the savannas'. Toussaint also became a coachman, but later he was put in charge of all the livestock on the estate. At the outbreak of the Revolution he was forty-five years old.

Toussaint was loyal to France and played little part in the rising of 1791. However, he wanted emancipation more than anything else and when the possibility of this arose, he was prepared to fight France to secure freedom for the slaves.

In 1792 France declared war on Spain and Toussaint joined the Spanish forces as a mercenary because he thought that the French would preserve slavery. The Spanish allowed him to command his own force of 4,000 blacks, by whom he was called 'Physician to the armies of the King' because of his knowledge of herbal medicine. Other black leaders like Biassou had joined the Spanish, and they provided the core of the Spanish armies in Hispaniola.

When the Convention government in Paris abolished slavery in 1794, Toussaint felt that he had to join the French republican forces in the west. He fought his way out of the Spanish army, defeating Biassou in the process. By 1795 he was in command of 20,000 black soldiers in the north of St Domingue, fighting against the British for freedom from slavery. Toussaint's army was formidable because it was not just the black rabble that had been roaming the north before, but a well-disciplined, well-armed force.

Toussaint had become known abroad and he won the friendship and support of John Adams, the Vice-President of the United States in 1795, and President in 1797. Through Adams, Toussaint imported 30,000 guns for the black forces in St Domingue, and ships and other supplies were sent to help against the British. As he distributed the guns he told his black forces, 'The gun is your liberty'. They knew that they had to win or become slaves again.

Toussaint soon became the real leader of the French forces. He drove the British from the right bank of the Artibonite River and he threatened their stronghold of St Marc to the south. By 1798 the British were in a desperate position, as a result of disease and Toussaint's attacks. Colonel Maitland, the commander of the British forces, was forced to make an armistice with Toussaint. The British would withdraw from St Domingue, if Toussaint would agree to protect the French inhabitants, refrain from attacking British trade and from trying to spread the revolution to Jamaica. Toussaint himself kept the terms honourably. By October, 1798, the British, who had lost 40,000 men from fighting and disease in a five-year campaign in St Domingue, withdrew from their last town, Mole St Nicolas.

Toussaint's domination of St Domingue

After the British had evacuated St Domingue, Toussaint turned against the mulattoes and French in the west and south. He sacked Rigaud's base at Les Cayes, then the blacks turned on the mulattoes, and mutilated and murdered thousands in 1799 and 1800. On top of this horrible massacre, the autumn rains never stopped and the irrigation dams on the Artibonite and Cul de Sac Rivers burst and flooded the Cul de Sac Plain. People lost their land, evacuated the area and never returned.

In 1799 the government in France, powerless to do anything about it, accepted that Toussaint was in control of St Domingue and appointed him Governor-General. Toussaint's followers called him 'L'Ouverture', because he had 'opened' the door to freedom. In 1800 Toussaint stopped the widespread slaughter. He wanted stability and economic recovery for St Domingue and he even managed to persuade some exiled whites to return and resume planting. Unfortunately, his only answer to the labour problem on the estates was forced labour. However, there was a slight economic revival between 1800 and 1802.

Toussaint's Constitution

In 1801 Toussaint issued a constitution for St Domingue which he put into operation without waiting for approval from France. He made himself Governor-General for life with the right to nominate his successor. There was to be a Central Assembly for St Domingue composed of two delegates from each department chosen by the municipal administrations. Members of the municipal administrations were to be nominated by the Governor from a minimum list of sixteen names. The Central Assembly was to make the laws, but they had to be initiated by the Governor. An important point was that laws would not need approval from France, in spite of the fact that the constitution affirmed that St Domingue was part of the French empire. This made St Domingue self-governing, which was an entirely new idea in empire in those days. Slavery was abolished for ever and there was to be no colour distinction in the civil service.

Under this constitution Toussaint claimed the whole of Hispaniola. By the Treaty of Basle, 1795, the Spanish had transferred their part of the island to the French, but the transfer had never been effected. Toussaint made the French claim a fact by taking Santo Domingo in 1801.

3

Haitian Independence

Napoleon

The attempted 'pacification' of St Domingue

Napoleon's attitude to Toussaint

Napoleon Bonaparte took over the government of France from the Directory in 1799 and set up the 'Consulate', with himself as First Consul. In 1802 he made himself Consul for life with the right to nominate his successor. Finally, in 1803, he became hereditary Emperor of France.

Napoleon was unwilling to accept two rulers within the French empire and tried to bring Toussaint back under his rule. He regarded Toussaint as an upstart, and referred to him as a 'gilded African'.

The points at issue were:

1 Toussaint's constitution of 1801 which made St Domingue independent of France. Napoleon was particularly upset because Toussaint had put it into effect without his approval.

2 Napoleon was planning to rebuild the French empire in North America around St Domingue and Louisiana. Spain had ceded Louisiana to France in 1800 and Napoleon now wanted St Domingue under his control. He felt that St Domingue, as a supplier of tropical products, was indispensable to his North American plans. It was also important strategically because it was in the centre of the Caribbean and could guard the approaches to the Gulf of Mexico and the mouth

of the Mississippi. Toussaint stood in the way of these plans.

3 The biggest point at issue was slavery. Toussaint had made it clear to the Directory in 1799 that he would resist slavery to the last drop of his blood. Napoleon thought that the re-introduction of slavery in St Domingue was essential for the revival of the economy. He also felt that an independent black republic was not a good example to the rest of the empire and that it was dangerous to let it continue.

Leclerc's expedition to St Domingue

In December, 1801, Napoleon sent an army of 20,000 veteran soldiers from France to St Domingue under the command of General Leclerc, the husband of Napoleon's favourite sister, Pauline. The mulatto generals in St Domingue, Rigaud, Boyer and Pétion, joined Leclerc's staff.

At first friendly messages were sent to Toussaint in the hope that he would co-operate, but there could be no co-operation over such an issue as slavery. When the French landed at Cap Français, Toussaint was in another part of the island and they were resisted by Henri Christophe. He burnt most of the town before the French could take it, saying to his men: 'We will blow in the wind like ash, rather than submit to a new slavery'. When Toussaint finally received the French overtures he replied that he would not submit to the French.

Leclerc brought forward Toussaint's two sons, Issac and Placide, and asked them to choose between France, where they had been educated, and their father. They chose their father. Leclerc then denounced Toussaint and his followers as traitors and the war began.

The French quickly captured the principal towns, including Santo Domingo and Port-au-Prince. Some of the black commanders surrendered without fighting. Leclerc defeated Toussaint and he took over the Governor-Generalship.

Christophe and Dessalines take over

Toussaint accepted an amnesty for all his men. He was allowed to retire as a General with his own guard to his estate at Ennery on the western coast. Christophe, Dessalines and Maurepas were taken into the French army as generals. All native officers were allowed to keep their ranks in the

Henri Christophe

French army. Finally Leclerc promised liberty to all. By May, 1802, the fighting was over.

Then in June, 1802, Toussaint was taken prisoner, put on board a French warship and taken to France. Toussaint said to his captors: 'In overthrowing me, you have cut down in St Domingue only the trunk of the tree of liberty. It will spring up again by the roots for they are numerous and deep.' His prophecy quickly came true. Christophe, Dessalines and the other black generals were so shocked at this betrayal of Toussaint that they escaped from French service and began fighting again. Napoleon's decree of May, 1802, re-instituting slavery in the French empire, also increased the determination of the blacks. The desperation with which they received this news was best shown in Guadeloupe where there was a mass suicide of 400 ex-slaves in August.

The war was fought bitterly on both sides. The French obtained bloodhounds from Cuba and Eastern Hispaniola to hunt down the blacks, but their resistance was fiercer even than before and this time the French did not win. They could not live off the land and had to buy all their supplies at inflated prices from the United States. Then, in the Autumn of 1802, a terrible yellow fever epidemic struck St Domingue, killing 40,000 French soldiers and 60,000 blacks. Leclerc himself died and General Rochambeau succeeded him. The French army was now very weak, but there was no hope of re-inforcements as France was again at war with England early in 1803. Napoleon decided that he needed all his men in Europe. He gave up his idea of a new French empire in North America, sold Louisiana to the United States and virtually abandoned St Domingue.

Rochambeau had no hope of winning, but he fought ferociously. The British blockaded all the ports of Hispaniola and cut off food supplies so that the French retreated to Santo Domingo, Mole St Nicolas and Cap Français. In November, 1803, Rochambeau was besieged in Cap Français by Dessalines' army while the British prevented a French escape by sea. Rochambeau knew that Dessalines would slaughter his garrison to a man, so on 30 November the French garrison of 8,000 put to sea and surrendered to the British who took them to Jamaica as prisoners. Four days later the French garrison at Mole St Nicolas did the same.

Independence

On 29 November, 1803, Dessalines, Christophe and Clerveaux, the commander of the black forces in eastern Hispaniola, declared the independence of St Domingue. Then on 1 January, 1804, at a meeting of blacks and mulattoes at Arcahaye, Dessalines, the General-in-Chief, renounced all connection with France and renamed St Domingue 'Haiti' (the Arawak word for 'Land of Mountains'). He tore the white out of the Tricolour, the French flag, and left the red and the blue. He replaced the letters, 'R.F.' *(Republique Française)* with the words, 'Liberty or Death'.

In May, 1804, Dessalines was made Governor-General for life and during his two-year regime the remaining whites were assassinated. He was an extremely ruthless and bloodthirsty man who had been brought from Africa to be a slave on a plantation of a free black. In the rising of 1791 he had murdered his master and taken his property and his name. He soon became the scourge of the mulattoes and the whites, leading the massacres in the south in 1800.

The price of independence

Loss of life

In the fighting in 1791, 10,000 blacks died; another 30,000 died before the end of the century in the various wars against the mulattoes and the British; and 60,000 blacks were killed in the campaigns of Leclerc and Rochambeau. Apart from the deaths in the fighting, thousands more were murdered or starved in the anarchy which followed the fighting. Then in 1802, a yellow fever epidemic broke out which resulted in the deaths of over 60,000 blacks. Thus between 1791 and 1803, about 200,000 blacks died. This was between a third to a half of the population.

The mulatto population also suffered terribly from both the blacks and the whites. A few lost their lives in Ogé's rising of 1790, and many more in Sonthonax's terror of 1792-3. Many mulattoes were killed fighting in Rigaud's army against the British between 1794-5. After the British withdrawal, Toussaint turned against the mulattoes and Dessalines massacred many of them when Rigaud and Pétion attempted resistence. Between 1798 and 1800, about 10,000 mulattoes were killed. Most of the mulattoes under Rigaud, Pétion and Boyer joined Leclerc's army and more were killed. After the amnesty and the threat of the restoration of slavery, the mulattoes joined the blacks and, in spite of further deaths, some mulattoes survived the Revolution, most notably Pétion and Boyer.

Creole whites in St Domingue virtually disappeared. In 1791 they numbered between 30,000 and 35,000 but, by the end of Dessalines' rule in 1806, there were almost none. Thousands were killed in the uprising of 1791 and many went into exile in 1791, 1793-4 and 1795-8. Whites had evacuated the north from 1791 onwards and those who had stayed on, or who returned in the relative peace of 1800-02, were massacred by Dessalines. However, Christophe invited 2,000 white British planters into the north of the island to re-establish the plantations in 1814.

The loss of life to foreign armies was also high, due to both fighting and yellow fever. Between 1793 and 1798 there were about 80,000 British soldiers in St Domingue, of whom about 40,000 died, 20,000 from yellow fever. The French lost about 50,000 soldiers, many in the yellow fever epidemic of 1802.

Pétion

Political chaos

After independence there was political instability in Haiti. Dessalines was crowned Emperor Jacques I in October, 1804. In 1806 he was assassinated by the soldiers of Pétion. The eastern part of Hispaniola seceded and came under Spain again. Haiti itself was divided into a kingdom in the north under Henri Christophe who was crowned King Henri I in 1811, and a republic in the south under General Pétion. In 1812 the north and south were at war with each other and Pétion captured Port-au-Prince. However, they made peace in 1814 as they feared another invasion from France.

In the north Christophe created a medieval-type monarchy, building himself a huge fortress at La Ferrière. He was very friendly towards Britain and proposed an alliance against Napoleon. The independence constitution had abolished slavery, but people were forced to work on the sugar estates to try to revive the export trade. His tyrannical and cruel regime made him so unpopular that there was a revolt against him and he committed suicide in 1820.

In the south Pétion was not prepared to face the unpopularity of forced labour and he gave way to the peasants, allowing them to set up smallholdings which became the pattern of Haiti's

agriculture for the future. In 1818 Pétion died and was succeeded by Jean Pierre Boyer, his nominated successor. On the suicide of Christophe, Boyer became 'life regent' of the whole of Haiti. In 1822 Boyer re-occupied Hispaniola and the Spanish part remained under Haiti until 1844.

In 1815 Louis XVIII had tried to persuade both Christophe and Pétion to put themselves under the legitimate rule of France once again, but they refused and maintained Haiti's independence and freedom from slavery. In 1825 France recognised the independence of Haiti on condition of payment of compensation. Haiti started to pay this compensation, but only a fraction of the full amount was actually paid. In 1826 Britain recognised Boyer's rule of an independent Haiti, but the United States withheld recognition until 1862 because they thought that it would encourage their own slaves in the southern states to rebel.

Economic ruin

The revolution of 1791-1803, and the subsequent disorder, brought disaster to Haiti's economy. Before this period she had been the leading sugar producer in the West Indies. In 1791 St Domingue exported 73,000 tonnes of sugar. By 1804 this had dropped to 20,500 tonnes and by 1825 she exported under one tonne. Coffee exports did not decline so dramatically. They fell from 30,500 tonnes in 1791, to 14,000 tonnes in 1804 and

Christophe's palace

10,000 tonnes in 1818. Thereafter there was a slight recovery and by 1825 she was exporting 26,000 tonnes. Coffee did not collapse completely because it could be grown on the peasant small-holdings which sprang up during the Revolution.

Independent Haiti could not support large estates because the ex-slaves were not willing to undertake plantation labour. Therefore, peasant smallholdings for subsistence living, with a little coffee produced for export, became the basis of Haiti's economy. Organised labour was disrupted and this led to the failure to maintain the irrigation works in the Western Plain, and to the floods of 1800. In this way, some of the most productive land in Haiti was lost. It suffered repeated flooding and erosion and was allowed to return to bush.

However, the new subsistence economy of Haiti enabled independence to be preserved and made Haiti the first country in the New World to abolish slavery successfully, an achievement which was worth economic sacrifices. At first, Britain, France, Spain and the United States put an embargo on trade with Haiti. When this was lifted, she had lost her means of production and her markets, and never recovered them.

The boost to foreign sugar producers

The collapse of St Domingue's sugar industry boosted sugar production elsewhere. It brought the results that British sugar planters had been hoping for since the Seven Years' War. A reflection of the expanding sugar trade of the British islands was the opening of the West India Docks in London in 1800. Prices for sugar on the London market rose from 54/3d per cwt in 1792 to 69/2d per cwt in 1796. Then they fell, but rose again in 1807. After another drop they reached 96/- per cwt, some sales actually topping 100/- per cwt, by 1814.

Sugar from the British islands sold extensively in Europe, and in 1794 the British islands took over part of St Domingue's trade with the United States. Impetus was also given to sugar production elsewhere. In 1794 Etienne de Bore started the sugar industry in Louisiana and by 1800 there were eighty-one sugar plantations there. The Indian sugar industry had been established before the collapse of St Domingue, and William Pitt, the British Prime Minister, thought that India should take over the European sugar market. The first sugar exports from India had reached Britain in 1791, and by 1800 they had reached 10,000 tonnes per year. In Europe, Prussia started the sugar beet industry at this time with the encouragement of the King. However, it was Cuba which really became the successor to St Domingue as the world's leading sugar producer and ruined many British planters in the nineteenth century.

Effects of the Haitian Revolution on other countries

The Haitian Revolution was a symbol for millions of slaves and people fighting for their liberty throughout the world. It was the inspiration of Simon Bolivar in his independence struggles in Venezuela and other parts of South America.

All countries with slaves feared that the Revolution would spread and so they opposed it. Countries which were monarchies, like most of the European countries, were against it because it was republican. Countries with colonies feared it because it would lead to the breakdown of their empires. On the other hand, some countries, like Britain and Spain, welcomed it because it weakened France, their chief colonial rival. The United States was in a dilemma. They had only recently fought for their own independence, but they had a huge slave population in the south and they did not want slave revolts there. They had also built up a considerable trade with St Domingue which was being ruined. When the Revolution began, John Adams persuaded the United States to support it because its aims were independence and freedom, and because of the embarrassment it was causing France, Britain and Spain. However, when it proved successful the United States thought again, and saw the dangers of a similar revolution in its Southern States. Therefore they placed an embargo on trade and withheld recognition from the newly-independent Haiti.

The Revolution directly affected the Spanish part of Hispaniola which shared its border with St Domingue. Cuba, separated from it by less than 100 kilometres of sea, was unaffected but in Jamaica the Maroon War broke out in 1795. The authorities in Jamaica, conscious of the nearness of St Domingue and of how easily a full-scale revolution could spread, suppressed the rebels ruthlessly. The Maroons were conscious of the troubles in St Domingue and the absence of British forces, and they timed their rising accordingly.

Although the situation in Martinique and Guadeloupe was somewhat similar to St Domingue at the outbreak of the French Revolution, the differences were significant enough to stop them following the same pattern. The white populations of Martinique and Guadeloupe had been established longer and were more unified. Racial hatred was not as strong. However, there might have been a revolution but for the arrival of the Jacobin Commission in 1792. The effect of this was that the white planters called in the British who captured both islands in 1794. Guadeloupe enjoyed a longer period of freedom than Martinique, but finally both islands were restored to France in 1814.

The white exiles from St Domingue went to the United States, Puerto Rico, Cuba and Jamaica. This exodus began after the arrival of Sonthonax's Commission in 1792, although there had been a small evacuation from Cap Français to Jamaica in 1791. (When Toussaint captured Santo Domingo in 1801, 2,000 Spaniards fled to the United States.) The French planters from St Domingue usually became planters in their new homes; for example, they took their coffee planting to Jamaica and were responsible for raising Jamaica's coffee exports to over 6,000 tonnes in 1812.

The Revolutionary Wars

British policy at the start of the war in 1793 was directed by Henry Dundas, the Secretary for War. He decided that the best way to protect the British West Indies and the sugar trade was to occupy the French islands. He thought Britain would be able to do this easily because of the collapse of the French navy at the beginning of the Revolution, and with help from royalist planters which, however, later proved to be very disappointing. Although Dundas's ideas were basically correct, his plans suffered a setback when the Jacobin Commissioners persuaded people to fight for their freedom in the French islands and the British were temporarily driven out. By 1796 the British began to dominate the Caribbean again.

In 1793 the French sent eight ships to the Caribbean. The English answered by sending an expedition under Rear-Admiral Gardner to protect the English planters. He was recalled after three months, but he left two ships to protect Jamaica's trade, and six frigates to guard the

Leewards. The British captured Tobago, but after landing troops at Martinique, Gardner decided that St Pierre was too strongly fortified and he re-embarked. However, another expedition under Admiral Jervis and General Grey arrived in the West Indies in January, 1794. They captured Martinique, St Lucia, Les Saintes and Guadeloupe within ten weeks.

In June, 1794, Victor Hugues, a mulatto ex-innkeeper from Guadeloupe, arrived in the West Indies as a Jacobin Commissioner to enforce the decrees of freedom and equality passed by the Assembly. He was a bloodthirsty revolutionary who stirred up the people to drive out the British and royalists from Guadeloupe and the other islands. The recovery of Guadeloupe was disastrous for the British because the French then used it as a base for spreading the Revolution to nearby islands, and for attacking British colonies. The British in Dominica withstood an attack from Guadeloupe in June, 1795 but St Lucia was re-captured. In Grenada a mulatto, Julien Fédon, led a successful revolt of the French and mulattoes until reinforcements arrived in March, 1796, and the rebels were defeated. Victor Hugues' agents encouraged a revolt in St Vincent with the help of some French troops from Guadeloupe and the British experienced heavy losses until reinforcements arrived in June, 1796.

General Sir Ralph Abercromby relieved Grenada and St Vincent in 1796. He spent the rest of the year recovering the other islands with the exeption of Guadeloupe which remained in French hands. In the rebellious islands most of the French, free blacks, and mulattoes, as well as the Black Caribs from St Vincent, were deported to prevent further trouble.

In 1796 Abercromby turned against the Dutch colonies in Guiana where at least half the planters were British. Demerara, Essequibo and Berbice surrendered. The Dutch were allowed to continue their administration under the protection of the British. In 1799 Surinam surrendered, and in 1800 and 1801 Curaçao and St Eustatius surrendered to the British rather than fall into the hands of the French.

The Spanish had declared war on England in 1796 because of the presence of a British army in Hispaniola, the capture of Dutch colonies in South America where they did not want a large British presence, and an insult to the Spanish flag in Trinidad. An expedition under Abercromby

Battle of Trafalgar

quickly captured Trinidad (the Spanish Admiral, Apodoca, surrendered with little fighting) and then went on to attack Puerto Rico. However, it was decided that Puerto Rico was too strong and the attack was abandoned.

In Central America the Spanish prepared to attack the British settlement of Belize. The Baymen decided to defend it even though the British were able to send only 200 soldiers from Jamaica. With only about 350 men, Belize was successfully defended against a force of 2,500 Spaniards.

From Sweden and Denmark the British acquired St Bartholomew, St Thomas, St John and St Croix. Thus Britain held nearly all the colonies of France and her satellites, with the notable exceptions of St Domingue, Guadeloupe and the larger Spanish islands. However, in the Treaty of Amiens, 1802, Britain agreed to restore all these colonies to their former owners, except Trinidad which Spain ceded to Britain. Trinidad remained British until independence, although it retained much of its Spanish character.

The Napoleonic Wars

War between Britain and France was resumed in March, 1803. A strong force under Leclerc was sent out by Napoleon to curb the rebels in the French islands and to re-impose slavery.

The British set about recapturing what had been lost by the Treaty of Amiens. In 1803 St Lucia and Tobago were taken. Later in the year Demerara, Essequibo and Berbice surrendered, as did Surinam in 1804.

Napoleon then planned a full-scale attack on the West Indies under Admiral Villeneuve. Apart from the conquest of the British islands, he was instructed to attack the sugar convoy from Antigua in order to divert British ships from Europe to the Caribbean. Villeneuve achieved little. He began attacking the sugar convoy and had taken a few ships when Nelson arrived. Villeneuve hurried back to Europe where later Nelson caught him and decisively beat him in the Battle of Trafalgar, in October 1805, off the coast of Spain. This great victory gave the British conclusive command of the sea. The principal French colonies, Martinique and Guadeloupe, fell in 1809 and 1810. By 1810 all the French islands, with the exception of St Domingue, were in British hands. The Dutch islands of St Martin, Saba and St Eustatius surrendered in the same year.

In the Treaty of Paris, 1814, Britain restored to France all the captured colonies except St Lucia and Tobago. The Netherlands ceded Demerara, Essequibo and Berbice to Britain on payment of

£5,000,000. France gave back to Spain the eastern part of Hispaniola. The Treaty of Paris is noteworthy because it decided the possessions of the colonial powers in the Caribbean without further change until the independence movements of the 1960s.

The effects of the Revolutionary and Napoleonic Wars

The economy of the British West Indies was helped by the wars, but afterwards there was a slump which pointed to future difficulties.

The effect of the vacuum in trade left by the collapse of St Domingue has already been discussed. Exports from the other French islands were also cut. The British West Indies filled most of this vacuum. By 1794 the output of tropical products from the British West Indies had doubled, and prices were high and rising higher. New species of sugar cane, the Otaheite and Bourbon varieties, had been introduced into the British islands and they helped in the expansion of output. This produced a glut of sugar by 1806 and prices fell sharply. The situation was made worse by the Berlin Decrees of 1806 by which Napoleon closed the ports of Europe to British products. There was far too much sugar left in Britain for home consumption. However, leaks gradually appeared in Napoleon's system and British products found their way into Europe and sugar prices rose again. Foreign sugar, being carried in foreign ships, chiefly American, was also reaching Europe and depressing prices. The war between Britain and the United States between 1812-14 stopped this trade and helped British sugar prices reach all-time records.

Coffee became an important export for Jamaica for a short time during the wars with France. By 1796 output and prices for coffee had doubled, but they crashed in 1799 when other parts of the world increased their production and could undersell Jamaican coffee.

From 1790 to 1810, cotton in the British West Indies enjoyed a boom. It was expensive, sea-island cotton, fashionable for women's clothes, men's shirts and night-wear. At one time the British West Indies supplied nearly three-quarters of the cotton on the British market. However, in 1793, Eli Whitney invented the cotton gin which made it possible to clean the green seeds from the

Eli Whitney's original cotton gin

much hardier, short-staple boll which could be grown profitably throughout the southern United States. The gin could replace the labour of fourteen slaves. By 1810 South Carolina and Georgia cotton made up a quarter of all the exports of the United States, and British West Indian cotton declined sharply.

From 1810 to 1814 there was one more sugar boom for the British islands. In 1814 Britain restored nearly all of her conquests, and competition from the French islands began to build up again, but very slowly. Guiana and Trinidad were now British and they could have been used to produce sugar more cheaply than the other British islands, but they could not import slaves as the slave trade had been abolished after 1807. Moreover the high duties which had been levied in wartime and which were easily paid in periods of high prices, were continued after the war and crippled the sugar industry when prices dropped.

Jamaica benefited most from the wars. By 1812-13 she was exporting three-quarters of all British West Indian exports. This was because Jamaica was one of the only British colonies with vacant land on which to expand production. She also benefited from the increased trade with the Spanish after 1808. Spain herself was overrun in the Peninsular War and the supplying of her colonies was taken over to a large extent by Britain via Jamaica; for example, Cuba was open to British goods between 1812-14 because the United States was prevented from trading with Cuba by the war.

Punishment of slaves

4

The Control and Treatment of Slaves in the West Indies

The law and the slave

On the whole, slaves were treated better in the colonies of the Catholic and Latin countries, Portugal, Spain and France, than in those of the Protestant and Teutonic countries, the Netherlands, Denmark and Britain, for three reasons:

1 The link between the Mother Country and the colonies was much closer because of their strong centralised government. For example, Spain, Portugal and France all produced detailed slave codes of law. The Spanish code was particularly mild and explains why many British runaways tried to reach Spanish territory. In the British colonies there was a large measure of self-government by assemblies of white settlers who passed laws, such as the Barbados slave code, which were extremely stringent.

2 The clergy not only influenced the metropolitan authorities in drafting the slave codes, but they also tried to exert their authority over the slave owners on the spot. This influence was considerable through the pulpit, the confessional and, ultimately, excommunication. For example, the Catholic Church encouraged the marriage of slaves and opposed the separation of slave families. In many British islands the law expressly forbade slave marriages.

3 The Portuguese and Spaniards had far less race or colour prejudice than the British. Mating between white and black was common in all their

territories. Everywhere the rule was that the child took the status of its mother, but in Latin colonies the master usually manumitted the children and, sometimes, the mother. The best example of racial toleration in the New World was in the Portuguese colony of Brazil. Even before the liberation of 1888, free persons of African descent had reached positions of eminence. In British possessions, a person with the smallest strain of African blood was 'black' whether slave or free. It was rare for a master to manumit children born of a white father and slave mother, and he almost never manumitted the mother. In fact, in some British colonial codes, manumission was prohibited or made very difficult.

The French position was somewhere between the Spanish and the British. The French slave code was lenient in that it acknowledged that a slave had certain human rights, but in practice the more lenient provisions of the code were ignored. Moreover, the original more lenient code of 1685 was greatly modified in the eighteenth century. For example, by a law of 1730, manumission could only be granted with the written permission of the Governor and the *Intendant*. Intermarriage was very common in some French colonies, for example, St Domingue, but on the other hand the French authorities saw the racial line as clear. In 1766 the French Minister of Marine said of mulattoes: 'Slavery has imprinted an ineffaceable brand in their posterity; descendants of slaves can never enter the class of whites'.

In the British islands

The British islands considered slave legislation their own affair. In the early nineteenth century, when the British government tried to persuade colonial legislatures to pass amelioration measures, their proposals were largely ignored. For example, in response to the British Parliament's proposal that each island should keep a Register of Slaves, the Jamaican Assembly said in 1815: 'The Registry Bill assumes a right of legislation within the island upon a subject of mere municipal regulation'. The Barbados Legislature issued a petition containing the following words: 'We beg leave to deprecate in the strongest terms all legislative interference between master and slave, as leading to consequences directly opposite to the proposed object of those deluded philan-

thropists.......' In other words they were saying that they knew best about slave laws.

The fundamental difference in the legal position of slaves between the British and the French or Spanish islands was that in the former the slave had no rights under law. In some islands there was an official known as the 'Protector of Slaves', usually a local magistrate drawn from the planter class himself. The slave was unlikely to get any satisfaction from such a man in an appeal against his master.

The basis of the slave laws was fear. The severity of the laws increased as fear grew with the increase in the number of slaves. There had been Deficiency Laws which tried to keep a 'safe' ratio of 10:1 between slaves and whites, but these had been disregarded by the eighteenth century. In Jamaica the ratio was already 15:1 by 1700 and later in the century it passed 20:1. With so few whites holding down so many slaves, the fear of revolt was very great and any leniency was regarded as weakness.

Occasionally there were humanitarian governors and slave masters, but they were at loggerheads with the legislatures. In 1699 Christopher Codrington, the Younger, became Governor of the Leewards. He issued instructions 'to endeavour to get a law restraining inhuman severities, and punishing the wilful killing of negroes with death, and also to encourage the conversion of negroes'. This met with no response from the Legislature.

Joshua Steele was an humanitarian slave master who owned three plantations in Barbados from 1773 to 1790. He improved conditions for his slaves, allowing them to rent land from him and repay him with labour, and even paying them for some of their services. In 1783 he abolished arbitrary punishments on his estates and set up a system of trial by a jury of older slaves. In 1789 he manumitted many slaves who had worked loyally for him. His experiments had satisfactory results, but his death in 1791 was greeted with great relief by the other planters in Barbados.

Punishments were very severe. Slaves were executed or mutilated for relatively minor offences. The most cruel treatment of slaves was in Jamaica. It seems that where the planters enjoyed most prosperity, as in Jamaica, St Domingue and Cuba, the slaves were treated worst. At the opposite end must come Belize where the slave conditions were comparable to those of the free whites who were generally poor. Slaves and whites often worked

Inspecting slaves

shoulder to shoulder in logwood cutting and became comrades, so much so that in 1798 the slaves defended Belize side by side with their masters against the Spanish and showed no inclination to revolt or escape. Many were rewarded with their freedom. Although Barbados had a harsh slave code, in practice, the slaves were treated comparatively well.

The powers and responsibilities of the master over the slave

Although slave laws varied from island to island, basically a master had absolute authority over his slave with some important reservations. A slave was a property, a 'thing'; a law of 1674 in Jamaica spoke of slaves as 'goods and chattels'. A chattel is defined as a movable possession, or something to be used for a mortgage for a debt. Slaves were referred to as if they were inanimate things, for example, 'one tonne or three slaves' in a contract of 1676. The slave was the personal possession of his master who had almost absolute power over him. He could sell his slave, transfer him as payment of a debt, use him as security for a debt, and make all these transactions against the will of the slave. Usually the value of an estate included the slaves on it, and a slave was sold with the land, buildings and equipment.

The power was 'almost' absolute, because the master did not legally have the power of life and death over his slave. Some planters found this an unwelcome interference with property rights which in the West Indies were regarded as inviolate. It was not a capital offence for a master to kill his slave wilfully. In 1724 Governor Hart of Antigua tried to have it made a capital offence, but the Antiguan Legislature would not agree. The 1724 Act in Antigua tried 'to prevent the inhumane murdering, maiming and castrating of slaves by cruel and barbarous persons (as has been much practised) by laying a fine on those guilty'. However, the offence was so lightly regarded that the usual fine in Antigua was between £100 and £300. A law passed in Jamaica in 1739 said,

> Whoever shall kill a slave out of wilfulness, wantonness or bloody-mindedness, shall suffer three months imprisonment and pay £50 to the owner of the slave. If the party so offending be a servant he or she shall have on the bare back thirty-nine lashes.

Later, however, the killing of a slave became a capital offence. The first hanging of a white planter for murdering a slave in the British West Indies was in 1776 in Grenada, but a more famous case was that of Arthur Hodge in 1811. He was a slave owner from Tortola and a member of the Council

33

of the Virgin Islands, who was notorious for his cruelty to slaves. He murdered a slave through excessive punishment and was brought to justice. Governor Elliott feared that justice would not be done by a jury of Hodge's fellow planters, so he went to Tortola in a warship to observe the trial. After twelve hours the jury returned the verdict of guilty, but a majority recommended mercy. Elliott quickly proclaimed martial law because he could see that the white inhabitants would not carry out the death penalty. He ordered the execution and Hodge was hanged in May, 1811.

In an equally famous case, another planter was allowed literally 'to get away with murder'. This was the case of Edward Huggins of Nevis. In 1810 he marched twenty of his slaves to the market place in Charlestown and had them whipped by two expert whippers in the presence of his two sons. One female died and several others were mutilated by the lashes. Edward, but not his sons, was brought to trial. It was stated that one man had received 365 lashes, and another woman 292 lashes. Huggins was acquitted. Five magistrates who had witnessed the whippings, but had not intervened to stop them, were deprived of their offices. In 1817 Huggins was again acquitted for cruelty against slaves. These two cases show that, even after abolition, whites were not ready to

Owners with new acquisitions

regard the murder of a slave as a capital offence although the law held that it was.

Some planters also felt that they could mutilate their slaves at will. The law stated that a master could not legally 'maim, emasculate, dismember or mutilate' his slaves. Fines were imposed for these offences. Some councils had tried to legalise mutilation, although the British authorities were against this. For example, a Bermudan law of 1705 was banned by the Council for Trade and Plantations as being 'inhumane and contrary to all Christian laws'. In the 1730s a law was passed in the Bahamas which laid down that a person mutilating a slave had to pay £2 to the church. In Jamaica the mutilation of slaves was allowed by law and a bill attempting to ban it in 1784 was rejected by the Assembly.

Responsibilities went with power. Masters were legally responsible for the slaves' food, shelter, clothes, medical treatment and care in old age. In times of plenty, slaves were usually given an adequate and varied diet because it was in the master's interest to keep his slaves healthy and strong. In times of famine they always suffered first. Slaves usually received salt beef or salt fish every day, as well as other food. Housing the slaves was the master's responsibility, and he provided the materials with which the slaves built their own quarters. Usually these were mud and wattle huts. Two working suits of clothes made of a coarse, cheap cloth called 'Osnaburg' were provided per year.

There was no law that said a master should provide his slaves with their own provision grounds, but this was almost universal practice, especially in the large islands like Jamaica, Trinidad and Guiana. Even in Barbados, where land was very scarce, it was common practice. According to Bryan Edwards, writing at the end of the eighteenth century, the Jamaican slave law required a master to set aside one-tenth of his acreage, quite apart from grounds, for slave provisions - Jamaica could afford to. It was in the master's interest to provide grounds because they were useful in supplementing the food rations of the slaves without costing anything. They also increased the variety of the slaves' food, as the slaves usually chose to grow choicer food crops. They helped the master by keeping the slave happy, giving him an interest, and keeping him out of trouble in his free time in the evening. Usually slaves were permitted to sell the produce

Jamaican market

of their grounds in a Sunday market and this was exceedingly popular, both as a means of raising a little money with which to buy personal items, as a pleasurable recreation, and as a way of passing on news.

Legally a slave could not own any property but they often had a few possessions, such as extra clothes or jewellery. A Jamaican law of 1711 forbade slaves from keeping any livestock. This was the general rule throughout the islands. A slave could not grow or sell sugar, cotton or coffee on his own account, but could sell things made with his own labour like baskets, ropes and earthenware pots. A slave did not own his own labour, of course, and he could not hire himself out without his owner's permission. If the master did hire out his slave, the fee belonged to the master. In the case of artisan slaves, hiring out became common before abolition, and in many cases the master allowed the slave to keep some of the fee. These slaves were known as 'jobbing' slaves.

A slave had no rights of his own in law and no redress of grievance against his master. The evidence of a slave against a freeman was not permitted in a court of law except when special provision was made, as in a Special Act in Antigua in 1737. The justification for denying a slave these rights was that because of his 'baseness' a slave could not be trusted or expected to tell the truth.

A case could be brought on behalf of a slave by another freeman, but this was rare. The cases against Huggins and Hodge were brought by the authorities for political reasons, to show that amelioration measures were being taken in their islands.

On the estate, justice for the slave was arbitrary as it was in the hands of the master. This was contrary to the principles of British justice: the need to show that an offence had been committed; the right of a fair trial; and fixed penalties for certain offences if guilty. A slave could be charged in court if the offence concerned the public outside the estate. If he was found guilty and a punishment was imposed which deprived the owner of the slave's labour, whether by death, mutilation or imprisonment, the owner received compensation. This was usually between £35 and £50, depending on the time and the value of the

35

slave. In a terrible case in Barbados in 1693, Alice Mills was paid ten guineas compensation for carrying out the sentence of the Commissioners and castrating forty-two of her slaves. Sentences imposed by the courts were often carried out by the owners of the slaves.

Manumission

Slavery was for life in the British islands and manumission was entirely dependent on the owner. In Barbados, by a law of 1739, deposits had to be paid before slaves could be manumitted. This was copied by Antigua in 1761 and St Vincent in 1767. Later in the century, it became a universal condition for manumission in the British islands, both to discourage it and to make sure the slave did not become a burden on public funds. From the £100 deposit required in St Vincent the manumitted slave was paid a dole of £4 per month, so there was an humanitarian side to it as well.

Manumission was not always popular with slaves because life was very hard for them. By a Jamaican law of 1717, manumitted slaves had to carry a certificate of freedom and wear a badge with a blue cross on their right shoulder at all times. It was very easy to lose the certificate or for the authorities to find fault with it, and it made it difficult and dangerous for the manumitted slave to move from one parish to another. It was made illegal for a freed slave to work alongside a slave as it was felt that this would lead to resentment and rebellion.

A slave could buy his manumission with his owner's consent, and the price was fixed by the owner. This was in complete contrast to the Spanish law on manumission which allowed it to be done without the owner's consent at the price of the slave at the time of purchase. The manumission of slaves too old and feeble to work was frowned upon, but it did take place and was one reason why the authorities insisted on deposits before manumission. By law, owners were required to maintain their slaves when too old to work.

Slave marriage

In the British islands the law prohibited slave marriage. This was denying the slave a basic human right, one upheld in Christianity. There were four chief reasons why colonial legislatures would not allow slave marriage:

1 It was an extension of the principle of the slave having no rights outside those that his master permitted him. A slave, therefore, had no right to a wife and a family.
2 It would give the slave the security and love that come from family ties and take away his dependence on, and control by, his master.
3 It was another step in degrading the slave by denying him basic human needs and feelings.
4 The law held that a slave could not enter into any contract or promise. Therefore, in law, a slave marriage had to be null and void. However, on estates with strongly Christian masters, slave marriages were permitted. The offspring of slave marriages or casual unions were slaves. But very few slave children survived infancy.

A slave woman often had to accept a union with a freeman, because the proportion of white women to men was very small and it was considered unnatural for a white man to live by himself. These unions were casual or semi-permanent and marriage was either illegal or banned by convention.

Education

In most islands slaves were not allowed to be taught to read and write. This was difficult to enforce as the slaves saw education as a means of bettering their position, and some masters realised that education would improve the service their slaves could perform and increase their value. However, the general feeling amongst the planters was that slaves would be more subservient if kept ignorant.

Reading and writing for slaves was resisted in law right up to the time of emancipation. For example, in 1817, General Murray, the Governor of Demerara, told John Smith that he would be banished from the territory if he taught a slave to read. Slaves did learn to read and write, and as the planters feared, it made ideas like freedom and equality current among them. 'Daddy' Sharpe, the Jamaican hero, is a very famous example of a literate slave who used his education to spread the message of freedom in 1831 and 1832.

Christianity

In nearly all the British islands the law expressly forbade slaves to become Christians. This was one of the most hotly-debated issues between the Mother Country and the planters, who thought

Missionaries and slaves

to convert the slaves to Christianity but they were persecuted by the planters, especially in the larger islands. In 1786, in Barbados, the Methodist Meeting House was stoned. In 1793 the St Vincent Legislature passed an Act against itinerant Methodist ministers by forbidding anyone to preach who had not been resident on the island for at least a year. The Consolidated Slave Act of 1808 in Jamaica forbade Methodist and Nonconformist missionaries from having slaves in their chapels, but this act was overruled by the King. The strongest statement against missionaries came from the Governor of British Guiana in 1812. He wrote that they were 'ignorant and hot-headed fanatics anxious to convert everything into persecution.....they degraded the white inhabitants.... they produced discontent amongst the negroes'. As emancipation drew near, the struggle intensified until it erupted into widespread violence against the missionaries in Jamaica in 1832-33.

that Christianity would lead to emancipation, or deprive the owner of full rights over his slaves. The planters also argued that missionaries spread dangerous ideas like freedom and brotherhood. In 1698 the Bermuda Assembly argued that they wanted slaves to be converted to Christianity, but that it led to 'insolence, obstinacy and incorrigibleness'. A law of Jamaica of 1696 said that slaves could be baptised, but it would not make them free.

Ligon, an early traveller in Barbados, reported a discussion he had with a planter on this subject in 1650. The planter said that he could not make a Christian a slave by the laws of England. Ligon pointed out that he was asking it to be done the other way round, making a slave a Christian. The planter replied that there was no difference. If he was a Christian, he could not be a slave.

Opinion in the Mother Country held that it was the duty of the planters to convert their slaves to Christianity. In 1685, King James II of England resolved that all Negroes should be baptised and considered that their masters were sinning in not allowing it.

The Anglican Church was not involved as it was the Church of the planters and took their side. In 1658 the first Quaker missionaries arrived to convert the slaves. In 1676 the Barbados Assembly passed a law prohibiting Quakers from having slaves at their meetings. In the eighteenth century, Baptist, Methodist and Moravian missionaries tried

Punishments

Both the punishments meted out on the estates and those imposed by the courts were very severe. Their aim was to deter others and not to make 'the punishment fit the crime'.

The death penalty was awarded for relatively minor offences. An extreme example of this was a law of Barbados in 1688 which made slave thefts of more than one shilling punishable by death. The death penalty could be inflicted in many barbarous ways apart from hanging. Breaking slaves into pieces and burning them was recorded in Montserrat in 1699; being hanged, drawn and quartered was also a common punishment for runaway slaves. In Jamaica in 1740 a punishment for a slave striking a white man was burning to death.

Although the Mother Country decreed that mutilation was contrary to all Christian laws, it was nonetheless permitted. A common punishment for striking a white man was cutting off the hand. The two chief crimes that these horrible punishments were intended to deter were running away and rebelling. There was a scale of punishments for running away, according to how long the slave absented himself from work. For example, in 1717 the Barbados Legislature prescribed cutting off a foot for one month's absence, rising to death for a year's absence. Penalties for harbouring runaways were also severe. In St Vincent, by a law of 1767,

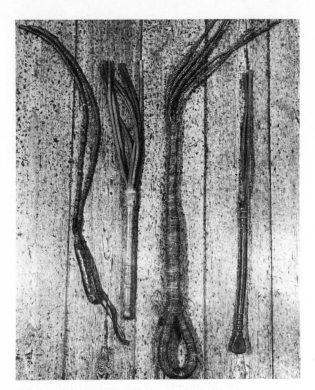

Instruments of torture

fifty lashes were prescribed for the first offence, rising to 150 lashes for the third offence.

For revolt, or even plotting revolt, the maximum penalty, death by being hanged, drawn and quartered, was inflicted. One of the earliest slave revolts in the British West Indies was in Barbados in 1649. Eighteen of the rebels were executed.

Of course, the most common punishment, even for trivial offences, was whipping. If a slave did not step aside for a white man in the street, he could be whipped. It was meant to be restricted to thirty-nine lashes for one offence at one time, but many more lashes were given and such uncontrolled whippings led to mutilation or death. For obvious reasons fining or imprisonment were not punishments applicable to slaves.

In the French and Spanish islands

The Code Noir

The control and treatment of slaves in the French West Indies was dictated from France. In 1685, all the previous slave laws were collected into a single code called the *Code Noir* (Black Code). It was inspired by the ideas of Colbert, although he was dead (1683) before it was finally produced. It lasted until 1804 when it was replaced by the *Code Napoleon,* the basis for the legal system throughout the French empire. The *Code Noir* was meant to be strictly applied, but in practice the milder measures were disregarded, and many modifications were made to the separate clauses in the following century.

However, basically the code survived in its original form.

1 All slaves to be baptised.

2 Slaves not to be worked on Sundays or Holy Days.

3 Slave marriage to be encouraged. The owner's consent must be given.

4 Sexual intercourse between master and his slave to be punished by the confiscation of the slave. If between another man and the slave, a fine to be imposed. Children of such unions would take the status of the mother.

5 Rations and clothers to be provided. Old and sick slaves to be fed and maintained.

6 Slaves to be forbidden to own property and anything they acquired to belong to their owner.

7 Promises, contracts and gifts made by slaves to be null and void.

8 Slaves to be forbidden to sell sugar, or any other produce, without their owner's permission.

9 Death penalty to be inflicted for striking master or mistress, and in some cases any free person.

10 Absenteeism of one month to be punished by cutting off ears and branding on the shoulder. Absent two times in one month to be punished by cutting off the buttock and branding the other shoulder. Absent three in one month to be punished by death.

11 Owner to be compensated if slave executed on owner's own denunciation.

12 Torture and mutilation to be prohibited under penalty of confiscation of the slave.

13 Slaves to be regarded as movable property, and liable to be sold apart from the rest of their family.

14 The plantation and the slaves to be regarded as one.

15 Owners and drivers to treat slaves humanely.

16 Owners to have the right to free a slave after twenty years' service.

17 Manumitted slaves to have the same rights as free persons.

Thus, in general, the *Code Noir* was more humane than British law. For example, Christianity, marriage, manumission and humane treatment were expressly ordered. Rations and clothing were precisely fixed. Mutilation was expressly forbidden. However, punishments were equally harsh and in many other ways French laws were similar to those in the British colonies, although the slaves were not so much at the mercy of their owner because the rules of treatment were more clearly prescribed.

The Spanish Code

The Spanish had a slave code for their European territories before they acquired possessions in the New World and they simply transferred this code to the Indies. It was drawn up in the thirteenth century and based on the Code of Justinian, a Christian Roman Emperor. The Spanish slave code was called *Las Siete Partidas*.

The basic difference between the Spanish slave code and other slave laws was that the Spanish acknowledged that slavery was contrary to natural justice and that it was an evil, but a necessary evil for the economic development of the colonies. This admission caused endless trouble in the Spanish colonies, as it implied that freedom was the natural state of man and gave the slaves their justification for revolting. The first slave revolt was recorded in Hispaniola as early as 1522 and, thereafter, there was a steady stream of revolts in Spanish territories. The authorities recognised the right of slaves to seek their freedom, so they tried to remove the danger of revolt by other means than repressive legislation.

Charles V attempted to enforce a ratio of 3:1 or 4:1 slaves to freemen. He also tried to enforce a minimum proportion of female slaves and, by encouraging marriage, to create a settled family life for the slaves and make them less inclined to revolt. The Spanish slave laws promoted more humane treatment for slaves and led to a far larger proportion of free blacks and mulattoes. For example, in Puerto Rico by the end of the eighteenth century free coloureds outnumbered slaves, and in Cuba they were nearly equal in numbers.

A slave could appeal to the courts against illtreatment. He could purchase his freedom without the consent of his owner merely by repaying his purchase price, if necessary by periodic repayments. The slave had a right to his ground with the consent of his owner. He had the right to marriage without the consent of his owner.

The master had to instruct the slave in the Christian faith and set aside certain days for this purpose. Slaves had to be given Sundays and Holy Days free from work. The master had to provide clothing and food, and care for the slave in his old age. The owner could not kill his slave or ill-treat him to the point of suffering. Specifically, he could not overwork or underfeed his slaves.

Finally the Spanish code required all judges to promote liberty because liberty was natural. In Spanish possessions, consequently, the slaves could find the courts on their side. This could never be the case in the British islands.

Other forms of slave control

A slave was restrained in many other ways than by the law. In the West Indies there was little need to restrain a slave physically, that is, by chains, but it could be done if necessary. Geography usually provided all the physical restraint that was needed. The small islands were like prisons in themselves, and only in the large islands could a slave escape with any hope of remaining free for long.

It was common to lock up slaves at night. Chaining slaves during the day was a punishment which was avoided if possible, because a chained slave could not work so well. Chaining was almost always restricted to field slaves. Popular ideas of slaves being chained together are misleading. The ball and chain round a slave's leg was more common. These physical restraints were not necessary in the fields because field slaves were always under the eye of a driver with a whip. Factory slaves were more trusted, but often the overseer was present or some free artisans. In any case, factory slaves were regimented in what they were doing and could not easily hide disaffection or troublemaking.

Colour was also a physical restraint for a slave. In the British islands, especially, to be black was to be a slave. In a small island with very few free coloured people, an escaping slave would have little chance of remaining free. In a very small island, like Grand Cayman, every slave would be personally known. Thus the size of the island was an important factor in slave control.

A socio-economic system was used by slave owners in the West Indies to control slaves. This was a class system whereby obedience, loyalty and good service could be rewarded by promotion. A slave may have had no chance of freedom, but he could make his life easier by hard work and good behaviour and be given an easier job. The classes of slaves from bottom to top were: field slaves; factory slaves; artisan slaves and domestic slaves. Within these classes there were also different grades. An artisan slave might hold a more prestigious position than a domestic slave so there could be overlapping. For example, an artisan slave might be used as a jobbing slave, being hired out because of his special skill. In some cases he might be allowed to live out in town, be allowed to keep a share of his fee and arrange his own accommodation. This was a very coveted position and the reward for loyal service and trustworthiness. By this scale of promotion and rewards, slave owners could control their slaves and expect good work and obedience from them. One of the best examples of a well-rewarded and highly-trusted slave was Toussaint l'Ouverture, entrusted by his master, Monsieur Breda, with all the livestock on the estate.

Socially, domestic slaves carried the most prestige as they often worked unsupervised. They could be entrusted with the master's valuables and could look after his children. They were allowed to wear better clothes and female domestics could often wear necklaces, earrings and bracelets. They learned to sew and cook, and possibly to read and write. Domestic slaves were usually loyal and the least willing to rebel because they had the most to lose.

On an estate the owner was like the father of a huge family. The dependence of a slave on his 'father' enabled the owner to exercise another form of social control. Not only did the owner provide shelter, food and clothing, but he also ordered the whole life of the slaves, in and outside working hours, and the lives and futures of slave children. A kind master could bend the law and permit marriage, Christianity and education, which made a difference to the slaves' life and happiness. For free time, festivals, music and dancing, the slaves were dependent on the goodwill of their master. Unfortunately in the British West Indies, the patriarchal nature of slave society was often missing because of absenteeism, and the slaves suffered from being under the ultimate control of an estate manager or attorney who did not regard them as his 'family'.

The greatest force in restraining a slave from seeking his liberty was probably economic. The economic responsibilities facing a free man of finding food, clothes and shelter for himself and his family did not apply to the slave. It was the argument put up in favour of the apprenticeship system in 1833; that a period was needed for the slave to adjust to fending for himself. It was also a reason why manumission was so uncommon. A manumitted slave had difficulty surviving in a slave society and thus many did not want manumission.

In a British West Indian slave society it was very hard for a manumitted slave to find a wage-earning occupation. In the eighteenth century, he could not expect to earn more than two shillings per week unless exceptionally talented, and he could not live as well as he had done as a slave. It was economically impossible for an ex-slave without other means to fend for himself in town. Subsistence living was the answer, but in many islands an ex-slave could not own real estate, but only lease it.

A Negro festival

A slave could be conditioned psychologically to accept servitude. Everything about his life reminded him that he was inferior in society. This was partly by deliberate design. Planters wanted to humiliate slaves in order to crush their spirit and make them submissive. In most cases it worked. Slaves began to feel inferior, as if there was something innate in their minds and bodies which fitted them to slavery.

But there was a danger in this kind of psychological control. Some slaves could not be broken mentally and, instead of submissiveness, the opposite resulted. The continual restriction of freedom and attempts to enforce a feeling of inferiority would cause smouldering resentment which would break out into rebellion, as in the case of a slave like Boukman.

Planters used culture to force inferiority on slaves. First of all, they created the idea that Africa was uncivilised, and that the slaves were taken from the 'jungle' or 'bush', and that they were 'savages'. This idea quickly won acceptance. Creole slaves regarded 'guinea birds' or 'bozals' (slaves fresh from Africa) as inferior. They were often more servile and bewildered in a strange new world. However, some bozals never gave this impression. The Joloffs from Senegambia were regarded as an 'incorrigible race' from the very beginning of the slave trade.

But if the slaves from Africa were really inferior, why was there the need to destroy their cultural identity as soon as possible? This was the second stage in which culture played a part in controlling the slaves. Their African cultural inheritance was deliberately destroyed to make them more controllable; an admission of its strength. African culture was broken by the separation of tribes as soon as possible in the barracoons, on the ships or in the markets; definitely before the slaves reached the estates. African slaves had usually lost their African names, languages, religions and customs after one generation in the West Indies. With the passing of these they lost their traditions, security and confidence and accepted the slave system. The slaves did not try to preserve their culture from Africa because the planters had succeeded in persuading them that it was inferior.

The third stage in using culture to control the slaves lay in not substituting a new culture in place of the one which had been destroyed. The slave was left in a cultural vacuum which he filled by substituting a culture of his own, a West Indian culture. For example; slaves in the British islands were legally denied Christianity. Therefore they evolved a mixture of beliefs, Christian, African tribal and superstitious. Slaves were also denied reading and writing. The language they heard in place of their tribal tongue was English in a mixture of orders and abuse, including plenty of cursing. Amongst the slaves there developed a patois, a mixture of English, French, Indian, African tribal and Creole. After generations this had a right to be called a language with its own words and grammar. However, in the period of slavery, the West Indian cultural forms lacked self-confidence and could not break the feeling of being neither one nor the other.

The slave was thus controlled by culture in that his African cultural inheritance was destroyed, and he was not allowed to participate fully in the white man's world. The cultural vacuum was unbearable for the slave. He had to grasp some culture so that he felt he belonged to society. Usually he tried to grasp the white man's culture and to do this he had to obey the white man's rules and accept his station in life in the white man's world.

Samuel Sharpe

5

Resistance and Revolt

Response to slavery

Submission

There were about fifty major slave risings spread over 300 years, representing only about two risings per territory. Of course, some territories like Jamaica had many risings, while others had none at all. Submission was obtained in two ways. Firstly, it was enforced by harsh suppression. The punishments for running away and rebellion were so brutal that it is surprising that there were any risings at all. They were acts of desperation and prove how much West Indian slaves hated slavery and would resist it. Secondly, owners offered various incentives to encourage submissiveness.

In the West Indies, the Ashanti were rated the best slaves for hard work, obedience and loyalty. However, even they had their limits. In 1701 Christopher Codrington, Governor of the Leewards, wrote to the Lords of Trade and Plantations that although they were the most faithful, they could also be the most revengeful if they were wronged. Slaves from the 'Popo' region west of Dahomey who were embarked at Whydah were reputed to be both hard-working and submissive. They were nicknamed 'pawpaws' in the West Indies.

Colonial historians of the planter class point to the cheerfulness of slaves as evidence of contentedness with their lot. For example, in his *Speeches on the West Indies, 1833,* Barrett says 'There is not a

A slave hunt

7 Refusal to work, which was much more serious. This was not often attempted by individuals, but by groups of slaves, or the whole labour force in the form of a 'strike'. However, the consequences of such a strike could be dire if it was construed as a conspiracy or plot to rebel for which the punishment would be mutilation or execution.

Legally in the British West Indies a slave could not complain about his treatment. However, as a form of passive resistance which was really a strike in disguise, the slaves would make a mass protest to a magistrate. In Spanish and French islands complaints were allowed in law and were a frequently used device for disrupting the slave system.

8 Running away, which was the only way to escape slavery. This could only be attempted with any hope of success in the large or mountainous territories like Cuba, Hispaniola, Guiana, Puerto Rico, Jamaica, Trinidad, Guadeloupe, Martinique and Dominica, and even in most of these islands chances of remaining free were very slim indeed.

9 Slave suicide which was common from the beginning. The most famous example of slave suicide was that of 400 slaves on Guadeloupe who, in 1802, put themselves in a fort and blew it up rather than submit to the re-introduction of slavery. Slaves most prone to commit suicide were reputed to be the Ibos from the Eastern Region of Nigeria.

Slaves saved their children from the horrors of slavery by infanticide. Slave children were frequently neglected and died as a result. The parents often looked on this as a merciful release and made little effort to prevent it.

peasant in the world that walks abroad with a more contented countenance and a more confident bearing than the colonial slave'. Others drew their evidence from occasions like the landing of slaves after the Middle Passage, or slave festivals at Christmas or Easter. Writing of a slave's happiness was often a deliberate falsification of his conditions. No slave submitted voluntarily to his servitude; submission was only apparent and not real.

Passive resistance

In order to defeat the slave system the slaves used various kinds of passive resistance. Examples of such methods are:
1 Slow working and malingering.
2 Pretending ignorance.
3 Deliberate carelessness, or carelessness resulting from a casual attitude which usually went undetected but caused trouble later.
4 Pretending to be ill.
5 Telling lies to avoid doing something or to create confusion.
6 Carelessness with the owner's property.

Active resistance

Major acts of active resistance were rare because of the penalties, but there were many major acts of sabotage.
1 Damaging and destroying the owner's property by disabling the farm machinery, from breaking machetes to burning the mill and the ripe cane. It was difficult to detect the culprit unless he was actually observed.
2 Maiming and killing of livestock. Again a slave could easily get away with this.
3 Petty stealing of estate property caused inconvenience and expense to the owner as well as personal gain to the slave.
4 The maiming or murdering of other slaves was not so common, but it did go on. To prevent this,

and to guard against even more serious offences, slaves were not allowed to carry offensive weapons, even large sticks, except under close supervision.

5 Murdering the whites on the estate. Many slaves wanted to do this but their chances of getting away with it were very remote and they could expect no mercy if even suspected of such a crime.

Revolt and marronage

If we take the definition of a revolution as being a successful revolt, there were only three revolts in the West Indies which could possibly be termed 'revolutions'. These are the Maroon Revolt in Jamaica, the rising of the Bush Negros in Surinam and the Haitian Revolution.

There were many revolts in West Indian history which did not turn into revolutions for the following reasons.

1 Slave revolts were often acts of desperation undertaken by slaves who knew that they had no chance of success. This is particularly true of many risings in Jamaica, for example the 1754 revolt in Crawford Town.

2 Slaves took advantage of times of war or times when the authorities had other difficulties on their hands to revolt, but when conditions returned to normal the revolts were easily suppressed. Examples of such revolts are Tacky's Rebellion of 1760 and the Second Maroon War of 1795.

3 Inadequate preparation on the part of the slaves was a frequent cause of failure. Many slave revolts were spontaneous, perhaps arising from an act of brutality in the fields, and can hardly be called revolts. But they often spread.

The rising in St John in the Virgin Islands in 1733 was one in which the slaves achieved their immediate objectives and even enjoyed a short time of freedom before the inevitable force arrived to suppress them.

4 Frequently revolts failed because a slave remained loyal to his master, perhaps to ingratiate himself and be rewarded. The two famous examples of this are Tacky's Rebellion in Jamaica in 1760, and the 1823 Rebellion in Demerara. The former began successfully, but was sabotaged by a slave from the Esher Estate warning the authorities. The Demerara rebellion was betrayed at the outset by Joseph Packer, a house slave who informed his master who informed the Governor. House slaves were the least likely to take part in rebellion and consequently the most likely to betray the other slaves.

Negro insurrection

44

5 Often the ringleaders of the rebellions could not agree amongst themselves. Frequently the split was between extremists and moderates. The extremists wanted the extermination of the whites, blacks to take over the properties and even complete independence under black government. The moderates wanted non-violence (an almost impossible hope in a slave rising) and pressure on the authorities to introduce better conditions. Moderates were out of place in slave risings. The authorities certainly would not compromise or show mercy to slaves in rebellion, and they were not interested in distinguishing motives and aims.

The two rebellions in Guiana illustrate this. In 1763, Coffy only wanted the partition of Berbice, probably on the lines of Surinam where the blacks held the interior and the whites the coastal lands. Akara realised that no compromise with the whites was possible and wanted to inflict total military defeat on them. Again, in the 1823 rebellion, Quamina was a moderate who wanted non-violence. Many of the slaves of John Smith's mission followed him but others were more realistic and saw that there could be no half measures. This division made the rebellion lack strength and direction and it was suppressed.

6 The basic reason why revolts did not succeed was simply that the authorities had superior arms and forces. Slaves had no military training and many could not use firearms even if available. Sooner or later the rebel slaves would come up against a disciplined, well-armed force which could easily put them to flight.

The Haitian Revolution succeeded partly because Toussaint trained his black troops in the Spanish army; his supplies of weapons came from outside and could always be renewed (at one time he received 30,000 guns from the United States) and the slaves had enough time and campaigns to develop into seasoned troops.

Revolts against slavery

This is not intended to be an exhaustive list, but was selected to show the spread of the revolts in the West Indies during the years of slavery.

1522 Hispaniola

This was the first slave revolt in the West Indies. Numbers of slaves had exceeded the ratios recommended by Charles V, and the Spaniards were expecting trouble. Several Spaniards were killed,
but the slaves were quickly brought under control and some were executed.

1639 Providence

This was the first slave revolt in the British West Indies. In spite of Providence's being a Puritan settlement, some masters treated their slaves badly. The revolt was a surprise as there were only about ninety slaves to 500 whites on the island at the time. Obviously the revolt could not succeed, but it made the British elsewhere conscious of slave/white ratios and of the need to maintain militias.

1649 Barbados

This revolt could have been serious. The slave population of Barbados had been allowed to grow without check. There were serious difficulties in supplying such large numbers and slave conditions, generally, were poor.

1685 Jamaica

This was a serious slave revolt in which several white settlers were killed. Some slaves, who had escaped into the mountains, defied the militia. Martial law was proclaimed and kept in force for several months.

1687 Antigua

This occurred in spite of Antigua's good treatment of slaves. Its suppression was brutal as the slaves were hunted down on horseback and taken dead or alive.

1725 Nevis

A plot for a slave rising was discovered and two slaves were executed.

1733 St John

This was a very serious rising in this Danish island, where conditions were particularly bad. Forty whites were killed. English volunteers from Tortola and St Kitts failed to put down the rising. Eventually a strong French force from Martinique succeeded and many slaves were executed.

1760 Jamaica

Tacky's Rebellion. This was the most serious revolt in Jamaican history to date. It broke out in St Mary and spread throughout the island. Tacky was formerly an African chief from Ghana. He planned the rising carefully with some of his fellow Ashanti, and oaths were taken. They killed about sixty whites, mainly at the beginning of the rebellion. Then they faced the militia bravely, encouraged by the obeah-men who gave them a powder which they said would make them immune to injury. When it did not work many slaves surrendered, but Tacky and twenty-five others took to the hills where they were hunted down by Maroons. This caused ill-feeling in the future between slaves and Maroons. About 400 slaves lost their lives in the various risings in Jamaica at this time. About 600 slaves were deported to the Bay of Honduras and sold to the Baymen.

1773 Belize

Two whites were murdered on the Belize River in May, 1773, and the revolt was not put down until November. About fifty armed slaves were involved. They killed eight whites altogether and captured five settlements.

1770,1771,1774 Tobago

There was a series of serious slave risings in Tobago which eventually ended when the ring-leaders were brutally executed. The likelihood of revolts was great in Tobago as the slave/white ratio was over 20:1.

1763,1772 Surinam

There were two slave revolts in this Dutch colony. The first revolt had links with the more serious rising in neighbouring colony of Berbice and can really be considered as the same revolt. Both the 1763 and 1772 revolts were serious, especially the former which nearly succeeded.

Revolts became more frequent throughout the British West Indies as emancipation approached. Many slaves mistook abolition for emancipation, and many thought that emancipation had been granted by the British government, but was being withheld by their owners. In Jamaica in 1803, 1807 and 1831 there were slave risings for these reasons. In Trinidad there were risings in 1819,1825 and 1829. Again, emancipation was the chief reason, but the shortage of slaves also meant that the existing slaves were very overworked. The mort-ality rate of 1 in 23 per day was very much higher than in any of the other islands. There were revolts in Barbados in 1804 and 1816.

Marronage

The word 'maroon' is a corruption of the French word 'marron' which in turn comes from the Spanish, 'cimarron' which means 'dweller on a mountain top' (Sp. *cima*, 'mountain top'). The Spaniards first applied the word to Indians, but gradually blacks predominated amongst the Maroons and so the usage changed.

Maroons originated in Hispaniola. Very early on, slaves ran away to the mountains and forests, intermarried with Arawak women and allied with the Indians against the Spaniards. From then on they were a constant problem to the Spanish authorities. A typical example was the Arawak *cacique*, Henriques, who rebelled in 1519 and took refuge in the mountains of Hispaniola. He defeated several parties of Spaniards sent out to capture him. Soon other Arawaks and runaway slaves joined him. Finally, in 1533, the Spanish authorities made a treaty with Henriques which gave him a grant of land and a guarantee of freedom. In return he promised to surrender escaped slaves.

Thereafter the Maroons in Hispaniola were strong enough to maintain their freedom. As early as 1545, their numbers had reached 7,000 and outside Santo Domingo they were a considerable force to be reckoned with. The early history of the Maroons in Hispaniola is interesting because it established both the pattern of Maroon settle-ments in Jamaica and Surinam and the response of the authorities to them.

Maroons overran the Spanish island of Puerto Rico after the emigration of whites to the mainland in the 1520s and '30s. The escaped slaves inter-married with Carib women from the neighbouring islands of the Leewards. Again they became a formidable force in the island.

However, the largest numbers of Maroons in the Spanish territories surrounding the Caribbean were in the Isthmus of Panama, where the escaped slaves from Darien and the towns of the Isthmus found refuge. They were joined by slaves captured by the pirates from the Spanish islands and rel-eased on the coasts of the Isthmus. They lived in small towns and isolated villages in the Panama forests. Drake found a Maroon town surrounded by a moat and a thick mud wall. Inside were three streets and fifty-five houses. The Spanish actually recorded a larger town of 217 large houses. The population must have been considerable because many families lived in one house.

The Maroons of the Isthmus gave invaluable help to Francis Drake on many occasions. In 1573 they advised him of the convoy of treasure for

Nombre de Dios. Twenty-five Maroons actually joined him on his raid. Later they showed Drake the Pacific Ocean.

There were Maroons on Dominica at a much later date. These posed problems for the English after they had assumed control. In the War of American Independence, the French supplied arms to the Dominica Maroons who killed many whites. The English had to recruit a special force to bring them under control in 1786. However, they remained a problem into the next century as their boldness and ferocity increased. In 1812 the new Governor, George Robert Ainslie, offered freedom to those who would surrender, but in vain. The successes of the Maroons made it difficult to control the slaves, and in the end Ainslie gave orders for their extermination. This was done, but as a result he was recalled in 1814. In Dominica, unlike other parts of the Caribbean the Maroons did not manage to hold out until emancipation.

The most famous Maroon territory in the New World was not in the Caribbean, but in Brazil. This was the Palmares Republic, so called because of the palm trees the inhabitants hid among. In 1650 Palmares was declared an independent black republic. The Portuguese recognised its independence in 1678, but the treaty was never observed. Later Palmares was led by Zumbi who tried to hold out against the Portuguese, but in 1694 they captured the capital of Macaco and hunted down and killed Zumbi two years later. At its peak the Palmares Republic had a population of 200,000.

The Bush Negroes of Surinam

In the Dutch colonies on the Wild Coast it was easy for escaped slaves to keep their freedom in the forests of the interior. The Dutch tried to ally with the Indian tribes to outflank them and sometimes the Indians co-operated, but the Bush Negroes survived in Surinam and even, on a much smaller scale, in Berbice. They did not like being driven into the interior, but preferred to stay on the fringe of European settlements as part of their way of life consisted of raiding the plantations.

Some of the Bush Negroes were African-born slaves who had revolted and moved into the bush to resume the subsistence living they had known in Africa. They subsisted on plantains, yams, and eddoes. However, others were much more revengeful. They were rebels who moved to the bush to plot the murder of the whites and to raid the plantations. They were organised under leaders in a quasi-military life, with the lowest ranks performing the menial tasks of subsistence and plundering the plantations by night.

The Bush Negroes of Surinam lived in circular clearings in the forest with their dwellings in the middle and their crops around. Nearest the huts were the lowest growing crops, rising to the banana trees at the outside of the circle. This was to give them cover as well as food. A more permanent settlement would be surrounded by a moat concealed by grass and reeds, with sharp stakes in the sides and bottom below the water level. However, their greatest protection came from the thick forest of the interior which could only be penetrated by the rivers. Further into the interior these rivers had rapids, and beyond them the Bush Negroes felt safe.

After several expeditions into the interior had failed, the Dutch made a treaty with the Bush Negroes granting them freedom and the right to occupy the interior provided that they would not stir up slave revolts or raid plantations. The Bush Negroes kept the peace for thirty years, but in 1795 they were stirred up by the agents of the republican Victor Hugues, who was preaching freedom amongst the slaves of the Eastern Caribbean.

Taking advantage of the disruption caused by the Revolutionary Wars, they moved against the European plantations in West Demerara in April, 1795. Their night raids continued until September and put considerable strain on the finances of the colony. The Dutch failed to bring them under control until they used Indian guides to help the white soldiers track them down. Finally a large party of soldiers, slaves and Indians brought in the ringleaders for execution, but groups still remained in the forests in West Demerara and were still there when the free villages began after emancipation.

The Maroons in Jamaica

When the British invaded in 1655 Ysasi, the Spanish commander, made an alliance with the Maroons to help him against them. Totalling less than 1000, they were led by Juan Lubolo (Juan de Bolas) in the St John district of St Catherine. They attacked Spanish Town, burned houses and killed British soldiers in their quarters. Then in 1658,

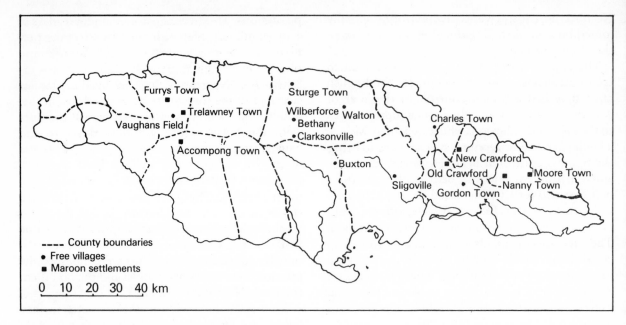

Map 4   Jamaica: the Maroon Settlements and Free Villages

they stopped the British forces reaching Rio Nuevo, where Ysasi had landed, by holding the overland route. Even after the Spanish had left Jamaica, the Maroons did not surrender and, although few in number, continued to menace the British.

This traditional defiance of the British continued into the eighteenth century. There was not only danger from the Maroons, but also from the slaves who were encouraged to revolt by their presence. Moreover Jamaica's failure to keep a regular militia encouraged defiance.

Jamaica was excused the 4½ per cent export tax, but still expected Britain to make arrangements for her defence. Further friction was caused as British plantations extended into the traditional Maroon areas. It was easier for slaves to escape and for the Maroons to raid these outlying plantations.

Parties of armed whites found it very difficult to operate in Maroon areas. In 1720 the King of the Moskito Indians of Central America was asked to send fifty Indians to hunt them down, but they had little success. There was peace for a few years but then raids began again and the Governor reported in 1726 that he could not raise men to serve against the Maroons as the Militia Act had expired. By 1730 the position was again very serious. The Maroons were bold enough to raid a plantation in March and carry off six women slaves; they defeated several successive forces sent to apprehend them.

The authorities believed that the Spanish were supplying the Maroons with arms in preparation for a Spanish invasion. They did not trust the militia which was composed of white indentured servants, including many Irish who were, themselves, suspected of encouraging revolt. Therefore the Jamaica Assembly asked for armed assistance from Britain and two regiments were sent. Their living conditions were very poor and they suffered a high death toll from disease. The remainder were withdrawn as the authorities considered that the danger had passed.

The First Maroon War

There was no clear-cut beginning to the First Maroon War. In March 1732, the militia captured the three chief Maroon settlements, but in 1733 further armed parties were defeated and the captured towns had to be abandoned. An appeal was made to the British Admiral in command of Jamaican waters, who sent 200 sailors to assist the militia. They were led into an ambush and defeated. There was clearly a war now.

At last the Assembly voted the money to raise a force to tackle the Maroons. Two hundred Moskito Indians and companies of free blacks and mulattoes were recruited. The Maroons were much more aggressive because of their recent successes, but gradually the superior forces of the government wore them down by persistent attacks and a scorched earth policy, and forced them to seek peace.

On 1 March, 1739, Articles of Pacification were signed with the Maroon Chief, Cudjoe, and other leaders from Trelawney Town. The Maroons were given freedom and the possession of all the lands lying between Trelawney Town and the Cockpits, amounting to about 600 hectares, for ever. In return they promised not to attack white planters, to give assistance to the government against external enemies or internal revolt, and to return all runaway slaves for a reward. Two white superintendents would live with them 'to maintain a friendly correspondence'. Similar agreements were made with other Maroons at Accompong, Crawford Town and Nanny Town.

This agreement formally acknowledged the areas the Maroons had been using for years. St James was their principal parish, but they spread into Trelawney in Cockpit Country, especially when it was necessary to avoid the authorities, and into St Elizabeth north of the Black River. The Maroons of Crawford Town and Nanny Town, although referred to as 'wild negroes', did not give the authorities so much trouble as they were too cut off from the main body in the north-west. In fact, the Maroons of the east co-operated in handing over runaway slaves in 1760 and afterwards were distrusted by the slaves for this. The 600 hectares allotted to the Maroons was typical of the system of 'reserves' which the British employed in their colonies throughout the world. The amount of land was very small in the case of the Maroons, and took no account of population expansion, thus there was bound to be trouble later.

The Second Maroon War

Two thousand Maroons were expected to subsist in the area designated by the land grant of 1739, and by 1795 they were feeling restricted. A second grievance was the replacement of a white superintendant, Captain Craskell.

The spark which set off the trouble could probably have been extinguished peacefully if the Maroons had not already been dissatisfied with the government's attitude. In July, 1795, two young Maroons from Trelawney Town were convicted of stealing pigs from a white planter and sentenced to thirty-nine lashes. The Maroons did not object to the sentence, but to the fact that the whipping was given by the black overseer of a slave prison in front of runaway slaves whom the Maroons themselves had handed over to the authorities. The onlookers

Trelawney Town

jeered and the insult to the Maroons was more than they could bear. They threatened to kill Captain Craskell and attack other whites. The government replied by mobilising the militia and sending mounted troops to the area. They could have calmed the Maroons by replacing Craskell with James and compensating them for the insult sustained. However, in view of the black revolution in St Domingue, the government decided to show firmness.

On 20 July a meeting between some prominent whites and Maroons was called to discuss grievances. Three hundred armed Maroons came in a belligerent mood and demanded the removal of Craskell and the redress of the indignity suffered by the two whipped men. The whites promised to lay their requests before the governor.

The Maroons then tried to incite the slaves to rebel, but luckily for the whites they had little success. Jamaica was poorly defended because most of the troops had been sent to Hispaniola and the remaining regiment was under orders to sail. There is no doubt that the Maroons knew this and were waiting for the regiment to sail from Port Royal, which it did on 29 July. They began mobilising and the slaves were restless and on the point of revolt. A boat was sent to intercept the regiment at sea and it was brought back to Montego Bay, thirty-two kilometres from Trelawney Town, on 4 August. The whites were very relieved. The arrival of the troops quietened the slaves, but could not stop the Maroon war.

Lord Balcarres, the Governor, proclaimed martial law and sent a message to Trelawney Town warning the Maroons that they were surrounded. He summoned them to meet him at Montego Bay on 12 August and to submit to His Majesty's mercy. If they did not do so, their town would be destroyed and a price would be set on their heads. On 11 August some of the older Maroons surrendered, but the young ones decided to fight and began by burning their town themselves. On 12 August they attacked the outposts of the troops and inflicted a severe defeat on mounted troops and militia, actually killing the colonel in command.

Then they drew back into Cockpit Country and began raiding white plantations and killing all the whites they could find, men, women and children. On 12 September they ambushed another force, again inflicting heavy casualties. The government decided to send for large hunting dogs from Cuba, which arrived on 14 December. The dogs were never used, but their very presence may have had an affect on the Maroons.

A new commander, Major-General Walpole, adopted the policy of starving the Maroons out. They were forced to raid slave grounds which made them very unpopular. It is not certain whether it was the arrival of the dogs or the cutting off of supplies which made the Maroons surrender. General Walpole said that if they gave themselves up within ten days from 21 December, together with all the runaway slaves, they would not be executed or deported. Only twenty-one surrendered in time, but General Walpole extended the period to the whole of January as he considered that the original ten days was too short. The troops then moved in to take the remainder, most of whom surrendered, but some held out until midMarch.

The government betrayed General Walpole's promise to the Maroons. The Legislature voted twenty-one to thirteen that those who had not actually surrendered by the end of the year 1795 should be deported. So in June, 1796, 556 Trelawney Town Maroons were sent to Nova Scotia. After four years there, it was decided that the climate was unsuitable and they were transferred to Sierra Leone. Some of the old ones, and some descendants of the deportees eventually found their way back to Jamaica in 1841 as labourers on the sugar estates, but most remained in Africa. General Walpole was bitterly disappointed and refused to accept the sword of honour which the Legislature voted him.

Thereafter the Maroons of Trelawney Town lived peacefully and remained free. Most of their young men had been deported and the rest felt that they could not hope for any improvement in their conditions.

The 1763 rebellion in Berbice

The causes of the slave uprising in Berbice in 1763 are very confused because different groups had different reasons for rebelling, and even the man who became leader of the rebels, Coffy, said later that he had not wanted to rebel in the first place! Some slaves desired revenge because of their terrible treatment and injustice. The Berbice Association economised on the imports of foodstuffs, the planters did not grow enough provisions on the estates and some slaves were underfed. The estates were often left in the hands of managers

Coffy

the slaves. However, as soon as the rebellion started on 23 February 1763, at the Plantation Magdelenenburg on the Canje River, van Hoogenheim lost sympathy with the slaves and was determined not to give in, even though the cause of the whites seemed hopeless and many of them wanted to evacuate the colony. He had only twelve soldiers at his disposal, so he recruited twelve sailors from a ship in the harbour and sent them to defend the Canje plantations, but to no avail, and the rebellion spread.

By March the rebellion had spread to the Berbice River, and two plantations close to Fort Nassau had been raided. Fort Nassau was the key to the colony and the extremists amongst the slaves were anxious to attack the Fort. But Coffy, whose aims were more moderate, had became the leader and the attack on Fort Nassau was put off. Coffy wanted a partition of Berbice with the whites on the coast and the blacks in the interior, on the lines of Surinam. He referred to himself as 'Governor of the Slaves'. Plantation Peerboom, where some whites were taking refuge, was attacked by 600 slaves. Food and water were running out and they accepted a guarantee of safe conduct to the river from Cosala, the slave leader, if they would surrender the estate. In spite of his promise many whites were killed.

The morale of the whites was very low and they forced van Hoogenheim to agree that the colony should be abandoned. Here Coffy made his mistake if he had really wanted a black takeover. Van Hoogenheim, his most resolute opponent, had been over-ruled and was on the point of abandoning Fort Nassau which Coffy could have taken with ease. But he hesitated and allowed van Hoogenheim to outmanoeuvre him, by stalling him until reinforcements arrived. Coffy realised van Hoogenheim's strategy too late. Coffy's hesitation may have been influenced by the behaviour of some of the slaves. After their initial successes, they were unwilling to accept the discipline and hard work which he realised was necessary for the new black colony to succeed. His position was further weakened because some of the Creole slaves were ready to surrender.

A British ship from Surinam landed 100 soldiers at Fort Andries and van Hoogenheim was able to attack for the first time. He left a small force at Fort Andries, sent twenty-five soldiers up the Canje to defend his position from that side, and he himself led the main party up the Berbice to

and overseers who did not give a thought for the welfare of the slaves. Coffy himself, in a letter to the Governor, gave this as a cause of the rebellion. He blamed a few evil planters and managers, including his owner, Barkey of the Plantation Lilienburg.

However, many of the leading rebel slaves were well-treated and were domestic and artisan slaves like Coffy. Their motive for rebelling seems to have been to gain permanent freedom. This group was sub-divided into those who would have settled for a black reserve in the interior, like the Bush Negroes of Surinam, with a treaty guaranteeing freedom, and those who wanted to exterminate all the whites and take over the colony themselves and make an independent black state.

The Governor of Berbice, van Hoogenheim, sympathised with the plight of the slaves before the rebellion and in 1762 he had been asking the Berbice Association to send more provisions for

Plantation Dageraad, which he had wanted previously to make the key to his defence. He fortified the plantation and had ships in the river train their guns on the possible line of attack. Akara, Coffy's second-in-command, realised that the longer the delay the stronger the whites would become, so he attacked Dageraad, but his three attacks were all beaten back.

Coffy sent a letter to van Hoogenheim suggesting a partition of Berbice. Van Hoogenheim asked him to wait two months for a reply from Holland. Van Hoogenheim's motive was to delay until more troops could arrive. He did not want a partition, but wanted to defeat the slaves once and for all. Coffy waited all through April, 1763.

Gravesande, the Governor of Essequibo, not wanting the slave revolt to spread to Demerara which he was trying to open up, evacuated most of the women and children from Demerara to St Eustatius. He then planned a three-pronged relief of Berbice. He ordered the Commander of Demerara to organise the Indians to attack the slaves in the rear from the upper reaches of the Demerara River. Secondly, he secured help from Barbados: an eighteen gun ship, two armed brigantines, 100 marines and arms and ammunition. Thirdly, he asked for help from the Zeeland Chamber, the Berbice Association and St Eustatius. Two well-armed ships with 158 soldiers arrived from Holland.

At the beginning of May, Coffy realised his mistake and began an all-out attack on Dageraad. On 13 May 2,000 slaves attacked the 150 whites who were heavily defended in the plantation and from the river. The fighting lasted five hours and eight whites and fifty-eight slaves were killed. Coffy failed to take Dageraad. He was also troubled by the serious divisions in his own ranks between African slaves and Creoles, and especially by the challenge to his leadership from Atta who was an extremist. Atta took over, and Coffy killed his close followers and then committed suicide. However, Atta was now leading a lost cause as the whites were recovering and more help was coming. In December a large force arrived by ship up the Berbice River to coincide with an attack on the slaves to the rear from Upper Demerara. Most of the slaves ran away into the forests and the rest were hunted down and killed.

The rebellion had lasted for ten months. If an immediate attack had been made on Fort Nassau in March 1763 the slaves probably would have succeeded in driving the whites out of Berbice, although the success could only have been temporary as the Dutch would not have given up Berbice. Sooner or later a strong force would have been sent to retake the colony. This is evident from the determination of officials like Van Hoogenheim and Gravesande.

It is unlikely that Coffy and the slaves could have held off an attempt at re-colonisation because revolutionary spirit was waning. The Creole slaves were not enthusiastic and some remained loyal to their former masters. Other slaves had turned their attention to looting and pleasure instead of securing their position. Finally, the leaders of the slaves were divided in their aims and power struggles amongst the leaders weakened their cause. Therefore we can conclude that the rebellion had little hope of success in the long term, but was a remarkable demonstration of the desire of the blacks for freedom and even for their own independent country.

When Guyana became a Republic on 23 February, 1970, that day was chosen because it marked the anniversary of the Berbice Slave Rebellion, and Coffy was chosen as a national hero. Coffy had been born in Africa and brought to Guiana at an early age. In the rebellion he was realistic, not trying to achieve too much too soon, and not making demands which he knew would not be met. This showed his wisdom and statesmanship, as did his attempt to organise the blacks to lay the foundations of their country by hard work and the readiness to defend their land. His mistake lay in thinking that he could treat with Van Hoogenheim and in allowing himself to be tricked into waiting. Coffy became a martyr in the independence struggle and an inspiration for the future.

The 1816 Revolt in Barbados

A registry Bill similar to the ones that had been introduced in Trinidad in 1812 and St Lucia in 1814 was passed for all the British colonies in 1815. It It merely required slaves to be registered, but its reception in the West Indies was startling. The whites were furious at what they considered interference in their domestic matters and the slaves misinterpreted it as emancipation, or they chose to interpret it as such. In Barbados the slaves hear about the Bill and felt that their masters were withholding their freedom. This was one of the causes of the slave revolt of 1816. When the British Parliament realised this reaction they asked the Prince Regent to issue a proclamation announcing

His Royal Highness's highest displeasure at the daring insurrection which has taken place in the island of Barbados; (and declaring) in the most public manner, His Royal Highness's concern and surprise at the false and mischievous opinion which appears to have prevailed in certain of the British colonies, that His Royal Highness has sent orders for the emancipation of the negroes.

The whites in Barbados attributed the revolt to the Nonconformist missionaries, especially the Wesleyan Methodists, the Baptists and the London Missionary Society. They had been very strong in Barbados and had preached the ideas of freedom, equality and brotherhood, although they had always urged the slaves to refrain from violence and to wait for freedom to come from England.

Some slaves wanted independence. The commander of the troops who put down the rebellion believed that this was its cause, and he wrote to the Governor, 'they stoutly maintained, however, that the island belonged to them, and not to white men'. It was possible in Barbados, more than in any other colony, for the slaves to think of the island as a black man's land. The preponderance of blacks in the community was so marked and its history so long that it seemed to many to be their island.

The revolt began on 14 April when the slaves on some plantations in St Philip's Parish started destroying the planters' property. It quickly spread to the parishes of St John and St George. Sixty estate buildings were destroyed and canefields set on fire. The revolt was crushed on the second day when Colonel Edward Codd in command of the Barbados militia and some regular British troops mobilised quickly and rounded up the rebels. Some accounts say that no whites lost their lives, others that one died. It seems, therefore, that no violence against the whites was intended and that the slaves were just trying to secure their own emancipation which they believed was legally theirs.

As usual the vengeance of the authorities was terrible. Several hundred slaves were killed by the soldiers and many were executed afterwards. The whites turned against the missionaries in Barbados, chapels were damaged and ministers threatened.

The most famous, William Shrewsbury, was forced to leave and take refuge in St. Vincent.

The 1831 Revolt in Jamaica, 'The Baptist War'

In Jamaica, white public opinion was opposed to amelioration in any form, but the British government was prepared to put financial pressure on the Jamaican Legislature to pass it. By the end of 1831 even Jamaica accepted that emancipation was inevitable and the Assembly concentrated on the question of compensation. There is no doubt that the slaves knew roughly what was going on, but they did not know the precise details. One slave in Montego Bay, Samuel Sharpe, could read and write, and from his master's newspapers he learnt that emancipation was very near and that wage labour would come to Jamaica. He spread the word amongst his fellow slaves. The Christmas holiday was approaching and he told the slaves not to return to work after Christmas unless they were paid. This strike began on 27 December, as most slaves were not required to work on Christmas Day and Boxing Day. The masters and the authorities realised that someone well - acquainted with political developments in England and Jamaica had incited the slaves, and they blamed Sharpe. He was also a prominent member of the Baptist Church, another cause of suspicion. However, Samuel Sharpe was not to blame for the rebellion that followed. He had not planned it and was opposed to violence.

The situation in the north-west of Jamaica was explosive. When a husband was forced to watch the brutal flogging of his wife, he struck the whipper. The overseer ordered the slave to be arrested, but the other slaves refused. Thus the revolt began. The first plantation to be attacked was the Kensington Estate in St James. Quickly the revolt spread to other plantations in the neighbourhood and soon the parishes of St Elizabeth, Manchester, Portland and St Thomas-in-the-East were involved. By January 50,000 slaves were in revolt because they believed that their masters were withholding freedom.

Another name for this revolt is the 'Baptist War' because the whites felt that the Nonconformist missionaries had encouraged the slaves. This was not true. William Knibb of the Baptist Church knew about the strike and revolt beforehand and

William Knibb

This was the most serious rebellion ever experienced in Jamaica, but it never had any chance of success and was confined to the north-west. The revolt did not reach Spanish Town and Kingston, where the authorities had troops stationed and a fully armed merchant ship at the end of every road and lane leading to the waterfront.

After the revolt the British government gave £200,000 compensation to estate owners. The whites felt that this was 'conscience money', as the Assembly reported in 1832 that the interference of the British government in local laws, and the irresponsible expressions of British ministers and individuals in the House of Commons, were to blame for the revolt. They maintained that 'false and wicked reports of the Anti-Slavery Society were being circulated throughout the island.'

The whites turned their vengeance against the missionaries, especially the Baptists, Methodists and Moravians. William Knibb was arrested on a charge of inciting the rebellion. Several other ministers were assaulted. In January, 1832, some whites formed the Colonial Church Union, a so-called religious body, to prevent the dissemination of any other doctrines apart from those of the Churches of England and Scotland. In a few weeks they destroyed fourteen Baptist and Wesleyan chapels. Later in the year, the Colonial Church Union was dissolved by royal proclamation.

The 1831-32 revolt in Jamaica was a very ill-advised attempt by the slaves to try to better their conditions. It served no useful purpose because the British government was already determined to enforce emancipation throughout the colonies, and even the Jamaican Legislature had accepted its inevitability and was just trying to get the best terms it could for the slave owners. It was a sad event, costly in human lives, and it embittered the already bad relations between whites and blacks.

Samuel Sharpe and William Knibb were the heroic figures of the revolt. Sharpe was a Jamaican martyr who became affetionately known as 'Daddy' Sharpe to the people. He was an inspiration to men like Paul Bogle forty years later. Knibb was a fine example of everything a missionary should be; utterly devoted to his flock and ready to make any personal sacrifice for them.

tried to stop it. However sympathetic a white missionary was, the slaves believed that when loyalty was put to the test he would side with the whites, therefore they did not heed Knibb, nor Bleby, a Methodist missionary, who warned the slaves that the authorities would win.

The slaves did not set out to kill the whites, but to destroy property. In all, only fifteen whites were killed which was not many in such a large rebellion. Many whites evacuated the estates until the authorities had regained control. Retaliation by the authorities had begun before the end of December, 1831, when a militia company of coloureds defeated some of the rebels but then, instead of putting down the rebellion, they retreated to Montego Bay, leaving the slaves in control of St James and Trelawney. On 1 January Sir Willoughby Cotton, in command of regular troops, arrived. He offered a free pardon to all slaves who would surrender, except the ringleaders. Most of the slaves gave themselves up, but there was severe fighting in the wild bush country of St James and Trelawney before the revolt was finally crushed. In the fighting 400 slaves were killed, 100 others, including Samuel Sharpe, were executed, and another 100 were flogged.

Slave medallion

6

Slavery Challenged

Attitudes towards slavery

Pre-eighteenth century attitudes

Slavery has, in the past, been part of the normal order of society in most countries. In some ancient and feudal societies, it was very difficult to draw the line between 'slave' and 'free' in the lowest ranks of society. There were slaves, but there were also free peasants who were tied to the soil. In Russia, until the mid-nineteenth century, the term 'serf' would have seemed to an outsider to embrace both classes.

Slaves could be acquired legally, either in war or as a penalty for a crime. It was considered just to enslave a man who had taken up arms against you, and a person who had committed an offence had to pay for it by loss of freedom, giving his labour in compensation. Greeks, Romans, Chinese, Turks, Africans and Europeans took slaves in this way. Even in the nineteenth century, enslavement as a punishment for a crime was considered just in some countries. But people were having doubts about the justice of the enslavement of captives.

African slaves were acquired in three ways: in war; as a punishment for a crime; and by purchase. Europeans entering the West African slave trade regarded the first method as just if it really was 'in war', but later doubts were cast on this. However, these moral problems did not trouble Europeans until the seventeenth century. Then an English philosopher, John Locke, said that this method of acquiring slaves was justified only if the war was just.

Some Catholics before the eighteenth century, questioned whether slavery was right, but they still practised it. They argued that slavery, although wrong and contrary to the natural rights of man, was a 'necessary evil'. Ferdinand and Isabella of Spain tolerated slavery because they believed that the empire could not be developed without it. To mitigate this 'necessary evil', the Spanish made the conversion of slaves compulsory. They also acknowledged the right of slaves to seek their freedom.

Among the English before the eighteenth century, there were only rare examples of the condemnation of slavery. According to their doctrines the Puritans should have been against slavery, but Puritan congregations in Bermuda and Providence Island practised slavery.

However, anti-slavery feelings were common amongst the Quakers. They were very unpopular in the West Indies because they would not bear arms in the militia, and also because they sometimes freed their slaves and always converted them to Christianity.

There was the genuine conviction that it was better for an African to be a Christian slave than a free pagan. In the case of the Catholics, this was sincere as they did attempt to convert their slaves to Christianity. Protestants also used this argument, but did nothing about making their slaves Christians.

Another justification given for enslaving Africans was that the slave's life was being saved by being brought to the West Indies. This was a very artificial argument to satisfy a guilty conscience.

The unpleasant racial attitude that Africans were a degraded race and so deserved their slavery was widespread in England and France, but not so common in Spain. Such phrases about Africans as 'the baseness of their condition', 'cannibals all', or even 'dirty, stinking animals' were common. Europeans with this attitude thought that they were helping the Africans they enslaved by raising them from their natural degraded condition.

A completely contradictory attitude had arisen before the eighteenth century, but it was widely held only amongst intellectuals. This was the idea of the 'noble savage'. This varied from embracing all Africans as being noble because they lived in a perfect state of nature uncorrupted by any government or laws, to applying only to certain Africans who had to be carefully distinguished from the others who were not noble.

Different attitudes towards slavery arose because the usual authority on all moral issues in those days—the Bible—was ambiguous on this subject, and it was used to support views for and against slavery. Those who supported slavery cited the Old Testament, and the passage about the curse on Ham and his posterity, and their 'blackness' giving them inferiority and making them slaves for ever. Even in the New Testament, justification for slavery was found by Bishop Bossuet, the confessor of Louis XIV, who said that the Holy Ghost, speaking through St Paul, was telling slaves to accept their status.

On the other hand, the idea of Christian brotherhood made Christians condemn slavery. Du Tertre, the seventeenth-century French missionary in St Kitts, held that Christians could not be slaves. They were all children of God and, if baptised, they were the brothers of the whites. The Quakers held that if slaves were men they had immortal souls which were as capable of salvation as the souls of whites.

From the Bible the planters took the doctrine of 'obedience' and used it to reconcile slavery with Christianity. Men owed obedience to the commandments of God; a subject owed obedience to his king; children owed obedience to their father; a slave owed obedience to his master—this was how they argued. A man could be a good Christian and a good slave if he practised 'obedience'.

Eighteenth century attitudes

Many of the old attitudes remained in the eighteenth century, but there was also a great increase in anti-slavery feeling, especially in the second half of the century in England and France. Even in the West Indies and North America, there were slave owners who were prepared to admit that slavery was wrong. Nevertheless, as soon as their way of life was threatened by the anti-slavery movement, the planters closed their ranks and defended slavery.

In France anti-slavery was a secular movement, not based on the revealed work of God in the Bible, but on man's reason. It culminated in the Declaration of the Rights of Man in August, 1789, when 'Liberty, Equality and Fraternity' was the slogan. In England, on the other hand, anti-slavery was founded in the evangelical movement. The Evangelicals and Nonconformists believed the Gospels' teaching that salvation came from faith and good works, and one of the good works they took up was to rid the world of the evil of slavery.

The decline in prosperity of the English sugar islands caused some people to question the economic necessity of slavery. If 'free' grown sugar from the East could compete favourably, perhaps slavery was wrong for economic as well as moral reasons. Many industrialists felt that if the slave economies changed into wage economies, the workers would have money to buy British goods.

Much controversy was aroused by the attitude that blacks were slaves because they were inferior to whites. The supporters of this view held that blacks were inferior because they had achieved little in thought, word or deed. Thomas Jefferson, the President of the United States in 1801, found himself in a terrible dilemma over this. His attitude was that blacks were inferior because of their lack of achievement, but he had to speak against slavery because he thought that it was morally wrong and contravened the 'inalienable rights of man' as stated in the Declaration of Independence. However, he did not want the mixing of free blacks with whites in American society, nor did he want the creation of a 'black belt' in the South. His solution to these conflicting attitudes was to propose the return of all blacks to Africa, once freed from slavery.

Others denied that blacks were inferior, and argued that they had not reached eminence in arts, sciences and ideas because they had not had the opportunity. Adam Smith, the great English economist, insisted that great qualities existed in blacks which would be realised when they were freed from the domination of their masters.

Another attitude to slavery which could not be resolved, but was debated vigorously, was the view that slavery was economically unsound. The defenders of slavery and the slave trade argued that the economies of the West Indies would collapse without slaves. They showed that the initial costs of buying the slaves were high, but thereafter, because there were no wages, the costs were low. Their opponents held that the costs of slave labour were always high because mortality was high and replacement expensive. Sickness, carelessness and wilful damage also made costs high. It was not possible to prove that slave labour was cheaper than wage labour or that it was more productive. On balance, the attitude of most writers was that the cost of slave labour was lower, but so was their productivity.

The French thinkers of the eighteenth century strongly condemned slavery. Probably the strongest condemnation of all came from Jean-Jacques Rousseau. He held that man was born free and, according to natural law, could never be enslaved. Very similar views existed in England, but they were not based purely on reason. They were held by men like John Wesley, who said in 1774, 'Liberty is the right of every human creature, as soon as he breathes the vital air; and no human law can deprive him of that right which he derives from the law of nature.'

There was also the attitude in France that although all men were equal and it could never be legal for one man to own another even as a prisoner of war, slavery was necessary for the plantation islands which could not function unless white masters could rule black slaves.

Planters and slave traders in the late eighteenth century were on the defensive against these well-reasoned attacks from philosophers, economists and evangelicals. Two West Indian planters, Edward Long and Bryan Edwards, were historians who tried to convince the outside world that the

Jean Jacques Rousseau

Caged prisoners being transported to Australia

blacks deserved to be slaves. They pictured blacks as dishonest, immoral, lazy, cowardly, lustful, cruel, supersitious, in fact possessing every vice imaginable.

The planters also followed the theory that 'the best means of defence is attack'. In particular they attacked the British government. They said that if slavery was morally wrong, it was not just wrong at the end of the eighteenth century, but had always been wrong. Yet it had been approved by governments in the past, and through all changes of political parties. Secondly, they pointed to the Englishman's right to property which it was the duty of the government to uphold. They said that the abolition of slavery was a denial of this right. Thirdly, they attacked the British government for the transportation of criminals to Australia; for the conditions for sailors in the English navy; for prison conditions in England; even for the standard of living of the workers in English industrial towns. They claimed that West Indian slaves lived

in blissful conditions by comparison. They maintained that slave laws were the concern of colonial legislatures, not of the British Parliament.

The planters and their supporters were helped by two events which changed people's attitudes to slavery and turned them against abolition. These were the French Revolution and the Haitian Revolution.

At first the French Revolution was enthusiastically received by abolitionists because it proclaimed liberty and equality, but when it turned to violence and bloodshed many changed their minds or at least withdrew their support temporarily from abolition.

The Haitian Revolution had an even greater impact on abolition in the West Indies and the Southern United States. Chateaubriand, a famous French writer who had previously supported abolition, said in 1802 'Who would dare still to plead the cause of the Negroes after the crimes they have committed'. He was referring to St Domingue.

58

Many people in England and France, however, regarded the Haitian Revolution as a great achievement.

Arguments for slavery

1 Slavery was supported by the Scriptures and was not incompatible with Christianity.

2 Blacks were unprepared for freedom and would be harmed by it. When free they would be more abused and discriminated against than when slaves.

3 Men were not born 'free and equal'. It was nonsense to talk of 'inalienable rights' for slaves because they were from a degraded race. Negroid Africans were considered a different species to whites and could be treated like animals.

4 Slavery was a kind of benevolent socialism in which the blissful plantation slave was nurtured from the cradle to the grave. In a capitalist society without slavery, the blacks would be poor and downtrodden and this would lead to revolution.

5 There was a paternalism in a slave society which benefited the slave. Slave owners valued their slaves highly and wanted to look after them well.

6 The temperament of blacks enabled them to adjust to their life of drudgery and menial work and be happy in it.

Then there were the 'necessary-evil arguments'. These accepted that slavery was morally wrong, but that it was better to keep it, since it already existed, than to end it. Also they held that its benefits outweighed its evils.

7 Sugar, cotton and certain other tropical crops had to be grown on plantations which were worked with slave labour. Slavery might be wrong, but it was necessary for the production of these crops.

8 Slavery provided the basis for a superior culture There had to be a class of slaves to perform the menial duties so that the white, leisured class could confine itself to government and culture.

9 Slavery already existed in Africa, so Europeans were not introducing a new evil. New World slavery was better than African slavery.

10 Slavery might be wrong, but it gave the opportunity for conversion to Christianity.

There were a group of arguments on economic grounds.

11 Slavery provided a cheaper labour force than wage labour. Also slaves were cheaper than machines, or even sometimes than animals, as a means of production.

12 Slavery was not necessarily suitable only for a plantation economy. It could be adapted to a manufacturing economy.

13 Slavery could lead to diversification in agriculture. Slaves were as capable of producing food crops as plantation crops. They were also capable of handling cattle.

14 Slavery did not necessarily lead to soil exhaustion. It was the small size of the plantations and the limited size of the islands in the British West Indies which caused this.

Finally there were arguments put forward by whites that slavery was necessary for the preservation of white society.

15 If the slaves were freed, the whites would become a minority.

16 Successful planters could make huge profits and become the leaders of society economically, politically, socially and culturally.

17 Slavery was the means by which small planters could rise in the world and emulate the big planters.

18 Poor whites were committed to slavery and racial-superiority theories in order to preserve the little status they had. The threat of free blacks to white privilege made the poor whites hate the blacks more than anyone else.

Arguments against slavery

These arguments were put forward by people who attacked slavery. They were not necessarily mere contradictions of the other side's arguments, although this was sometimes the case. There were many arguments based on moral grounds.

1 Slavery was contrary to reason, justice, nature, the principles of law and government, the whole doctrine of natural religion and the revealed voice of God. (This was the general argument on moral grounds which was used by Thomas Clarkson, the abolitionist).

2 It was morally wrong for Christians to traffic in, or keep, slaves.

3 If people bore in mind the maxim, 'do unto others as you would have them do unto you', they would condemn slavery.

4 Slavery was a denial of civilisation. In a slave society a minority might appear civilised, but it was impossible for them to be really so while

denying civilisation to others. 'Civilisation' and 'slavery' were contradictory terms.

5 Freedom is the true, natural state of man. Only with freedom can man attain true greatness.

6 It was admitted that in free societies the poor suffered, and if free the blacks would probably be poor, but the horrors of slavery far outweighed the horrors of poverty.

7 Slavery made the whites lazy and ignorant. William Byrd II, a wealthy Virginia planter, said 'Blow up the pride and ruin the industry of the white people, who, seeing a rank of poor creatures below them, detest work for fear it should make them look like slaves'.

There were many arguments against slavery on economic grounds.

8 Slavery led to economic instability and held back technological improvements in agriculture.

9 Slavery led to monoculture which was dangerous to the economy.

10 Intensive cultivation by slaves led to soil exhaustion.

11 Slavery prevented the development of a manufacturing industry.

12 Slavery limited the size of markets and the flow of goods and circulation of money.

13 Slavery led to the exodus of white yeomanry from the community.

14 The profits of plantation owners were not reinvested in the local economy, but spent abroad.

15 The slave system was inefficient, wasteful and unproductive. There was always the problem of a high rate of mortality, wilful or careless damage, the maintenance of very young and old slaves and ever-rising replacement costs.

16 Slavery made slaves a reluctant labour force. Slaves felt that their labour was useless as all the profits went to the masters.

An argument against slavery which had great practical force amongst whites was that it was against their interests.

17 Slavery brought fear and insecurity. The danger of slave revolt and massacre was ever-present.

18 Life in a slave society was unpleasant and uncomfortable for whites, surrounded by cruelty and suffering.

19 Some whites had a 'guilty conscience' about slavery and preferred to live in a free society.

20 Inevitably a slave society was socially restrictive.

The campaign for the abolition of the slave trade

The West India interest

London merchants and English landowners with interests in the West Indies had always had considerable influence at Court and with the Council for Trade and Plantations. At first their interest was not concerned with slavery, but with such matters as the selection of colonial governors and colonial policy.

The West India interest was a growing force in English politics. Some West Indians, or Englishmen with plantations in the West Indies, were members of Parliament. Others could control votes in the House of Commons through the system of patronage which existed in English politics in the eighteenth century. In 1766, there were forty members of Parliament who were either West Indian planters themselves, or were related to planters, or had concerns in the West Indies. Later in the century they could count directly on fifty votes and, with influence over other members, they made up the single most powerful interest group in English politics.

The strength of the movement against slavery took them by surprise. As late as 1783, they were chiefly concerned with the resumption of trade between the West Indian colonies and the newly-independent United States, and won concessions from the government to partially re-open this trade. In the same year Lord North, the ex-Prime Minister, said 'it would be impossible to abolish the slave trade for it was a trade which had in some measure become necessary to every nation in Europe'. When the West India interest realised the threat presented by the abolitionists they made slavery their chief concern and managed to defer abolition until 1807.

Realising that the battle was lost in the House of Commons, they relied on the House of Lords to protect their interests and the Lords did so until 1805, when they passed the Abolition Bill. The West India interest then realised that unless they did something quickly, emancipation would be passed as well. The planters in the West Indies and the West India interest in London differed over what to do. The committee in London advised the planters to ameliorate the conditions of their slaves as a last means of preventing complete emancipation, and actually drafted amelioration

West India Docks

proposals which were put before the Colonial Secretary, Lord Bathurst, in 1823. These were adopted by the British government, but the colonial legislatures made almost no attempt to enforce them.

Finally, by 1831, the planters realised that emancipation was inevitable and, in spite of their bitterness over the disregarding of their advice on amelioration, the West India interest persuaded the British government to turn a loan of £15,000,000 into a free gift of £20,000,000 to compensate the owners of freed slaves. The apprenticeship system was another palliative that they helped to secure.

Thus the West India interest was a powerful force which did not prevent emancipation, but succeeded in delaying it for about fifty years.

The Quakers

'Quakers' was a name given by outsiders to a religious group called the 'Society of Friends' founded by George Fox in 1648. They acted as a pressure group in the movement for the abolition of slavery. Until 1755 Quakers could legally own slaves, but it was against the principles of many to

do so. In 1755 they were forbidden to do so by the rules of their society, and they were required to use all their force to bring about abolition. Their strategy was to win over public opinion by carrying the arguments for abolition into every home in Britain through pamphlets, the Press and the pulpit every Sunday. When public opinion had been won over they would then introduce abolition into Parliament.

The Quakers' most enthusiastic worker was Granville Sharp who, from 1765, devoted his life to abolition and emancipation. In the second half of the eighteenth century, abolition became a religious crusade for the Quakers. When the 'Society for Effecting the Abolition of the Slave Trade' was founded in 1787, eleven out of twelve of its committee members were Quakers. The Society later became more representative, but the Quakers were always the leading force in the movement outside Parliament.

The Clapham Sect, or 'The Saints'

The Church of England was the established church in England and her colonies. In England it was

Granville Sharp

associated with the landowning gentry and the Tory Party, and in the West Indies it was the Church of the planters. In both England and the West Indies, it kept aloof from the abolition movement.

In the eighteenth century an evangelical movement grew up within the Church of England. The members wanted less emphasis on salvation through the sacraments and more on salvation through good works and morality. One group in this movement was known as 'The Clapham Sect', or 'The Saints', because they worshipped at the church of the Reverend John Venn in Clapham in the south of London between 1792 and 1813. Among them were William Wilberforce, Granville Sharp, Thomas Clarkson, James Ramsay, James Stephen and Zachary Macaulay, all famous names in abolition. Three of these men had considerable first-hand experience of the evils of slavery: Ramsay had been a clergyman in St Kitts for nineteen years; Stephen a lawyer in St Kitts for ten years; and Zachary Macaulay the under-manager on a Jamaican sugar estate for four years. They gave practical, supporting evidence to the other members of the sect who had considerable influence in public

affairs, men like Wilberforce, Lord Teignmouth and Henry Brougham. In Parliament the contribution of the Saints to abolition was great, and they complemented the Quakers who had done so much to arouse public opinion in the same cause.

However, the Saints were mainly concerned with the abolition of the slave trade. Some of them did not want to interfere with slavery on the plantations and left the movement before emancipation. Indeed, some of them did not want emancipation.

Industrialists

The abolition movement coincided with the Industrial Revolution in Britain.

The new industrialists were producing textiles, pottery, iron and steel goods more cheaply and in greater quantities. They were primarily interested in getting cheap raw materials, and they turned from British West Indian sugar to other sources which were cheaper. The flood of cheap goods they produced needed wider markets and, although the slave-populated islands of the West Indies did not provide a good market, the industrialists thought that after abolition they would do so. Whereas the commercial interests in Britain had strongly supported slavery in 1760, by 1800 they were becoming indifferent, and later were actively against it.

Historians who want to play down the humanitarian motive for the abolition movement in Britain emphasise the economic reasons for it. They argue that abolition was passed so that British industrialists and merchants could sell more goods and make more money, a purely self-interested motive. However, the humanitarian motive was present in many industrialists. They were members of the new Nonconformist Churches and their evangelicalism was strong. In the reformed Parliament of 1832 their representatives voted for emancipation. Humanity and economics for once went hand-in-hand.

The British anti-slavery movement

The campaign outside Parliament

The general public in Britain was indifferent to slavery, and the first task of the abolitionists was to win them over to support for abolition. Moreover, upper-class people had to be persuaded that slavery was not respectable. For example, even after all the propaganda against slavery, William Ewart Gladstone, later Prime Minister and renowned for his uprightness, spoke in support of slavery in his maiden speech in the House of Commons in 1832.

West Indian planters on leave in England, or retiring there, often brought slaves with them and there were a few thousand black slaves in England when the Law Officers of the Crown assured the planters that slavery was allowed in England in 1729. In 1749 the Lord Chancellor, Lord Hardwicke, ruled that a runaway slave could be legally recovered in England. In 1765 a Barbadian slave, Joseph Strong, had been abandoned in England as being unfit to work. Granville Sharp's brother, a doctor, helped Strong to recover, whereupon his master David Lisle, claimed back his 'property' and sold him to a Jamaican who put him on board ship for Jamaica. Granville Sharp rescued the slave and secured his release.

By 1770, it was calculated that there were 10,000 black slaves in England valued at over half a million pounds. Sharp wanted to establish that slavery was illegal in England and set these slaves free. His victory came with the case of James Somerset, a Jamaican slave who had been ill-treated and abandoned by his master. When he had recovered, his master claimed him back and Sharp took the master to court. The case was heard by Lord Mansfield, who had become Lord Chief Justice of England in 1756 and dominated the legal profession until his death in 1793. On 22 June, 1772, Lord Mansfield made the decision which is commonly known as 'Mansfield's Judgement', that slavery was illegal in England, in these words:

> The state of slavery is so odious that nothing can be suffered to support it, but positive law. Whatever inconvenience may therefore follow from this decision, I cannot say this case is allowed or approved by the law of England; and therefore the black must be discharged.

Mansfield was right about inconvenience. As a result of this decision there were over 10,000 ex-slaves in England without means of support. This led Granville Sharp to start his scheme for resettling them in Africa, and the colony of Sierra Leone was founded in 1787. In 1778 the Scottish judges faced a similar case with a slave, Joseph Knight, and followed the decision of Lord Mansfield.

These victories led Granville Sharp and the abolitionists to press for the emancipation of slaves throughout the British empire, but later they realised that emancipation was too big a step to expect and they settled for the abolition of the slave trade instead. This was a much more widely accepted cause and one for which public opinion was prepared.

The campaign in Parliament

The main task of the 'Society for Effecting the Abolition of the Slave Trade', founded in 1787, was to change the law on slavery. Some of its members were Members of Parliament who could introduce the abolition issue into debates in the House of Commons; the most famous of these was William Wilberforce.

William Wilberforce entered the House of Commons as member for Hull in 1780 at the age of twenty-one. Early in his career, he was converted to evangelical Christianity and joined the Clapham Sect. He even considered taking Holy Orders, but was persuaded to do his good works in Parliament instead. In 1787 he was approached by Thomas Clarkson to take up the cause of abolition, and he held Abolitionist Society meetings at his home in London. Clarkson furnished Wilberforce with evidence against the slave trade and Wilberforce

William Wilberforce

canvassed other members of Parliament to support abolition. He had many useful connections in Parliament, including friendship with William Pitt, the future Prime Minister. Wilberforce's influence in Parliament and his speechmaking were his great contributions to abolition. He spoke so regularly on abolition that it became known as 'the perennial resolution'. Abolition became his life's work.

The first motion against the slave trade came before the House of Commons in 1776 and was easily defeated. This made it clear to the abolitionists that much more preparation had to be done. In 1787 and 1788, 100 petitions against the slave trade reached Parliament and an impartial report by the Trade Committee of the Privy Council 'on the present state of the African trade' was published, which helped the cause by providing valuable evidence for Wilberforce. Thomas Clarkson provided more evidence in a pamphlet, 'A Summary View of the Slave Trade and the Probable Consequence of its Abolition'. On 9 May, 1788, William Pitt introduced a resolution against the slave trade in the House of Commons. Charles James Fox and Edmund Burke, two other great statesmen, spoke in favour of abolition. A resolution to consider the slave trade in the next session was carried. In the meantime, a law was passed to limit the number of slaves carried according to the size of the ship.

Most of the evidence against the slave trade was supplied by Thomas Clarkson, who could be called 'the eyes and ears' of Wilberforce. He was born in 1760, the son of the Reverend John Clarkson, a schoolmaster. In 1785 he won a Latin Essay Prize at Cambridge with *'Anne liceat invitos in servitutem dare?',* (Should men be given into slavery against their will?), in which he showed that there was no justification for slavery. In 1786 he published this essay in English and circulated it among influential people. From then on he devoted his life to abolition, to collecting evidence against the slave trade, and to urging people to take action against what was morally wrong. Clarkson was the one non-Quaker on the first committee of the Abolition Society, and he worked closely with the Quakers to abolish slavery. In 1788 he visited Liverpool, Bristol and Lancaster collecting evidence, and he continued to travel extensively until 1792 when his health failed and he had to retire.

On 12 May, 1789, Wilberforce condemned the slave trade in a masterly three-hour speech, but

Thomas Clarkson

the resolution was defeated. On 18 April, 1791, he introduced a bill abolishing the slave trade. Again it was easily defeated.

In 1792, 500 petitions poured into Parliament and the abolitionists had partial success when the House of Commons passed a resolution, 'That the Slave Trade ought to be gradually abolished'. In 1792, also, a bill was passed in Denmark abolishing the slave trade from 1802. This was a great boost for the abolitionists. However, the House of Lords blocked the bill for gradual abolition.

In 1792 the abolitionists' campaign suffered two checks. The first was caused by the French Revolution, followed by the Revolutionary Wars. Pitt and the government devoted all their energies to the war with France, and abolition was dropped. Wilberforce kept up his speeches in the Commons, and Pitt introduced a bill to abolish the slave trade in 1797, but support for abolition was half-hearted and proposals for abolition had no chance of success. This disillusionment with reform and abolition lasted until the horrors of the French Revolution had been forgotten.

The second was caused by the West India interest, which began a campaign of serious counter-propaganda in 1792. Its members organised their own opposition in Parliament and printed their own pamphlets for circulation. They found it difficult to attack Wilberforce as he was such a respected figure, and they concentrated their attack on people like the Reverend James Ramsay who had just published an essay on 'The Treatment and Conversion of African Slaves in the Sugar Colonies'. They spread tales of Ramsay's depravity in St Kitts and poured scorn on his campaign.

When the abolitionists' parliamentary campaign began again after 1802, they were strengthened by three new members from the Clapham Sect, James Stephen, Zachary Macaulay and Henry Brougham. The first two brought their West Indian experience, and the third his cleverness and influence. Surprisingly Pitt was now almost a handicap to the movement because there were some members in his government who were against abolition. He could not adopt abolition as his policy because it would split his government and bring about his downfall.

In 1804 Wilberforce introduced a bill for the abolition of the slave trade in House of Commons. The bill was carried in the Commons, but defeated this time in the Lords. An Order-in-Council was issued in September, 1805, which prohibited the slave trade in the newly-occupied colonies of Trinidad, St Lucia and Guiana. This measure showed the support of the Crown for abolition. Pitt died in 1806 and Charles James Fox was prepared to commit the new government to abolition. A new Abolition Act was passed by the Commons in 1806, and by the Lords in 1807, with substantial majorities in both Houses. The Act received the Royal Assent on 25 March 1807. The abolitionists had won their first great victory.

Difficulties in enforcing the abolition of the slave trade

The Act of 1807 declared all trading in African slaves from 1 January, 1808, to be 'utterly abolished, prohibited and declared to be unlawful'. However, British captains continued to trade in slaves because they were unlikely to be caught. If they were, punishments were not severe, only a fine of £100 for every slave carried. The British government set about remedying this. British warships were sent to search for slave ships. In Sierra Leone the British West Africa Squadron was based at Freetown to patrol the Gulf of Guinea. It had

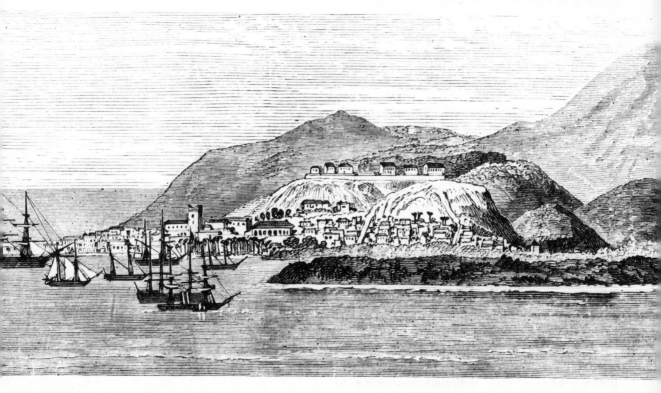

Sierra Leone

some success in the Gulf as slave ships could not sail away from the coast fast due to an unfavourable wind blowing into the shore, which came to be known as the 'Government wind'. Once out into the Atlantic, however, they could often outsail the government ships.

In the Caribbean, an international court known as the 'Mixed Commission' was set up at Havana to decide the legality of the captures made by British naval ships and to arrange for the disposal of the freed slaves. Up to 1834 they were usually taken back to Sierra Leone, but after emancipation they were more often sent to Jamaica, Barbados or Trinidad.

In 1811 the British government passed another Act laying down stiffer penalties for captains caught slave trading. Transportation was the penalty for the first offence and hanging for the second. These methods succeeded in deterring British captains from trading in slaves.

Another loophole in the law of 1807 allowed slave owners moving from one colony to take with them two 'domestic' slaves. In this way field slaves were moved, chiefly to Trinidad and Guiana where slaves were in short supply, and were sold there for high prices. Therefore, in 1812, an Order-in-Council was issued which made it compulsory for all slave owners in Trinidad to register their slaves by a certain date. Any blacks not registered would be declared free. This Order was ineffective. Finally no slaves from foreign countries were allowed to be imported into British colonies after 1 January, 1808.

The 1807 Act only applied to British nationals and to the British empire but, as Britain was the major slave trader, it caused the Atlantic slave trade to decline. Denmark was the only other country to have abolished the slave trade. The British government could only use diplomacy and persuasion to make other countries give up the trade. In 1813 Sweden, and in 1814 Holland, abolished their slave trade, but like Denmark, these countries were only small carriers of slaves. At the Congress of Vienna in 1814-15, all countries attending agreed to a British motion to stop the slave trade, but they did little to carry it out. France asked for a five-year interval before she abolished her trade so that she could re-stock her colonies! In 1818 France, and in 1820 Spain, made slave trading illegal, but in practice they did nothing to stop their nationals continuing to trade.

The British government then introduced the idea of 'Reciprocal Search Treaties', whereby the British navy had the right to search foreign ships, and foreign naval ships had the same right to search British ships. Reciprocal Search Treaties between Britain and Spain were signed in 1817 and 1835. However, the main Spanish slave trade was to Cuba and it was almost impossible for the British navy to search even the 3,000 kilometres of the coast of Cuba, let alone the rest of the Atlantic. In any case Spanish ships could evade detection by flying the flag of the United States.

The slave trade would not stop without the goodwill of all countries, and this could not be obtained. The only way in which it could be stopped was by an end to the demand for slaves through the abolition of slavery. Thus the slave trade continued until the abolition of slavery in the United States, Puerto Rico and Cuba.

Abolition of slavery in Jamaica

The Emancipation of Slaves

Amelioration

Attitude in the British islands

The abolitionists had thought that the threat to abolish the slave trade would make the planters treat their slaves better. In 1792 a new consolidating Slave Act was passed in Jamaica, which included heavy fines and imprisonment for mutilation, and the death penalty for the murder of a slave. After this Act came the following report from Jamaica attempting to show that slave conditions had improved.

> Jamaica enjoys the most undisturbed tranquility.. the slaves throughout the whole island signified by their uniform and peaceable demeanour, the utmost satisfaction with the blessings they possess from peace, plenty and humane masters.

In 1798, a Slave Amelioration Act was passed in the Leeward Islands which was considered very humane at the time. Finally, the treatment of slaves in Barbados was reported as being the best in the British West Indies.

All this belied the facts. The psychology of the planters seemed to be exactly the opposite to that postulated by the abolitionists. The planters, especially those in Jamaica, took the attitude that if abolition was coming the slaves must be made to suffer for it. They were more cruel, worked the slaves much harder and looked after them less well than ever before. In fact, some of the worst

Ill-treatment of slaves 1830

treatment of slaves took place in the first thirty years of the nineteenth century.

Many of the Clapham Sect had left the abolition movement because they did not want emancipation and the remaining abolitionists felt that they could not press for it immediately. They felt that the next step should be amelioration. This was supported by the West India interest which felt that better treatment of slaves would persuade the abolitionists to drop emancipation. By 1815 the British government, too, was in favour of this policy.

In the British West Indies there was a distinction between the new or Crown Colonies—Trinidad, St Lucia and the Guiana colonies—and the old colonies, sometimes called the 'The Legislative islands' of Barbados, Jamaica and the Leewards, which were almost self-governing. The British government by Orders-in-Council, could pass slave amelioration measures for the Crown Colonies, but only the local legislatures could pass such measures for the other islands.

The Registration of Slaves or Registry Bill, which was intended to stop excessive punishment as well as prevent the illegal sale of slaves, was passed for Trinidad in 1812 and for St Lucia in 1814. In 1815, the abolitionists began their new campaign against slavery. Wilberforce introduced a bill for the compulsory registration of slaves in all colonies, but it was met by protests from the colonial legislatures that the British government had no right to interfere with their slave laws. Wilberforce agreed to withdraw his bill when the Colonial Secretary promised to write a circular letter to colonial governors urging them to ameliorate their slave laws, and especially to pass registration bills. But this letter had little effect. The colonies regarded the dropping of the bill as a victory over the abolitionists.

In 1823 the 'Society for the Gradual Abolition of Slavery' was formed, aimed at making amelioration part of government policy. They campaigned for its immediate enforcement by law, followed by abolition 'at an early date'. In its first year the Society formed 200 branches in England which sent 750 petitions to Parliament. The most famous one was entitled, 'An Appeal to the Religion, Justice and Humanity of the Inhabitants of the British Empire in behalf of the Negro Slaves in the West Indies'. A publication called the 'Anti-Slavery Monthly Reporter' also appeared in 1823.

Thomas Buxton had taken over from William Wilberforce as the chief parliamentary spokesman for abolition. In 1823 Buxton introduced his famous resolution in the House: 'That the state of slavery is repugnant to the principles of the British Constitution and of the Christian religion and that it ought to be gradually abolished throughout the British colonies.'

Meanwhile, however, the West India interest was working hard to try to stop abolition. A committee of fifteen, including ten Members of Parliament, was formed to plan their campaign. They decided to 'take the wind out of the sails' of the abolitionists by proposing their own amelioration measures. Of course, the success of this policy depended on the West Indian planters carrying out the measures if they were passed. The West India interest put their own detailed amelioration proposals before the Secretary of State, Lord Bathurst, who accepted them. In the face of these seemingly reasonable proposals and good intentions, Buxton agreed to withdraw his resolution; George Canning then put foward an amelioration bill based on the West India Committee's proposals.

The suggestions for reform sent to the colonies of Trinidad, St Lucia and Demerara were largely ignored. For example, Governor Murray of Demerara

Thomas Buxton

received his instructions and did not publish them. The slaves got the idea that their freedom was being withheld and they revolted in 1823. Although the Reverend John Smith had told the slaves that the rumour about freedom was false, and urged them not to use violence, he was blamed for inciting the revolt, imprisoned for seven weeks, tried and condemned. He died of tuberculosis in prison before the news of his reprieve arrived.

A circular letter was sent to the Legislative islands urging them to adopt and effect positive measures for amelioration rather than have the British government force a law on them. In detail, the measures suggested were

a) no flogging of women;
b) a day should be allowed to elapse between the offence and the flogging;
c) records of all floggings of over three lashes should be presented to the magistrates at the quarter sessions;
d) slave families should not be divided;
e) slaves should not be sold in payment of debts;
f) adequate religious instruction should be given to slaves;
g) slaves should be allowed to give evidence in court if a minister would vouch for the slave's character;
h) savings banks for slaves should be set up to encourage thrift and enable slaves to buy personal possessions.

The failure of amelioration

Although the amelioration measures were the proposals of the West India Committee, once again the Legislatures of Jamaica, Barbados, Dominica and St Vincent ignored them. In 1826 the revised Slave Code in Jamaica forbade slaves to receive religious instruction, and also said that no church services could be held between sunrise and sunset. Slaves could be whipped or imprisoned for preaching without their owners' consent. These laws were directly contradictory to the Colonial Secretary's request, and he protested to the Jamaican Assembly, saying 'I cannot too distinctly impress upon you that it is the settled purpose of His Majesty's Government to sanction no colonial law which needlessly infringes on the religious liberty of any class of His Majesty's subjects'.

The reaction of the West Indian planters, together with the ill-treatment of William Shrewsbury and John Smith and the harassment of other missionaries, angered the abolitionists in England and turned public opinion decisively against the planters. Wilberforce called for an inquiry into the Smith case and much publicity was given to Shrewsbury, a Wesleyan minister, who was driven out of Barbados after his home and church had been destroyed.

It was finally recognised in England that the planters had no intention of ameliorating their slave laws. The policy of amelioration was deemed a failure after about 1826, and in 1830 was definitely abandoned in favour of complete emancipation.

Missionaries in the British West Indies

It is hard to assess the contribution of the missionaries in bringing about emancipation. Their reports in the last few years before emancipation were influential, and the treatment which they received turned public opinion against the planters. But most of the missionaries did not belong to the established church to which most Members of Parliament belonged and they had little direct influence.

The Church of England was the church of the planters and it did very little to help the slaves. In fact it acted against them in denying them religion. Its most effective activity in helping slaves came from the 'Society for the Propagation of the Gospel', founded in 1699. Christopher Codrington left this Society money in 1710 to found a college in Barbados, known as Codrington College. Apart from this, there was little missionary activity by the Anglican Church. Nearer emancipation, when the British government insisted on religious instruction for slaves, the Anglicans concentrated on the idea that it was possible to be a good slave and a good Christian. Bowing to public pressure from England, the 'Society for the Conversion and Religious Instruction and Education of the Negro Slaves in the West Indies' was set up in 1794, but by comparison with the nonconformist societies it did little to help the slaves.

In the Spanish islands the Roman Catholic Church was active in converting and instructing slaves. The planters had to allow Catholic slave schools and give the slaves time to attend. The *Code Noir* contained similar provisions for the French islands, but in practice the attitude of the Roman Catholic Church there was the same as that of the Anglican Church in the British islands. The French government demanded the conversion of slaves but, by the time of emancipation in 1848, few slaves had been converted.

Prior to emancipation the West Indies were generally irreligious. There were too few ministers or priests for the population. If they were conscientious they were overworked, but most of them were of poor calibre and there was little respect for the clergy. In 1799 a Methodist missionary in Antigua summed up the situation thus: 'I am in an enemy's country; women and drink bear down all before them'. The slaves had come not to expect religious instruction, although they wanted it. In many cases they developed their own beliefs and rituals when they were deprived of formal Christianity. These un-Christian beliefs were a serious challenge to the missionaries.

Nonconformist missions

Eventually the slaves found their religious guidance from the Protestant nonconformist missions, most of which were established towards the end of the eighteenth century as the result of religious revivals in Europe. These were evangelical movements, placing emphasis on the study of the Bible, morality and good works, and giving little emphasis to the sacraments apart from baptism.

The United Brethren or Moravians, founded in Germany, were the first to establish missions for slaves in the West Indies. The first was in St Thomas in 1732; followed by St Kitts in 1756 and Antigua in 1774, and by 1800 there were over 10,000 Moravian converts in the West Indies, 7,000 in Antigua alone. Their missions practised self-sufficiency, so that a close Moravian community developed when they took over a plantation 'lock, stock and barrel'. Their missionaries were expected to labour and this presented problems in West Indian society.

The Baptist mission was the most important for its work amongst slaves in the British West Indies. It was founded in Jamaica by two blacks, George Lisle and Moses Baker, in 1784. They had been brought from America, via the Bahamas, by Loyalists who left America after Independence. They built a large, brick church in Kingston and sent out preachers on horseback to reach the slaves in the fields who could not attend the main church. Their success was so great that in 1813 they applied to the Baptist Missionary Society in Britain for help, and famous missionaries like

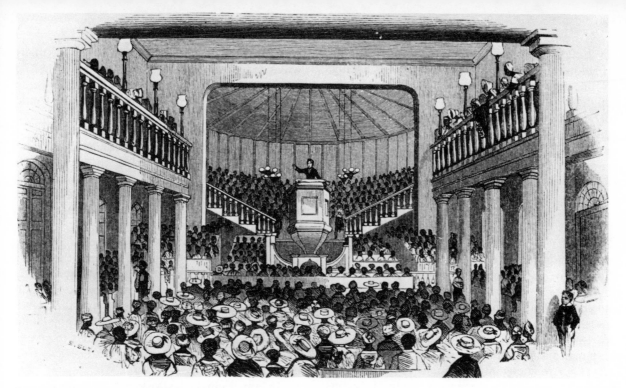

Interior of a Baptist chapel in Jamaica

William Knibb and Thomas Burchell arrived in the West Indies.

The Methodists began their work in Antigua in 1770 and spread through the Eastern Caribbean where they were attacked by the planters. In 1789 the Methodist Meeting House in Barbados was stoned and the slaves who attended were flogged. After a visit to Jamaica in 1789 by Dr Coke, a leading Methodist, twelve other missionaries were sent out from England.

After the Napoleonic Wars had ended in 1815, missionary work in the West Indies intensified. More Baptists arrived and the other denominations also stepped up their preaching and teaching to slaves.

The persecution of missionaries

The chief obstacle faced by the nonconformist missionaries, especially the Baptists and Methodists, was the hostility of the planters. Most planters were convinced that it was impossible to be a good slave and a good Christian. Moreover, the nonconformists preached other doctrines, like Christian brotherhood and equality before God, which the planters found unacceptable. Such doctrines were inflammatory in the planters' opinion, and in teaching them the missionaries were inciting the slaves to rebellion. The missionaries often insisted that the slaves be taught to read and write, so that they could have private Bible readings and prayers between Sunday services. The planters were very strongly against educating slaves, and so were the authorities. They felt that education would encourage disobedience to authority, and lead to deep discontent and rebellion.

The missionaries did not incite the slaves to rebellion, but they did have deep sympathy for the slaves and they did not like the existence of slavery. Unfortunately for the missionaries, their period of great activity amongst the slaves, 1815 to 1833, coincided with the anti-slavery movement, and the planters simply blamed the missionaries whenever there was unrest or rebellion. So the missionaries were persecuted. In fact, they advised restraint and always preached 'non-violence' to the slaves. They told slaves to wait patiently and their freedom would come. Unfortunately, by doing so, the missionaries often lost the confidence of the slaves who thought that they were taking the side of the planters because of their colour. The missionaries then found themselves hated by both sides.

In the Jamaica rebellion of 1831, William Knibb was in a dilemma. He could not openly support emancipation as that would be encouraging slaves to break the law. He wrote to the Baptist Headquarters in London for instructions, asking: 'While you are exerting all your energies at home, ought we to sit here idle all day?' However, in spite of his urging restraint, the planters blamed him for the rebellion and he was arrested. He was acquitted and left for England to make his report which contributed greatly to the passing of the Emancipation Bill in the following year.

Other obstacles faced by the missionaries

1   The law was used to make things difficult for the missionaries. For example, the St Vincent Legislature passed a law in 1793 which required a minister to reside in the island for one year before he could preach. The Consolidated Slave Act of 1808 in Jamaica forbade Methodists to instruct slaves or have them in their chapels. The 1826 Act in Jamaica forbade missionaries to take fees from slaves for religious instruction.

2   Right up to 1833, there were too few missionaries for the work they had to perform. They had to reach the slaves on the estates which necessitated travelling long distances on horseback in the hot sun. The death toll was high. William Knibb's brother died within five months of coming to Jamaica. William Knibb himself had to travel over 150 kilometres between the extremities of his mission, and he had to minister to congregations of 5,000 at some stations. There was just too much work to do.

3   Instruction of the slaves in English presented problems. Amongst themselves, the slaves were accustomed to use a 'patois'. The language they heard from the whites was often in the form of commands and abuse. The missionaries could not reach every slave with oral instruction, and they expected some slaves to learn to read and write so that they could instruct others. But education in reading and writing independent of religious education was not allowed, and so the slaves had no formal coaching in the English language.

4   Irreligion and immorality were widespread amongst the slaves. To counteract this, the missionaries were strict. They would not accept slaves into the Church unless they could pass certain tests to become 'ticket-holders' (full members) of the Church. To remain ticket-holders, every quarter the slave had to satisfy the Church of his good behaviour. A slave who showed an interest in the Church was known as an 'inquirer'. In the Baptist Church he would be questioned as to how many wives he had, and asked if he believed in God, and if he was sorry for his sins. Finally, if he answered some catechism questions satisfactorily, he would be baptised in a nearby river.

5   The slaves had rituals and superstitions which had grown up because they were denied Christianity. When the missionaries tried to superimpose Christianity on slave cults they often thought they had been successful, whereas the slave thought that the new religion and his old superstitions could survive together.

6   The Sunday Market was a special obstacle missionaries had to overcome. As it was the Lord's Day, the missionaries had to have Sunday for their services, but the slaves were reluctant to give up their beloved market. In Demerara the slaves suggested a Saturday Market so that they could keep the Sabbath, but the planters interpreted this as a trick on the part of the slaves to get two free days per week.

7   In Jamaica in the last year before emancipation there arose a group known as The Colonial Church Union. It was organised to resist the missionaries after the 1831-32 rising. Before this group was banned by the Governor in January, 1833, fourteen Baptist and six Methodist Chapels were destroyed and many missionaries were beaten up.

Conclusion

In spite of all these difficulties many slaves were converted and gave thanks to God on emancipation. Once freed, they turned to the nonconformist churches, especially the Baptists and the Methodists, who had done so much for them before 1833. The Anglican Church continued as the established church until it was disestablished in most islands between 1868 and 1870 but it failed to appeal to many ex-slaves. In all the islands except Barbados, where the Anglican Church was strong, the ratio of nonconformists to Anglicans became about 2:1 after emancipation.

The emancipation of slaves

Immediate causes

Amelioration had been rejected as being unworkable, and evidence of planter brutality came not only from the West Indies but also from

Mauritius. In May, 1830, at a public meeting in London a resolution was adopted for the immediate emancipation of slaves in the British colonies, and an intensive campaign began in 1831.

In Britain 'reform' was in the air; emancipation was just part of it. There was a strong movement to give more people the vote and increase parliamentary representation of the new industrial towns. These political reforms would help emancipation by increasing the parliamentary influence of the evangelicals and the new industrialists who were already changing their ideas about slave-produced sugar.

Extra impetus was given by the following.
1   The publication of a pamphlet by a man named Whiteley on his observations on the treatment of slaves in Jamaica;
2   The 1831-2 Slave Revolt in Jamaica and its brutal suppression by the authorities, especially the treatment of Samuel Sharp and William Knibb;
3   The arrival in Britain of William Knibb and Thomas Burchell who reported that to maintain slavery would promote a racial war;
4   A crowded meeting at Exeter Hall in London which sent a deputation to the Prime Minister demanding emancipation.

However, it was finally the attitude of the Jamaica planters which showed the British government that there could be no compromise with slavery. In 1831 they offered lower duties on sugar in return for amendments to slave laws by the colonial legislatures. Then they put forward the idea of compensation to the slave owners for freeing their slaves. This proved to be the incentive that the planters needed to accept emancipation. By 1831 even the Jamaica planters faced the fact that emancipation was inevitable.

The Emancipation Act, 1833

Thomas Buxton introduced the Emancipation Bill in 1833. Wilberforce, its former champion, was approaching his death. By the time he died on 29 July, 1833, he was assured that emancipation would go through, as it had already passed its second reading. The Act stated that: 'Slavery shall be and is hereby utterly and forever abolished and declared unlawful throughout the British colonies and possessions abroad'. However, in 1833 emancipation was not as complete as these words would suggest, because there were clauses in the Act

about an apprenticeship system which delayed complete emancipation until 1838.

The Bill originally proposed a loan of £15,000,000 to slave owners from the British government, and an apprenticeship period of twelve years. This meant that most slaves in 1833 were likely to die in slavery. These two clauses were amended and the final Act was basically as follows.
1   Slave children under six years old were to be freed immediately;
2   Slaves over six would have to serve an apprenticeship of six years in the case of praedial slaves, and four years in the case of all others;
3   Apprentices should work for not more than forty-five hours per week without pay, and any additional hours with pay;
4   Apprentices should be provided with food and clothing by the master;
5   Compensation in the form of a free gift of £20,000,000 should be paid to slave owners throughout the British empire on condition that the local legislatures passed laws to bring emancipation;
6   The apprenticeship period could be shortened, but no alternative to apprenticeship would be allowed.

On 29 August, 1833, the Act received Royal Assent. Emancipation was to come into effect on 1 August, 1834. Orders-in-Council enforced it on the Crown Colonies. In the other colonies, the local legislatures were expected to follow suit, and since they wanted their compensation, they enacted emancipation laws quickly. The Jamaican planters had been very worried when they first heard that compensation was to be in the form of a loan, but after this was changed to a free gift by the persuasive efforts of the West India Committee and the amount increased, they, too, passed emancipation quickly.

The Legislatures of Antigua and Bermuda decided to do without apprenticeship, so there the slaves had complete freedom on 1 August, 1834. The other islands accepted apprenticeship though it seemed hard for the slaves of St Kitts when their neighbours in Antigua were free. Complete freedom for all was scheduled for 1 August, 1840, but in the event it was brought forward to 1 August, 1838, when it was decided to end apprenticeship two years earlier.

On 1 August, 1834, 668,000 slaves were set free, or partially free because of apprenticeship. The slaves disliked the apprenticeship system, but they

Emancipation festival in Barbados

Compensation for a headman in British Guiana could be as high as £230. On the other hand, in Antigua where the output was low in relation to the numbers of slaves, compensation could be lower than £15. The following are figures for the average compensation per slave in some of the islands.

British Guiana, £52;
Trinidad, £50;
Jamaica, £20;
Barbados, £21;
St Kitts, £17;
Antigua, £15;
Bermuda, £12

The apprenticeship system

Antigua was the only British West Indian island not to have apprenticeship. Within two months, two-thirds of the ex-slaves there were working as free labourers on the plantations. This was because there was practically no unoccupied land for the freed blacks. Antigua's experience seemed a justification for the argument that free labour was more efficient than slave labour because within ten years fewer labourers were producing nearly twice as much sugar. Also the granting of complete emancipation immediately, made for good relations between blacks and whites.

Reasons for apprenticeship

There were many justifications given for apprenticeship. Probably in the mind of its author, James Stephen and his associates, they were sincere beliefs. However, in practice there was only one real reason—apprenticeship was used to soften the blow of emancipation by giving the planters a few more years of free labour, while conceding to the slaves their right to freedom. The earlier proposals of an apprenticeship period of twelve years show clearly that it was designed to appease the planters and 'trick' the slaves into thinking that they were free.

Humanitarians had accepted that apprenticeship was justified on the grounds that the ex-slaves would need time to adjust to looking after themselves, handling money and supporting their families. However, it was soon apparent that apprenticeship was not designed to do this because food and clothes were still provided by the master, and the

accepted it with patience. At midnight on 31 July, 1838, complete freedom was received with great rejoicing, but with little or no excessive exuberance in the form of drunkenness or violence as the whites feared. Indeed, many of the freed slaves went to church in thanksgiving.

Compensation

Of the total compensation of £20,000,000 for all the British empire, the British West Indies received £16,500,000. Most of the planters who received it, used it to pay off their debts.

Compensation to individual planters was worked out for each island from the ratio of the quantity of exports to the number of slaves; that is, a sort of assessment of the slaves' productivity in each island. In colonies where there were few slaves the ratio was high and compensation was high. For example, in Trinidad and British Guiana there were few slaves and output was relatively high.

slaves' opportunity for earning money was very limited.

It was also argued that the planters needed time to adjust to wage labour and there was certainly more foundation for this argument. There were no banks in Jamaica and planters were not used to transactions in cash. However, the planters did not use the apprenticeship period to adjust to a cash economy. Apprenticeship was over before the Planters' Bank in Jamaica, and the West India Bank in Barbados and the other islands, were established. Even by the 1860s, the planters had not adjusted to wage labour.

Apprenticeship at work

There were two drawbacks to apprenticeship, firstly that the planters would behave as if they still had slave labour and secondly, that the ex-slaves would think that they were completely free and refuse to work. The planters tried to exact as much work as possible from the ex-slaves. They were unwilling to pay for labour beyond the forty-five hours' free labour per week and tried to bring cases against ex-slaves so that they could be forced back into conditions of slavery. The ex-slaves often played into the planters' hands by refusing to work. Thus they were breaking the law and could be put in the workhouse or 'House of Correction', where they were treated as plantation slaves again.

In the apprenticeship period the treadmill, a new form of punishment for the West Indies, was introduced into the workhouses. Probably the Marquess of Sligo introduced it during his governorship of Jamaica, 1834-36, as an humanitarian punishment but, in practice, it was just the opposite. The ex-slaves were strapped by their wrists to a high bar with their legs working a revolving drum by continuous stepping on the steps. If they stopped the boards would come round and hit their shins a painful blow, so they just had to keep walking. A man with a whip stood by to keep them toiling.

Special Magistrates

The job of seeing that the apprenticeship system was not abused could not be entrusted to the justices of the peace, because they came from the planter class. New magistrates, called 'stipendiary'

The treadmill

or 'special' magistrates, were appointed. Soon there were 150 throughout the British West Indies, including sixty in Jamaica. Usually retired army or navy officers from Britain were appointed to ensure impartiality, but some West Indians had to be appointed to make up the numbers. For example, Richard Hill, a Jamaican of mixed race, was head of the special magistrates in Jamaica until his death in 1872.

Part of their job was to answer appeals from ex-slaves who complained of ill-treatment, although sometimes it was the planters who complained that the ex-slaves would not work. This entailed visiting the estates on horseback. In one month in Jamaica fifty-six magistrates visited 3,440 estates, and covered 22,720 kilometres. With this sort of hard work it is not surprising that twenty special magistrates died in the first two years. Moreover their salary was low; £300 per year in 1834, rising to £450 per year later, out of which they had to pay for their own accommodation and horses. Because of their work, and the fact that most of them were foreigners, they found themselves friendless, in a hostile environment.

No new laws were enacted for apprenticeship. Plantation discipline and punishment still continued, and the special magistrates had no jurisdiction in the plantations. It was up to an ex-slave to complain about his treatment, and there must have been many cases of cruelty which never came to light.

Special magistrates were unpopular with the planters because they listened to the appeals of the ex-slaves and frequently upheld them. But they could also be unpopular with the slaves for agreeing that the planter's punishment was justified. If the ex-slave broke the law, for example by refusing to work, he passed out of the jurisdiction of the special magistrate into the hands of the old magistrates from whom he could expect no mercy, and usually ended up on the treadmill. However, special magistrates probably favoured the ex-slaves because they felt that they were appointed to protect them.

The special magistrates were praised for their work by colonial governors, especially the Marquess of Sligo. They did a very good job under the most difficult conditions. They worked on two-year contracts and, therefore, could be dismissed if the authorities were not satisfied. Some were dismissed, but most continued in their jobs until their deaths, which shows how well the authorities were satis-

fied with them. Indeed, special magistrates were still at work in the West Indies long after the apprenticeship period had ended, even as late as the 1870s.

The end of apprenticeship

The apprenticeship system was judged a failure and brought to an early end. To the slaves, apprenticeship seemed just a continuation of slavery and it was unpopular with the planters, even though it was designed to help them. They often tried to make things worse for the ex-slaves by making them work on Friday afternoons and Saturdays, the traditional free times, or by taking away the 'grounds' of the slaves, or by removing other privileges.

In 1836 a Quaker humanitarian, Joseph Sturge, visited Jamaica and reported on the apprenticeship system. He emphasised the cruelty, especially in the workhouses, and even accused the special magistrates of corruption and siding with the planters against the slaves. In spite of its falsifications, his report had a very considerable influence on public opinion in Britain and on Parliament. *The West Indies in 1837* by Joseph Sturge and Thomas Hardy helped to bring apprenticeship to an early end.

In 1838 the British Parliament amended the Abolition of Slavery Act by forbidding the flogging of females or punishment on the treadmill, and by allowing colonial governors to supervise the treatment of apprentices in workhouses. However, they were still willing to keep apprenticeship, regarding it as an additional compensation to slave owners for the loss of their slaves. They would not agree to an early end to the system unless the colonial legislatures wanted it. The legal question of the status of artisan slaves finally decided the matter. Domestic slaves were to receive complete freedom in 1838. The artisan slaves, who maintained the machinery on the estates and did other specialised jobs, insisted that they should be classed as domestic slaves. However, without the labour of artisan slaves, the plantations could not keep running and so, when it was decided that artisans could not be forced to work after 1838, complete freedom had to be given to all slaves on the plantations, and apprenticeship came to an end. Everyone was pleased except those ex-slaves who had struggled hard to save enough money to buy their manumission, only to find that freedom would have been theirs without payment if they had waited a little longer.

One historian has stated that 'apprenticeship was the only practical way in which a great social reform could be effected'. This is doubtful. It was an experiment which the French and the Spanish chose not to repeat in emancipating their slaves. Victor Schoelcher condemned it both in its idea and its practice.

Abolition and emancipation in the French and Spanish islands

The French islands

Although slavery had been abolished throughout the French empire by the French Revolution, this was only effective in St Domingue. In 1803 Napoleon re-established slavery, and when the Bourbon kings were restored in 1815 they retained it.

In 1818 the French government promised to abolish the slave trade, but in fact the number of slaves in the French colonies increased. Like the British, the French had slave revolts demonstrating the resistance to slavery, especially in Martinique. There were revolts at Carbet in 1822 and 1824, and a large-scale revolt at Grande Anse in 1833. The French, too, decided to adopt a policy of amelioration before thinking about emancipation. Thus the French emancipation movement seemed to be following a parallel course to the British, although fifteen years later. However, many of the laws passed in Paris did not become effective in the French colonies due to local resistance by planters and officials, although there were no local legislatures. In 1832 the tax on manumission was abolished and the manumission process simplified, and in 1833 the registration of all slaves was made compulsory, and the mutilation and branding of slaves was abolished.

However, public opinion in France was not satisfied with amelioration and demanded complete emancipation. It was influenced by Victor Schoelcher who had personal experience of slavery in the Spanish colonies, and in 1830 he wrote *Letters about Mexico* in which he described slavery in Cuba. After a visit to the French West Indies in 1840, he was convinced that immediate emancipation was necessary.

In France, *La Société pour l'abolition de l'esclavage*

was formed in 1834, achieving a minor victory in 1836 when it was decreed that any slave setting foot in France must be set free. In 1838 it drafted an emancipation bill but the opposition from the West India interest in the French Assembly was much greater than in the British Parliament. The French West India interest defended slavery as economically necessary and socially desirable because of the savagery and idleness of slaves. Meanwhile the situation in the French islands was becoming desperate, for, after 1838, thousands of French slaves escaped to the neighbouring British islands.

Unlike the English abolition movement, it was not linked to any religious group. The French movement was rational and secular. In the early 1840s, the industrial workers of Paris and Lyons joined the movement. Schoelcher himself was an humanitarian, but not attached to any particular church group. He was personally very well informed about slavery, but did not approach abolition with the fervour of a religious crusade.

In 1847 a national petition from *La Société pour l'abolition de l'esclavage* called for immediate emancipation. On 27 April 1848, Schoelcher proposed the abolition of slavery throughout the French empire. The bill incorporated the idea of compensation and 126,000,000 francs were paid to the owners of 258,000 slaves in the French colonies of Martinique, Guadeloupe, Cayenne and Réunion. At an average of just under 50 francs per slave, it was less than the average amount received in compensation in the British islands. Schoelcher said that there could be no halfway stage between slavery and freedom like apprenticeship. All slaves emancipated in the French colonies had full freedom and also full rights of French citizenship immediately.

The Spanish islands

In the last twenty-five years of the eighteenth century there was a slump in tobacco production in Cuba and a boom in sugar. With increased sugar production slavery grew and, at first, the Cuban planters could not obtain enough slaves due to trade restrictions. Therefore, in 1791, the Cuban slave trade was declared open and duties on slaves were reduced. Traders from any country who imported slaves into Cuba were allowed to export any commodity without duty. By 1817 the number of slaves in Cuba had risen to 224,000, over a third of the population. The authorities became worried about the ratio of slave to free. They tried to attract European immigrants by offers of free land, but they did nothing to stop the slave trade.

At the Congress of Vienna, 1815, Spain promised to stop the slave trade and, in 1817, signed a Reciprocal Search Treaty with Britain. However, the Spanish had no intention of enforcing these measures which they interpreted as attempts by Britain to remove Cuban competition in the sugar trade. In 1820, the Spanish again formally agreed to stop the slave trade but with no effect. In some years after this, as many as 10,000 slaves per year were imported into Cuba. The Anglo-Spanish Commission Courts set up in Havana and Sierra Leone found it impossible to patrol the Atlantic,

or even the coast of Cuba. Spanish traders flew the United States' flag if they thought they were going to be searched. Philip Curtin estimated that between 1811 and 1870, 606,000 slaves were imported into Cuba and Puerto Rico, although for most of this time the Spanish slave trade was officially illegal! However, finally in 1865, the Spanish did abolish the slave trade effectively. Outside pressure had always been strong, but there was a growing abolition movement in Spain. In Cuba itself, the Creole Spaniards were worried about the great numbers of slaves and wanted the slave trade, which was in the hands of Spanish-born traders, suppressed.

There was increasing pressure from Britain, then nearing the height of her imperial power, to

Night chase of the brigatine slaver *Windward*

free slaves. Moreover the Spanish slaves knew the British slaves were free and the danger of slave revolts increased. In Cuba, by 1840, the majority of slaves were legally entitled to their freedom if they could prove to the Anglo-Spanish Commission at Havana that they had been imported after 1820, but as this was difficult all but a few remained slaves. In 1843 there was a series of revolts in the Matanzas region by slaves who thought that their freedom was being withheld. They were encouraged by some mulattoes. The brutal suppression of these revolts, including the execution of mulattoes, made more people in Cuba want to end slavery.

The fortunes of abolition in Cuba were linked to the independence movement. Many Creole Spaniards wanted independence, but while there was the danger of slave revolts they were dependent on Spain for protection. Even after the most unpopular regime of Tacon, the Cuban slave owners still clung to Spain and were despised for this by the liberals in Spain and Cuba. Others feared emancipation because they thought it would lead to a black republic like Haiti when independence came. Others feared that, without slavery, there would be a decline in the sugar industry, as in Jamaica. The extreme pro-slavery group even considered annexation by the United States if Spain could not protect them from slave revolts or was going to bring emancipation.

The British were urging emancipation in Cuba for humanitarian and economic reasons. Slave-produced sugar from Cuba was underselling the sugar produced in the British islands. Britain also wanted emancipation to keep Cuba out of the hands of the United States. If slaves were freed, there would be no more looking to the United States for protection. The United States had offered to buy Cuba in 1848. The British Prime Minister, Palmerston, thought that emancipation was essential to stop this happening.

The American Civil War, 1861-65, brought emancipation to slaves throughout the United States. There could be no thought of Cuba wanting to join the United States now. Cuba was on its own and the liberals urged emancipation and independence. The movement was supported by Cuban exiles in the United States who supplied guns and ammunition. In Cuba, Carlos Manuel de Cespedes led the independence movement. He started by freeing his own slaves in 1868 and the Ten Years War followed. The Spanish government was not able to put down the rebels until 1878 when the Treaty of Zanjon promised the gradual emancipation of slaves. In 1880 this policy was changed by a decree from Spain for emancipation without compensation. Emancipation for all slaves in Cuba was completed by 1886. The intervening six years had been used to allow emancipation to be accompanied by a policy of large-scale white immigration from Spain.

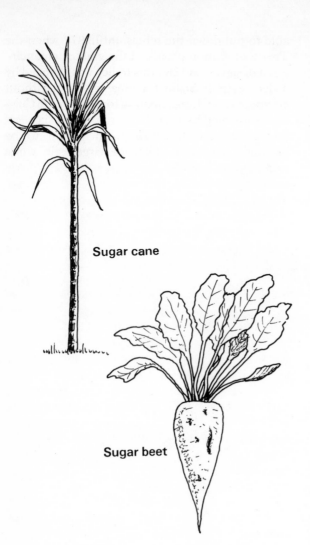

Sugar cane

Sugar beet

8

The Labour Problem after Emancipation

The immediate post-emancipation period

Before emancipation, all the territories in the British West Indies could be classed as plantation economies based on slave labour. After emancipation, the 'island separateness' developed, which led to island parochialism and pride, now so strong in the West Indies. Eventually, of course, this led to the islands becoming separate, independent nations.

Care must be taken when stressing this separate development. In a wider view, for example a comparison between the East Indies and the West Indies, the West Indian islands would all appear to be following a similar development, facing the same problems and finding the same solutions. Between 1838 and 1848 the British West Indies were still sugar islands with very little diversification of crops. The differences between some islands, for example Antigua and Barbados, were so slight as to be unnoticeable to anyone apart from the history student. Nevertheless, differences in economic development and social structure began to appear in this period which were magnified over the years into the great differences which exist today between two territories like Guyana and St Kitts.

The most important influence on separate development was geography. Basically the larger island, because they had more land available, had greater labour problems than the smaller ones. There was also the interaction between geography and other factors, like the size of the freed slave population, the attitudes of planters and ex-slaves and the policies of the island governments.

Let us compare the problems of Trinidad and Jamaica. Trinidad was large in area with a very small freed slave population, so it faced a grave labour problem, but the government was prepared to meet this with a policy of large-scale immigration. Jamaica was also large in area, but had a very large freed slave population which shunned plantation labour. The Jamaica government was not prepared to meet its labour problem with immigration on the Trinidad scale.

The territories which solved their labour problems with large-scale immigration had vastly different social and cultural development from the other islands. Even amongst the indigenous freed slave populations, the patterns for social development were set in this period, for example the village co-operativeness which is a feature of West Indian life.

The freed slaves in 1838

In the British West Indies the choices were:
a) wage labour on the plantation;
b) small-scale farming for subsistence;
c) a combination of wage labour and subsistence farming;
d) small-scale trading ('huckstering', or 'higgling' in Jamaica);
e) wage labour as artisans, e.g. in carpentry;
f) wage labour on the wharf or roads;
g) growing cash crops like sugar, arrowroot etc;
h) fishing for subsistence;
i) drifting into towns in the hope of work.

The freed slaves wanted to turn their backs on plantation labour, but in a small, densely-populated island like Antigua which had complete freedom without apprenticeship in 1834, there was no alternative but to accept wage labour on the plantations. Within two months of emancipation, two-thirds of the ex-slaves in Antigua were back on the plantations. Even in Jamaica, where the hatred of plantation labour was strongest, some ex-slaves found they had no alternative.

Pure subsistence living was possible in places like British Guiana and Trinidad. The pre-Columban crops, like cassava, maize, sweet potato, pineapple and paw-paw, were ideal for subsistence living. Added to these was the banana which had become a very important subsistence crop. There were also the 'new' crops which were introduced to feed the slaves in the second half of the eighteenth century, notably ackee which came from West Africa in 1778, breadfruit which was brought by Captain Bligh of the famous *Bounty* in 1793, and mango which came to the French West Indies in 1782, and was 'captured' by the British. Subsistence was possible on a diet of these crops but the ex-slaves missed their salt-fish and salt-meat. Money was necessary to obtain these and thus the pure subsistence life-style was modified, and a combination of subsistence with some cash income was adopted. The cash was obtained either from sale of produce, or by hiring out one's labour. In British Guiana and Trinidad freed slaves made up gangs for task work, going round the plantations contracting for work when it was most in demand. Some freed slaves began growing cash crops, for example, coffee in Dominica and arrowroot in St Vincent.

The increase in cash incomes meant that there were new markets to be supplied, and increased imports after emancipation provide evidence of this. Therefore, many freed slaves set themselves up as small traders, buying at low prices and selling at a profit. They served as the distributors between the ports and the new communities. Many had acquired skills when they were slaves and decided to expoit their skills, becoming carpenters, mechanics and general handymen.

There was a drift to the towns like St John's in Antigua and Port-of-Spain in Trinidad, lured by the prospect of employment. Some freed slaves, but not as many as contemporary writers suggested, turned to crime. The apparent rise in crime is correctly explained by the fact that criminals were no longer dealt with on the plantations but in the public courts.

Proper family life was possible after emancipation. The freed slave family often pooled their labour resources and shared the proceeds, thus achieving self-sufficiency and independence from the plantations.

The attitude of the ex-slave

The ex-slave's first thought was to turn his back on the plantation which he associated with slavery and cruelty. To do this he needed land of his own. Moreover, he had been indoctrinated by plantation society that land gave not only prosperity but also political power and social prestige. Thus land was the only path the slave knew to advancement.

Plantation slaves attending a religious meeting

There was also a very strong desire for education amongst the freed slaves because it would free them from bondage to the soil. Parents realised that it might be too late for them, but they wanted their children to benefit from education. Some of the new villages had schools, but the common attitude was that education could be more easily obtained in the towns.

In general, plantation society had exerted such a powerful psychological influence on the ex-slave that he could only think in terms of emulating the planters in some way, however small. Those who took to fishing, subsistence in the bush or trying their luck in the towns were considered to be 'opting out of the system'. Such people could never succeed in the plantation society's understanding of the term.

The attitude of the planters

Almost universally the planters feared that they would be faced with no labour force, or be ruined by having to pay excessively high wages. Many gave up their plantations before 1838. Those who remained urged their governments to adopt measures to ensure a cheap, adequate labour force.

The planters knew that the freed slaves hated plantation labour and would try at all costs to avoid it. Only a few planters were enlightened enough to try to make life and work on the plantations attractive and rewarding enough for free labour, and they faced very high labour costs. Most planters saw the availability of land for the freed slaves as the greatest danger to their labour supply. One Jamaican planter said, 'If the lands in the interior get into the possession of the Negro, goodbye to lowland cultivation and to any cultivation.'. But their pleas to the government met with little success and the blacks managed to get land in some way ; the planters just made it more difficult.

In some islands like Antigua, Barbados and St Kitts, there was almost no land available so the question of stopping blacks acquiring land was irrelevant. Nevertheless, in Barbados the planter government considered destroying all provision grounds, so that the blacks would be entirely dependent on their wage.

In the larger territories such as British Guiana, Jamaica and Trinidad, the planters also tried to stop the blacks acquiring land. They tried, unsuccessfully, to get the British government to ban the sale of Crown Land to blacks. They tried to prevent squatting on Crown Land and imposed heavy fines for doing so. For example, in British Guiana, squatting was punishable by three months hard labour. They imposed heavy taxes on land and would not allow the breaking up of large estates into small parcels. All territories insisted on cash sales only.

Nevertheless, blacks did acquire land. In Jamaica by 1860, nearly 40 per cent of the cultivable land was in the hands of blacks. In St Vincent, by 1857, 485 hectares were owned by blacks. Even in Barbados where there was almost no available land, by 1859 3,500 blacks had managed to buy estate land. They succeeded because:
a) the British government was willing to make Crown Land available;
b) there were always some planters who would sell their land to blacks;
c) squatting became an accepted, if illegal, method of acquiring land;
d) co-operation amongst blacks enabled them to pool their resources and buy whole estates if small parcels were not available;
e) the missions bought land if individuals or groups could not afford to;
f) land speculators bought large amounts of land, broke them up and sold them in small parcels.

The planters then tried to keep the freed slaves labouring on the plantations by making life impossible if they did otherwise. The measures taken in Jamaica were typical of those throughout the British West Indies.
1   The planters gave the freed slaves notice to quit the plantation, but they could stay on if they worked. The Jamaican Assembly passed the Ejection Act to evict freed slaves from their homes at a week's notice, and the Trespass Act, by which a freed slave could be imprisoned for reappearing on his home estate.
2   Freed slaves were allowed to remain on the estate, but they lost their grounds and had to pay rent for their cottages. If they did not labour on the estate the rent was very high.
3   Some planters paid high wages at first to keep their plantation labour, but later many found that they just could not afford to do this. A wage bill that was about two-thirds of the plantation's running costs was the maximum.

Having neither stopped the ex-slaves acquiring land nor found other means of keeping them as a reliable, permanent labour force, some planters turned to immigrant labour as the solution to the labour problem.

Large and small territories

Older writers distinguished between colonies, by describing those which had been in British hands since the early or mid-seventeenth century and had well developed plantation economies and large slave populations as 'developed'. Among these economies were St Kitts, Barbados, Antigua and Jamaica. Territories acquired in the mid-eighteenth or early nineteenth centuries, with only partially developed plantation economies and a small number of slaves, were described as 'undeveloped'. Among these were St Lucia, Dominica, Trinidad and British Guiana. This classification is misleading. A better one is simply 'large' and 'small' territories.

In both classifications, Jamaica presents a problem as it was both a 'developed' territory and one in which there was much land available. If the territory was small, there was little or no labour problem. If the territory was large, there was a big labour problem. Let us examine this in detail:

Classification	Territory	Area in sq. kms.	Nos. of freed slaves	Pop. density (per sq. km.)
Small	Antigua	280	30,000	125
	Barbados	430	83,000	230
	St Kitts	296	20,000	85
Large	British Guiana	215,000	83,000	0.5 (not inc. Indian)
	Jamaica	11,500	312,000	27
	Trinidad	4,800	21,000	4.5

Note. All figures are approximate. Population density is calculated on total population, not just freed slaves.

In Antigua, Barbados and St Kitts it was almost impossible for ex-slaves to acquire land, so they had to work for wages on the plantations. Usually they were allowed to keep their 'grounds', but due to the high density of population these were small, not more than twenty-eight square metres—not enough for subsistence independent of wages.

In British Guiana and Trinidad where it was relatively easy for ex-slaves to find land, either by buying Crown Land or by squatting on it, there was a desperate labour problem. Consequently British Guiana and Trinidad adopted the policy of large-scale foreign immigration.

Jamaica was a separate case. There was land available, but not so much Crown Land as in British Guiana and Trinidad, and it was not fertile. Planters were very reluctant to sell land to ex-slaves. Therefore there was a very large ex-slave population wanting land, but good land was scarce and all land was hard to obtain. Nevertheless, the labour problem was serious because hatred of plantation labour was strongest in Jamaica, and the ex-slaves were prepared to make do with poor land well away from the estates. They were encouraged to do this by the missionaries. The Jamaican government did not turn to large-scale, non-white immigration to the same extent as Trinidad and British Guiana and, therefore, Jamaica's labour problem persisted throughout the nineteenth century.

The small islands overcame their labour problems quickly and their sugar industries survived. The large territories suffered insurmountable labour problems in the short run, and their sugar industries collapsed. The following table shows how some of the small islands actually increased their sugar production in the decade after emancipation, 1838 to 1848, while the large territories suffered drastic declines:

The two extreme cases illustrate the point very well. In Barbados where they had no trouble keeping the labour on the estates, sugar production increased nearly two and a half times. In Jamaica where there was an acute labour shortage, sugar production dropped to a third of its former level. Trinidad, where there was plenty of land available, actually increased production slightly, because high wages kept labour on the estates and even attracted labour from neighbouring islands.

Wages and fringe benefits

The factors of supply and demand set the level of wages in most of the islands, but sometimes other forces were influential. In the small islands, the plentiful supply of labour made wages low and fringe benefits small. In the large territories, the supply of labour was scarce and wages were high with generous fringe benefits.

In the British West Indies, a plantation labourer was expected to work nine hours per day, five days per week. This consisted of working from sunrise to sunset with an hour's break about 9 a.m. and a two-hour break at mid-day. The table on page 85 shows the range of wages in some of the islands. Thus the average money wage in the small islands was under 1/- per day, and in the large territories it was 2/-. On the whole, the planters set the wages too low at first and found that they had to increase them. Before emancipation, planters had to provide food, clothing and shelter. After emancipation, there was no obligation for the employer to provide these, but the freed slaves still expected them and their labour often depended on them. Thus cottage and grounds were usually provided throughout the British West Indies, but whether rent was charged depended on the island. In Antigua, if a labourer took a rent-free cottage, he

Territory		Approximate yearly average in tonnes	
		Pre-emancipation	Post-emancipation
Small	Antigua	10,000	13,000
	Barbados	16,000	39,000
	St Kitts	6,000	5,000
Large	British Guiana	45,000	25,000
	Jamaica	90,000	30,000
	Trinidad	6,000	7,000

Territory		Wages
Small	Antigua	1/- (1834) rising to 1/6d (1839) (Planter/labourer relations were better than elsewhere)
	Barbados	9d (1838) rising to 10d (to combat threat of emigration to Trinidad)
	St Kitts	6d (1838) rising to 9d (1839)
Large	British Guiana	2/- (seven-and-a-half-hour day)
	Jamaica	1/- rising quickly to 1/6d (7½d was actually offered at first)
	Trinidad	2/- to 2/6d

was under contract to labour for a year according to law. If he wanted a shorter contract and a rent-free cottage, he had to give a written contract. Antigua also offered free medical attention. In Barbados a rent-free cottage and grounds were provided, but the grounds were small. If more land was wanted, rent had to be paid. In St Kitts usually no cottage was provided and even if it was, the labourer was liable to sudden eviction. Poor labour conditions account for the decline in sugar production in St Kitts, even though there was little alternative to plantation labour.

In the large territories the fringe benefits had to be much greater to attract and keep labour. In Jamaica it was the usual practice to charge rent for the cottage if high wages were paid, although it was rent-free if wages were 1/- per day. However, grounds were large enough for the labourer to be able to supplement his wage with the sales of some produce. In Trinidad, wages were the highest in the British West Indies and also the fringe benefits were the most generous. In addition to cottage and grounds, fish, flour and free medical attention were provided.

Contracts were hated by the freed slaves as they reminded them of slavery, but they were sometimes accepted as security against eviction. Of course, the planters wanted contracts to guarantee a reliable, permanent labour force. It was partly the resistance to contracts, which made planters turn to immigrant labour which could be contracted.

Sugar cultivation by independent blacks

After emancipation, freed slaves were encouraged to grow sugar in most territories, because the island governments were worried about the decline in sugar production. There were three ways in which blacks produced sugar.

1 By buying a sugar plantation and continuing its production. Freed slaves had often saved their earnings under apprenticeship, and they bought estates by pooling their money in a co-operative venture. This happened chiefly in Britain Guiana; for example, in 1839, six freed slaves raised £1,400 as a deposit on Plantation Northbrook. They soon paid off the remaining £700 and thus owned a going concern. Later, a much larger group from adjacent estates, about 150 blacks in all, bought the Orange Nassau Plantation for over £10,000. The co-operative spirit which had formerly existed amongst slaves was strengthened by these business ventures in which they pooled not only their money, but also their labour.

2 By the system of métayage, or share-cropping, by which the labourer worked in the fields and in the mill and took a share of the profits. This system was found in St Lucia and Tobago, but was more common in the French islands. The share-croppers' usual share was between half and two-thirds of the profits, and the planter accepted this because wages made up about two-thirds of the running costs.

3 By growing sugar on grounds, or small parcels of land, or on the disused parts of the plantation. In many islands the labourers were allowed to do this in their own time. After growing the cane, they took it to the mill where it was made into sugar at the planter's expense. Again two-thirds of the profit was the usual reward. This system was especially common in Barbados where the labourers rented extra land on which to grow their own cane.

This made little contribution to the total sugar output in any territory except British Guiana. There, by 1848, one in four blacks were landowners. Métayage had little sucess in the British West Indies. It was still felt that sugar had to be produced on large, undivided estates under individual ownership, with each estate having its own mill.

The 'free village' movement

During and after the apprenticeship period co-operative communities of ex-slaves were founded, sometimes spontaneously and sometimes at the instigation of the missionaries. Some writers have said that this movement laid the foundation for an 'independent peasantry' and a class of 'yeoman farmers' which became the backbone of agriculture in the British West Indies. This is more true of Jamaica at this time than of the small islands of the Eastern Caribbean. The free village movement, properly speaking, was confined to Jamaica, British Guiana and, to a lesser extent, Trinidad.

Free villages had existed in the West Indies before emancipation, for example, the isolated Maroon settlements in Jamaica and Bush Negro settlements in British Guiana were 'free villages'. Usually pre-emancipation settlements were illegal but after emancipation they were legal provided the land was properly purchased.

Free villages were not always isolated. Frequently they were on the fringes of the plantations, so that work was available for the villagers if they wanted it. Sometimes they were on the outskirts of towns, like those around Port-of-Spain in Trinidad. Only a few were completely self-sufficient communities like those in the interior of Jamaica or Dominica where the desire to move as far from the estates as possible was strong.

Free villages in Jamaica

Maroon settlements were the models for the free villages in Jamaica, which were usually sited away from the estates. Even before emancipation William Knibb of the Baptist Mission had urged apprentices to leave the estates and set up free villages. He wanted the ex-slaves to own their own plots of land as part of a movement to found an independent black peasantry. In Jamaica land was available for purchase, but it was usually inferior Crown Land or the unused land on the fringe of the estates. If the ex-slaves could not raise enough money for better land, Knibb advised them to settle on Crown Land. In Jamaica, many free villages were financed and directed by the Baptist Mission, bringing it, once again, into disfavour with the planters.

The first free village was Sligoville, built on ten hectares of land bought by the Reverend James Phillippo, a Baptist minister, in 1835. When emancipation came, 100 families were sent to settle in 'the first town to arise in the ruins of slavery'. Then in 1838 William Knibb obtained £1,000 from the parent Church in England to buy 200 hectares in St Ann on which to build Sturge Town, 'our little Birmingham' as he called it. Seventy families settled around a church and a school—a real English-style village. Other Baptist missionaries sent more families to this village and it soon grew to 3,000 inhabitants.

Sligoville Mission, Jamaica

Clarkson Town, Jamaica

The free village movement, under the influence of Knibb, Phillippo, Burchell, Dendy and Clark, grew fast. Knibb estimated that there were nearly 8,000 cottages in 200 villages by 1840. By 1845 there were 19,000 people in such villages, and according to Sewell, the correspondent of the New York Times, there were 50,000 black cottage-holders in 1859. By that time about 40 per cent of the cultivable land in Jamaica was held by blacks in smallholdings of between one-eighth and sixteen hectares. The free village movement in Jamaica was successful in establishing an independent yeoman class. A typical family in a Jamaican village would be growing starchy crops for subsistence, keeping a few goats, chickens and perhaps a pig, cultivating some cash crops and drawing water for irrigation in the dry season from the Lebitz-type tank which became a feature of the village scene.

Humanitarians and missionaries, as well as governors, were remembered in the names of these villages; for example, Wilberforce, Clarkson, Buxton, Sturge and Sligo. Biblical names were also chosen, for example, Bethany. According to Knibb, by 1845, most of these free villages were sited in Trelawney, but there were also ten or more each in St James, St Ann, St Mary's and St Thomas-in-the-Vale.

Free villages in other islands

In British Guiana, the usual term for free villages was 'Negro Colonies'; there was plenty of fertile land, and the blacks themselves took the initiative, pooled their resources and set up communities on the estates they bought. Frequently the labourers from as many as fifteen neighbouring estates combined in this way. Sometimes they did not buy unused estates, but settled up the rivers as the Bush Negroes had done, but there was not the same desire to move away from the estates as in Jamaica. Some Negro Colonies grew out of squatters' settlements on Crown Land though this was really illegal.

By 1848 there were almost 10,000 cottage-holders independent of white plantations in British Guiana. Even with an average family of four, this meant that half the former slave population was living on its own land.

In Trinidad the free village movement was not so strong, but in the Montserrat Ward in the centre of the island there were Negro Colonies similar to those of British Guiana. Around Port-of-Spain there were also settlements of freed slaves.

Of course the free village movement was not possible to any great extent in the small, densely populated islands of the Eastern Caribbean, especially in St. Kitts and Barbados. However, in the mountainous islands like Dominica and St Lucia, freed slave settlements in the interior did occur, but the cottages were often scattered and not grouped so that they could be termed 'villages'.

Post-Emancipation Problems in the British Islands

Territory	Land available Crown Land	Unused estate land	Plantation labour	Wages and fringe benefits	Sugar production	Free villages
Antigua	Practically none		Readily available	1/- Cottage, grounds, free medical service, schools	25% increase	Some around St Johns
Barbados	Practically none		Readily available	10d Cottage, grounds	More than doubled	
Dominica	Much inferior land		Unreliable	9d to 1/- Cash crops, fishing, cottage, grounds	Same	Settlements in interior
Grenada	Available for purchase in small parcels		Irregular Emigration to Trinidad	9d Sale of produce to Trinidad	50% decrease	Scattered small-holdings
Nevis		Much available	Hard to obtain	Profit-sharing	Very small decrease	Scattered cottages
St Kitts	None available		Unreliable	9d Tenuous hold on cottage Allowed to grow food on estate	Very small increase	Very few
St Lucia	Inferior land available		Available, irregular	1/6d Some metayage, cottage, grounds	25% increase	Small, bush settlements
St Vincent	Available in small parcels		Unreliable Emigration to Trinidad	9d Sale of produce, cottage, grounds	25% decrease	Plantation cottages abandoned, scattered cottages
British Guiana	Much fertile and infertile	Much for purchase	Very scarce	2/- Legal limit of 7½ hours	40% decrease	Many large 'negro colonies'
Jamaica	Inferior land only	Hard to obtain	Scarce and unreliable	1/6d Rent for cottage	Decreased by 3 times	Up to 200 free villages
Trinidad	Much fertile land		Very scarce	2/- to 2/6d cottage, grounds, fish, flour and medical services	20% increase	Settlements around Port-of-Spain

9
Immigrant Labour

Immigrant labour

Labour situation after emancipation

Emancipation ended the days of the permanent, unpaid labour force on the plantations. Most freed slaves were not prepared to go back to the plantations, however good the conditions, unless there was absolutely no alternative. But freed slaves who re-engaged as plantation labour proved that they would work hard for wages. In Barbados, the output per worker increased dramatically after emancipation. However, except when the island was small with no available land, the planter could not rely on a permanent labour force made up of freed slaves. Even in Barbados there was the possibility of labourers migrating to Trinidad.

Long-term contracts of a year or more could have secured a labour force to satisfy the planters. However, both the freed slaves and the British government were fiercely opposed to contracts. Only in a few islands were they permitted, and only in one, Antigua, could they be as long as a year.

Among both planters and slaves there were psychological forces at work. Some planters found it hard to accept the idea of a free, black, wage-earning labour force because they had been used to blacks as slaves, while others believed that blacks would not work without the constraint of slavery. Some blacks, on the other hand, would never work voluntarily for an old slave master.

Thus planters in most colonies, especially British Guiana, Trinidad and Jamaica where the labour problems were desperate, looked elsewhere for labour. They turned to contracted immigrant labour to supply them with a plentiful source of cheap labour. After experimenting with many schemes, East Indian labour seemed the solution to their needs. Once again Jamaica was a special case. The Jamaican government was worried about the black/white ratio in the island which was about fifteen to one after emancipation. Other colonies were also worried about their black/white ratios, but they did not let this stop them following large-scale, non-white immigration policies.

Government reaction

Whereas the planters were very enthusiastic about immigrant labour schemes, the governments, both imperial and island, were hesitant. West Indian blacks had already migrated from colony to colony in search of higher wages and land. This movement was chiefly from the Windward Islands and Barbados to Trinidad and British Guiana. In 1839, Trinidad received over 1,000 immigrant workers and British Guiana received over 5,000 in the apprenticeship period. This had been voluntary immigration by individuals who, at first, had paid their own passages. Later the planters paid the passages, but it was all on a private basis and there were no contracts. Then in 1839 the planters of British Guiana began a 'Voluntary Subscription Immigration Society' and this, together with existing immigration schemes, forced the government to take notice.

The British government was in a dilemma because it had to support the sugar economies of its West Indian colonies and maintain sugar imports into Britain. The West India interest, still active in London, urged acceptance of immigrant labour. But the government was also under pressure from the Anti-Slavery Society which regarded immigration as another form of slavery. Moreover, it did not want to be accused of hypocrisy by foreign governments in allowing a new slave trade while persuading other countries to stop theirs. So in 1838, James Stephen, a Colonial Office official, humanitarian and drafter of the 1833 Act, was appointed to draw up conditions for immigrant labour schemes which would make it clear that no new slave trade was being established.

Island governments were under even greater pressure from the planters to participate in immigrant labour schemes. In principle they supported them, but did not want to finance the schemes out of public funds. Of course, the planters hoped that

their governments would pay for the importing of immigrants and argued that they would be repaid by greatly increased revenue from sugar exports. In the end the island governments partially gave way and agreed to pay one-third of the cost, provided that the planters paid two-thirds.

The different schemes

There were a number of different immigration schemes in operation at the same time, often overlapping. For example in the 1840s Africans, Madeirans and East Indians were all entering British Guiana under different schemes. Individual governments had absolute control over their own immigration policies.

European labour

European labour was imported chiefly by Jamaica in order to increase its white population while at the same time providing plantation labour. It was a hopeless experiment. Between 1834 and 1838, thousands of Scots and Irish and a few hundred Germans came to Jamaica. Most of them soon died, as they lacked immunity to tropical diseases. Others refused to work when they saw what they were expected to do and understood that it was regarded as the work of blacks. They either sought other employment of asked to be repatriated.

Yet the Jamaican government tried again in 1841 and imported more whites from Britain. Two hundred also went to St Kitts. After most of them again died or asked for repatriation, the governments were finally convinced that plantation labour from Northern Europe was a hopeless prospect.

Madeirans and Maltese

Madeira is a Portuguese island in the Atlantic off Morocco. The labourers there were paid only three to four pence per day and were attracted by prospects of higher wages in the West Indies. Private importations of Madeirans began in 1835, but were suspended in 1839 while the British government examined the conduct and the morality of the schemes. In 1841 Madeiran immigration was re-opened on an official basis and large numbers went to British Guiana until 1848 when the scheme was suspended again. It was resumed in 1850, but never again on such a large scale.

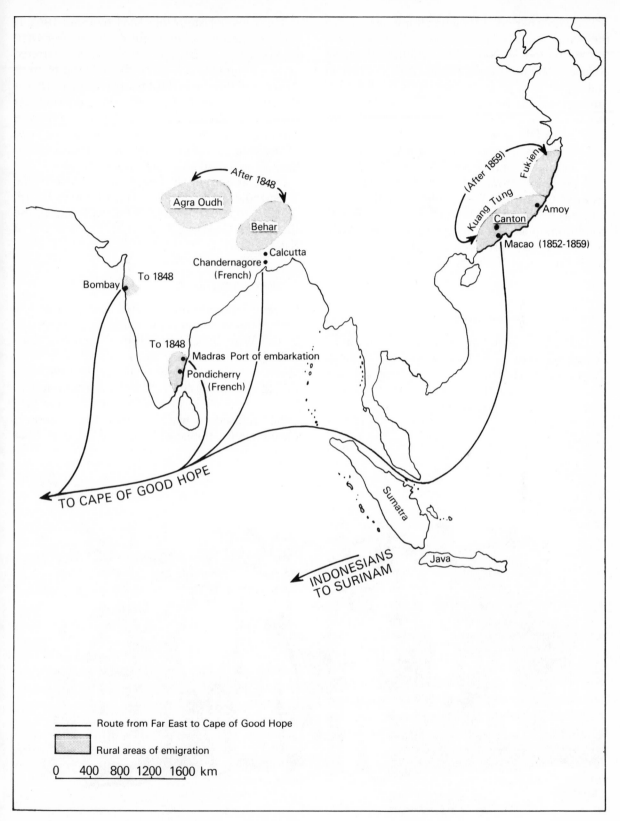

Map 5   Far East showing principal sources of immigrants

The whole period of Madeiran immigration into the British West Indies lasted from 1835 to 1882. In this period 36,000 came; 30,000 to British Guiana, 2,000 to Antigua, nearly 1,000 to Trinidad and only 100 to Jamaica. The rest were dispersed among Grenada, St Vincent, St Kitts and Nevis. It was an unsatisfactory scheme as it was irregular, the death rate of the new arrivals was high, and most of the Madeirans, especially in British Guiana, went into trading as soon as possible.

In the years before 1840 a few hundred Maltese entered the British West Indies, chiefly British Guiana and Grenada. The Maltese did not like the conditions and asked to be repatriated. Malta could never have provided enough immigrants to solve the labour problem on West Indian sugar estates.

Free African immigration

In 1841 the importation of Africans from Sierra Leone, the Kru Coast (just south-east of Sierra Leone) and St Helena, and Africans rescued from slave ships, began. Most of those imported were freed slaves or descendants of freed slaves, most notably of the Jamaican Maroons deported in 1796.

The scheme lasted from 1841 to about 1862. It was very popular at first, but declined after 1850 for two reasons. Firstly, private ships were chartered at the beginning to carry the emigrants from Africa, and this made the Africans think that it was slavery all over again. Secondly, the agents in West Africa undoubtedly lured the Africans with false promises of money and land. As soon as the news of the true conditions in the West Indies leaked back, it was hard to attract more Africans.

In all, about 36,000 free Africans came to the West Indies under this scheme; 14,000 to British Guiana, 10,000 to Jamaica, 8,000 to Trinidad, and the rest to Grenada, St Vincent, St Lucia and St Kitts.

Chinese immigration

Chinese immigration schemes lasted for a long period, but very large numbers did not come to the British West Indies, though they went to Cuba.

Early in the century there were two abortive schemes to obtain Chinese labour. In 1806, with the threat of abolition, Trinidad attempted to import some Chinese. Very few arrived and they either refused to work or were found entirely unsuitable for the labour required. Then in 1844

Chinese immigrants

British Guiana tried to attract Chinese who had previously emigrated to Malacca, Singapore and Penang. However, these Chinese were happy where they were and were unwilling to come to the West Indies

Large-scale Chinese immigration began in 1852 from the Portuguese colony of Maçao. The immigrants were convicts or prisoners of war and there were no women amongst them, which had unhappy consequences for the scheme in British Guiana. Therefore, in 1859 a 'family' immigration scheme was started. In 1860 British Guiana sent an agent to Canton to recruit Chinese families from the rural areas of Fukien and Kwangtung. In 1864 Trinidad joined the scheme and shared the cost of the agency. This scheme was more successful, but the agents undoubtedly practised some deception in recruiting because they did not tell the Chinese the nature of the work they were going to, and they made false promises about repatriation. The Chinese recruits were small farmers and market gardeners, not plantation labourers.

There were many problems as a result of Chinese immigration.

1   The Chinese government was opposed to it as it hurt Chinese pride, but having suffered a succession of defeats by the European powers since 1839, they were forced to accept it.

2   The immigrants would have settled more happily if Chinese women had been allowed to immigrate. It caused jealousy and resentment between the Chinese and the black populations and inter-breeding led to the mixtures of 'chigros' and 'chinidouglases' in different parts of the West Indies.

3   Chinese immigration was more expensive than other schemes because of the distance from China to the West Indies. It cost £25 to import a Chinese from Canton, but only £15 for an Indian from Calcutta.

4   China was not a British colony and the British government could only try to persuade the Chinese government to allow emigration. The Chinese, even when they allowed it, enforced all sorts of restrictions and conditions, such as the use of only certain ports for embarkation.

5   When the Chinese immigrants found that they had been misled about the kind of work, they frequently refused to work. As soon as they could they tried to obtain land of their own, or they asked to be repatriated, a very expensive business.

Thus the Chinese proved to be unsatisfactory physically, and unreliable as a permanent labour force on sugar plantations. It is hard to assess the total numbers of Chinese immigrants into the British West Indies, but a round figure of 20,000 in the period 1852 to 1893 is suggested. About 12,000 entered British Guiana up to 1879. Jamaica took nearly 5,000 up to 1893. Trinidad imported just over 2,500 between 1852 and 1872.

East Indian immigration

In 1837 John Gladstone, the owner of two plantations in British Guiana, applied to the Secretary of State for the Colonies for permission to import Indian labourers. In 1838, 396 arrived and the great flood of Indian immigration had begun. It was immediately proclaimed a success in British Guiana, but investigations by the Anti-Slavery Society revealed that many of the immigrants had died quickly. Some had been flogged and wrongly

Trinidad coolies at work

93

imprisoned, while others had not been paid what they had been promised. Therefore, in July 1838, the Indian government suspended emigration to the West Indies while a Commission of Enquiry made a thorough investigation into conditions in British Guiana.

Immigration resumed officially in 1844, and it lasted until 1917. In the 1840s the planters' demand for East Indian immigrant labour was very strong, especially in British Guiana where the government was spending £50,000 per year on immigration, mostly Indian. The British Guiana government was nearly bankrupt in 1848 because of this. However, a loan of £200,000 from the British government was put towards immigration, and the scheme continued. Trinidad and Jamaica were also importing Indians on a large scale, but the Jamaican government was unwilling to finance the scheme to the same extent as British Guiana and Trinidad. Consequently Jamaica took far fewer immigrants than the other two.

Up to 1848 the Indian immigrants, known as 'coolies', were drawn from the poor on the streets of the cities of Bombay, Calcutta and Madras. These cities always remained the ports of embarkation. After 1848 they were drawn from the provinces of Agra-Oudh and Bihar which always suffered terribly in the frequent famines. Many of these emigrants were peasant farmers.

India was a British possession and Britain felt a keen responsibility for her part in the scheme. In 1848, after giving loans to the governments of British Guiana, Trinidad and Jamaica, she wanted much stricter supervision over immigration. Britain was also allowing Indian immigrants to go to non-British colonies, the French, Dutch and Danish possessions in the West Indies. In these territories it was not possible to oversee the treatment of the immigrants and it was decided in 1876 to stop the transportation of Indians into all non-British colonies except Surinam, Guadeloupe and Martinique. In 1886 Guadeloupe and Martinique were also banned, and only Surinam continued importing Indians until 1917.

By 1917, 416,000 East Indian immigrants had entered the British West Indies. British Guiana received 239,000, Trinidad 134,000 and Jamaica 33,000. Another 10,00 went to the islands of the Eastern Caribbean, St Lucia, Grenada, St Vincent and St Kitts.

Although the scheme appears successful, in many ways it did not live up to expectations. From the moral point of view it had many failings; the indentured servant system deprived human beings of freedom for long periods of their lives; there was great mortality and suffering for the immigrants; grave social problems were caused in West Indian territories. Many people of Indian descent in the West Indies today, however, would not look back on the scheme as a failure. They now form half the population of British Guiana and over one third of the population of Trinidad.

The contracts

Some of these conditions apply to all immigration schemes, but chiefly they concern East Indian schemes.

At first black West Indian labourers moved from one island to another without contracts. When planters started paying the cost of the passage they insisted on contracts. However, as these contracts were signed on arrival, there was little a planter could do if the terms were refused. This frequently happened in British Guiana and Trinidad, where the workers had come for land.

For most of the 1840s, the British government would only permit contracts signed on arrival in the colony. When the immigrants were confronted with the hard conditions of plantation labour, they sometimes refused to sign. In 1848 the British Government gave way to planters and permitted contracts to be signed at the port of embarkation. This was better from the planters' point of view, but worse for the immigrants who had no protection against false promises.

The conditions of the contracts varied according to the scheme and the colony involved. With East Indian immigrants, the British government would allow contracts of only one year. In 1848 this was extended to three years and in 1850 the planters got what they had been pressing for from the beginning— five-year contracts signed at the port of embarkation.

The contracts stipulated the number of days to be worked, the number of working hours in a day, the daily wages and conditions about return passages. For example, a labour contract in British Guiana would run for five years from the day of arrival in the colony, every day of the year except Sundays and public holidays, and days spent in prison had to be made up at the end of the contract. A field labourer on a plantation had to work seven hours per day, and a factory labourer, ten hours. The wages were 1/- per day (later 1/6d) for a man over sixteen, provided that he was healthy, and 8d per day for a woman or boy under sixteen.

For the first three months after arrival food would be supplied to the immigrant and 4d per day could be deducted from his wages for this. The labourers were to be housed in 'barracks' rent-free, and would receive free medicine and hospitalisation. (N.B. contracts did not specify that work would be on sugar plantations).

The clause about free return passages was the most controversial. The planters and colonial governments did not want repatriation terms, which were insisted on by the governments of the country of the labourer's origin and by the British government. At first, immigrants were promised free return passages on completion of their contract. In 1854 they could claim repatriation only after living for ten years in one colony. This was to encourage 'reindenture'. In 1869 British Guiana had 30,000 Indians eligible for repatriation and, if they had all claimed it, the government would not have been able to pay. The government adopted the alternative of offering free land instead of return passages. In 1870 Trinidad adopted a similar measure. The government offered two hectare lots of Crown Land to immigrants on the expiry of their contract. In 1895 the British Guiana government modified the clause about return passages to require the immigrant to pay a quarter of the cost himself. In 1898 this was raised to a half.

The Labour Laws of 1864 greatly favoured the planter at the expense of the immigrant. A breach of the labour laws was regarded as a criminal offence and the immigrant could not, therefore, give evidence in his own defence when charged under them.

For minor offences such as failure to answer one's name at the muster roll in the morning, harsh fines of up to £5 could be imposed. Other minor offences were punishable by up to three months in prison. If a planter broke his side of the contract, such as failure to pay full wages, the immigrant had no recourse to the court, but could only go to the Petty Debts Department.

Organisation of Asian immigration schemes

Neither the Indian nor the Chinese government supported emigration or gave help in recruiting. With more government supervision in the Indian scheme after 1848, and in the Chinese scheme after 1859, recruiting agents responsible for contracts were appointed by colonial governments in the ports of embarkation. Sub-agents, paid by the West Indian governments, were employed in the districts and recruiters, paid according to the number recruited, worked in the fields. They were known as 'coolie-catchers' and were unpopular figures in the Indian village scene. Sometimes they were beaten up. They lured away the young and healthy, often with false promises, and they were particularly resented when they tried to attract women emigrants.

The emigrants were usually transported to the ports where they were kept in 'depots'. In Maçao, a Portuguese colony in China, the term 'barracoon' was used as in the days of the Portuguese slave trade in West Africa. The emigrants were medically examined before being embarked on ships, although many cases of diseases went undetected. The ships left India between October and February, in the days of sail, to catch the favourable monsoons blowing off the land mass of Asia. They sailed round the Cape of Good Hope, calling at Cape Town or St Helena for water, fruit and vegetables. The whole voyage from India to the West Indies took between eleven and eighteen weeks by sailing ship, and the voyage from China considerably longer. In the early days of the scheme, many did not survive the voyage. Improved conditions resulted from closer government supervision after 1848. Good ventilation, adequate food and medical attention, and warm clothing for southerly latitudes were required.

Two-thirds of the costs of the scheme were paid by the planters and the remaining third by the island government concerned. The actual handing over of the money to shipping agents and recruiting agents was done by the government, but the planters paid the wages of the immigrants and the costs of the medical services. The planters' share consisted of the costs of recruiting, the passage costs, wages and medical services. The government's share was the cost of the Immigration Department and return passages. The money for this was raised by a fee levied on the planter for each immigrant, and through export duties on all crops.

Between 1838 and 1917, West Indian governments spent a total of £20,000,000 on immigration schemes, an average of a quarter of a million pounds per year. By far the greatest share of this was paid by British Guiana.

'The New Slavery'

By definition, immigrant labour was not slavery because it was entered into voluntarily. The contract gave rights to the immigrant who was paid for his labour. There was a fixed limit to the period of indenture, and when it was over, the immigrant was free.

However, Joseph Beaumont, at one time Chief Justice of British Guiana, published a pamphlet in England in 1871 entitled 'The New Slavery', because he saw that, in practice, immigrant labour schemes were slavery under a different name. Although the emigrant from India entered into the contract voluntarily, he was often deceived about the conditions he was agreeing to.

In the West Indian colonies, conditions similar to those in the days of slavery existed. Workers were denied the natural freedoms of human beings outside their hours of labour. They were confined to their estates. Free Indians found it advisable to carry 'Certificates of Exemption from Labour' which allowed them free movement. In British Guiana, indentured labourers could be fined if found off their estates. Some colonies had strict vagrancy laws with harsh penalties. If a worker was absent from his estate for seven consecutive days he could be charged with desertion.

Immigrant labourers were certainly deprived of women. The root of the problem lay in India, where women were not emancipated because of the religious and social systems. The proportion of Indian women imported was only 3 per cent before the mid-1840s, rising to 18 per cent in 1845, 32 per cent up to 1870, and a legal minimum of 40 per cent thereafter. Up to 1870, immigrants had been denied the chance to lead normal family lives, and the problem of finding women in a strange country had caused many problems. In cases where Indian immigrants were married, their wives were sometimes taken away to be the mistresses of the plantation bosses as in the days of slavery.

Immigrants were also subject to arbitrary treatment by their employers. This sometimes involved flogging and imprisonment for trivial matters, and the immigrant dared not complain. To a certain extent this was checked by closer government supervision after 1848. Then the planters resorted to the tactic of 'summonses'. In two years, 1906 to 1907, nearly 40 per cent of the immigrant labourers in British Guiana received summonses for breach

of the labour laws. Pressure from the Indian government ended this abuse and the proportion fell to 13 per cent in 1915, and the maximum fine for breach of the labour laws fell from £5 to 10/-.

Planters hoped for 're-indenture'; that is, after the five year contract had expired the labourer would sign on for another five years. Various inducements were tried to persuade the immigrant to extend his bond, but after five years in 'quasi-slavery' most wanted their freedom. At first the prospect of freedom in a West Indian colony was not appealing and, before 1848, most immigrants asked for repatriation. As governments enforced better conditions, the proportion asking for repatriation fell.

After 1884 the proportion asking to be repatriated from British Guiana was one in four, but by then the immigrant had a definite promise of land at the end of his contract, and there were more Indian women in the colony. The trend was roughly the same in Trinidad.

One of the most powerful condemnations of the scheme for Indian immigration in British Guiana came from Des Voeux, an ex-stipendiary magistrate. When he was in St Lucia as Administrator,

Sir G. W. Des Voeux

he heard of trouble amongst the Indian workers on the Plantation Leonora in his old district of West Demerara in 1869. He wrote the famous 'Des Voeux' letter to the Secretary of State for the Colonies. His theme was that the whole 'establishment'—governors, agents-general, sub-agents, magistrates, medical officers, and, of course, the planters,—were against the immigrant. The officials who should have helped the immigrants were under the influence of the plantocracy, just as in the days of slavery when everything was against the slave.

The system depended on the officials in charge. They could check the abuses, and there were cases of colonial officials who did their utmost to secure fairness for the immigrants. Sir John Peter Grant in Jamaica and Sir Arthur Gordon in Trinidad worked on behalf of the immigrants during their governorships. In British Guiana there was a trio of officials, Joseph Beaumont, William Des Voeux and James Crosby, the Agent-General, who fought for the rights of the immigrants in spite of the obstacles placed in their way by the Governor, Sir Francis Hincks. In general, however, there was a lack of goodwill on the part of the planters and authorities towards immigrants.

Immigration to non-British colonies

The French, Spanish and Dutch colonies began schemes of immigrant labour before their emancipation acts had been passed. This was because the abolition of the slave trade had made it hàrder to obtain African slaves. Even Cuba, which was supplied with slaves by American traders after the Spanish had promised to abolish the slave trade, turned to immigrant labour to expand her sugar industry. As new markets opened to them with the passing of the Sugar Equalisation Act in 1846, every territory wanted to expand production.

Non-British colonies, apart from Cuba, had their own sources of immigrant labour in the East. The Dutch colonies had the Dutch East Indies, and the French had Chandernagore and Pondicherry, small enclaves in British India which they had been allowed to keep by the Peace of Paris, 1756. Although Cuba had no source in the East, she did have the Spanish Canary Islands. Nevertheless, the French and the Dutch came to rely heavily on British India as the source of labour for their sugar colonies. Cuba relied on the help of British agents

Hill coolies landing at Mauritius

in the Chinese parts of Canton and Amoy before turning to the Portuguese in Maçao. The British not only held the most plentiful source of immigrant labour in the East, they were also the best able to organise recruitment and transportation.

The Dutch colonies

The Dutch colonies, in particular Surinam, began to import labourers from Indonesia in the 1850s. At that time Dutch East Indian sugar plantations were at a disadvantage because of their distance from the European market. However, when the Suez Canal was opened in 1869 this distance was shortened by nearly 5,000 kilometres and Java became a powerful competitor to Surinam.

Emancipation had come to Surinam in 1863 and the freed blacks were reluctant to work on the plantations. Surinam thus faced a threefold problem: lack of cheap labour; competition from the East Indies; and the need to take her share of the expanding sugar market. The demand for immigrant labour was great. The Javanese who were imported were usually allowed to become small farmers and were lost to the sugar industry.

In 1870, therefore, the Dutch made an agreement with Britain for Indian immigrants. Britain was willing to allow Surinam to use this source as it arranged its immigrant labour scheme in much the same way as the British West Indian colonies. In

Surinam there was an Immigration Department under an Agent-General and the contracts were similar. Therefore, when Britain banned Indian emigration to French Guiana in 1876, she allowed Surinam to continue until the general abolition in 1917.

A total of about 32,00 Indonesians entered Surinam up to 1938, and nearly 36,000 Indians between 1871 and 1917. About one in four Indonesians and one in three Indians asked for repatriation after their contracts had expired. Over half the population of Surinam is descended from immigrants from the East.

The French colonies

The French took Congolese Africans prisoner and shipped them to Guadeloupe and Martinique where they were freed. This was a disguised continuation of the slave trade and lasted from 1830 to 1859. It was not a successful scheme and only about 17,000 Africans came to the French colonies under it.

After the French emancipation laws were passed in 1848, an immigrant labour scheme began from their trading stations of Pondicherry and Chandernagore in India. These two places were very small and supplied only about 10,000 immigrants to Guadeloupe and Martinique in ten years. This was not satisfactory, and in 1861 the French made an agreement with Britain to begin recruiting in British India.

About 68,000 Indians from British India came to Guadeloupe and Martinique between 1861 and 1886, and about 20,000 went to French Guiana up to 1876. However, the British government was not satisfied with the French treatment of immigrants. There was a high mortality rate and little government supervision. Therefore they banned the importation of Indians to French Guiana in 1876, and to Guadeloupe and Martinique in 1886.

Cuba

Although claiming to have abolished the slave trade in 1820, the Spanish authorities turned a blind eye on the continued shipment of slaves into Cuba by American traders. Moreover, slaves caught by anti-slave patrols were landed in Cuba and allowed to be re-sold into slavery.

In 1835, the new Reciprocal Agreement between Britain and Spain put an end to this practice by allowing a British Superintendent to reside in Havana to oversee the liberation of rescued slaves. The American slave trade into Cuba continued, but it was not adequate to supply the labour needs of the expanding Cuban sugar industry. The Spanish Cubans were worried about the increasing black-to-white ratio and they wanted another source of labour.

Immigrants arriving at Guadeloupe

Chinese immigrants in Cuba

Therefore Cuba began a Chinese immigrant labour scheme in 1847 which, through British agents in Amoy and Canton, involved the purchase of kidnapped Chinese or prisoners of war. The Chinese signed a contract before embarkation to give eight years labour, twelve hours per day, with pay of four pesos per month. It was really slavery, and when the base for the scheme was changed to Maçao, it was much the same. When the Chinese government sent inspectors to Cuba they found so much evidence of cruelty that they discouraged further emigration to Cuba, but it was hard to prevent it as Maçao was a Portuguese colony. In 1874 the Cuban government was persuaded to stop the scheme. Between 1847 and 1874 Cuba imported 125,000 Chinese. They were the mainstay of the expanding Cuban sugar industry until the great mechanisation of the 1880s.

The effects of immigration in the British West Indies

On the sugar industry

There is much controversy about whether immigrants helped the sugar industry or not. The figures for sugar production seem to suggest that, in those territories that imported labour, they helped the industry. In the decade after emancipation sugar production in British Guiana slumped to nearly 40 per cent of its pre-emancipation level. By the end of the ninteenth century, its sugar production was 250 per cent greater than at the pre-emancipation level. As British Guiana relied heavily on immigrant labour, it is tempting to conclude that the immigrants were responsible for this increased production. However there were other factors at work at the same time. More land was brought under sugar cultivation and more mechanisation was introduced into the sugar industry in British Guiana.

In Trinidad it was nearly the same story. High wages and good conditions had prevented a slump in production after emancipation, but Trinidad's sugar output was still very low. By the end of the century it was four times greater than the pre-emancipation level. Again the credit it given to immigrant labour.

However, the only fair conclusion to draw about British Guiana and Trinidad is that immigrant labour was accompanied by increased sugar production; it was not necessarily the cause of it. Contemporary planters certainly attributed the rise in output to the introduction of immigrant labour. Modern writers have differed about the right conclusion.

Barbados, an island with no immigrant labour, had experienced an initial increase in output of 250 per cent over its pre-emancipation level by 1848. But by the end of the century it had decreased by nearly 20 per cent of its pre-emancipation level. One is tempted to conclude that the decline in production was due to no immigrant labour. This is a false conclusion because Barbados, more than any other island, suffered from soil exhaustion and lack of mechanisation.

Grenada and St Vincent present an even more baffling conclusion. Both had substantial Indian immigration relative to their total population; Grenada 3,000 and St Vincent 2,700. In Grenada the export of sugar stopped completely before the end of the century, and in St Vincent it was five and a half times less than its pre-emancipation level.

The overall conclusion must be that immigration did not cause increased sugar production in the British West Indies, as there were so many other factors that could have been responsible.

On culture and society

The immigration of Indians into the British West Indies involved the introduction of completely different cultures and religions. They were Hindus or Moslems and the proportions, in the late nineteenth century, were roughly 86 per cent Hindu and 14 per cent Moslem. The Indians were remarkable for their cultural segregation and, indeed, remained very much a separate entity within West Indian society up to the present day.

The main reasons for this were:
1   The Indians were linked by a strong common bond of family friendship.
2   The immigration schemes by which they came to the West Indies isolated them on plantations and thus set them apart from the other inhabitants.
3   Even when free of indenture, many Indians remained in agriculture. Between 1885 and 1912, 37,000 hectares of Crown Land in Trinidad was sold or granted to Indians and 78 per cent of the Indian population worked in agriculture, about the same proportion as today. These free Indians established villages of their own and grew rice, cocoa and sugar cane. They re-established their Indian heritage, maintaining their separateness and giving Trinidad and Guyana an active peasant class.

4   Indians and Africans tended to despise each other in the nineteenth century. This did not bring them into conflict but rather tended to keep them apart. There was a great cultural void between the Indians and the West Indians. The latter regarded the Indians as inferior, partly because of their clothes, partly because they were not Christian and partly because they did the lowest paid jobs and occupied the lowest position in society. They were particularly despised by the blacks for accepting what the latter considered to be slavery.

Many of the Indians on the plantations and in free villages were unaware of this low social valuation and those who were aware of it did not accept it. They regarded the blacks as shiftless, uneducated layabouts. They disliked the low standards of morality in the West Indies, with its strong tradition of concubinage, preferring their own traditions of marital fidelity, especially on the part of the wife. They had no wish to become part of such a society.
5   Most of the immigrants spoke Hindi and continued to do so. Thus language was a real barrier which was only very slowly overcome. There was little association with other West Indians, apart from those Indians who were shopkeepers and traders. The Indians were unwilling to send their children to school because they feared conversion to Christianity. It was not until the late 1870s when separate schools for Indian children were established, mainly by the Canadian Presbyterian Mission to the Indians, that Indian children went to school and language barriers began to crumble.

To begin with, the immigrants had little family life, partly due to plantation life and partly due to the lack of women. Bride-price was more common in the West Indies than a dowry. But the traditional Indian idea of family re-emerged around 1870, with the establishment of free Indian villages. There were, however, notable changes. Although caste remained important, there were not enough women to maintain it and inter-caste marriages were common.

New links between those who had come on the same ship or lived in the same village developed. The idea of the extended family, including several generations and with a corporate identity, was very strong. This was one of the reasons why the Indian business and agricultural classes were so strong. A family council, of which every male over sixteen was a member, made all decisions on weddings, religious ceremonies and anything involving major expenditure. The eldest male was the head of the

Hindu temple in Trinidad

family and everyone contributed to a common financial pool.

In the mixed African/Western cultures found in the West Indies, religion was a separate compartment of life for most people. In Indian cultures, both Hindu and Moslem religion affected every aspect of life. Again, this contributed strongly to segregation.

Relations between the two Indian religions were good on the whole but this was not so with the Christian church. Christianity was the only socially acceptable religion in the West Indies and Hindu and Moslem religious practices were despised. For example, Hindu and Moslem marriages were not legal unless registered with the District Registrar and Indians were unwilling to do this. Thus most Indian children were illegitimate and this often made it difficult for them to inherit property and land.

Many Hindu temples and Moslem mosques were built and their festivals became part of the West Indian way of life. Among the most popular Hindu festivals was Divali, which commemorated the homecoming of Rama, his wife Sita and his brother Lakshman.

In music, drama and dance, the Indians brought their own art forms to the Caribbean and these have influenced West Indian music. The sarangi, the sitar, the dholak and the tabla are still popular musical instruments today.

The failure of Indians to integrate with the local peoples made them unpopular in the West Indies. There was a great lack of understanding on both sides. However, West Indian society was already so diverse, that it was able to absorb this huge Indian immigration without conflict.

Summary Chart of Immigrant labour brought to the West Indies between 1834 and 1917

Territory	Europeans (1834–1841)	Madeirans (1835–1882)	Africans (1841–1862)	Chinese (1852–1893)	East Indians (1838–1917)
British Guiana		30,000	14,000	12,000	239,000
Jamaica	5,000	100	10,000	5,000	33,000
Trinidad		2,000	8,000	3,000	134,000
Grenada		800	1,500		3,000
St Vincent		500	1,000		2,700
St Lucia		500	500		4,000
St Kitts	200	200	500		300
Antigua		2,000			
Totals	5,200	36,100	35,500	20,000	416,000

10

Problems of the Caribbean Sugar Industry

Richard Cobden and John Bright

British West Indian sugar before 1846

During the Napoleonic Wars, the British West Indies had enjoyed a near monopoly of sugar production and had charged increasingly high prices. It proved to be their only prosperous period throughout the century. After the war, with the emergence of new sugar-producing countries and the expansion of the older ones, their position became increasingly difficult.

The problems they faced were many, and among them was the labour problem caused by abolition. Because of this, the price of slaves on the internal market rose, and the only way they could combat increased prices was to raise the price of sugar. Emancipation made their labour problems even worse.

Another problem was competition from Indian and East Indian sugar. Hitherto, the West Indian planters alone had enjoyed low rates of duty on sugar. Pressure from the East Indian planters and a growing feeling in England against slavery, led to the extension of these low rates of duty to Mauritius in 1825 and India in 1836. This meant that Indian and Mauritian sugar were very real competitors.

Adjustment to a cash economy produced another very real problem. Before emancipation there had been relatively little circulation of money in the British West Indies. Planters obtained their needs, from machinery and slaves for the plantation down to personal and domestic requirements, from merchants in exchange for their sugar crop.

In theory, the apprenticeship period should have given the planters time to adjust to a cash economy. But they made little effort to do so and there was not enough money in circulation to pay the wages bills which were presented after 1838.

The level of wages, ranging roughly from 9d per day in Barbados to 2/6d per day in Trinidad, meant that planters could face a wage bill of just under £20 per week for 100 labourers in Barbados to just over £60 per week for 100 labourers in Trinidad.

These wage bills led to the foundation of the Planters Bank in Jamaica in 1837 and the West India Bank in Barbados, with branches in many islands. These banks were founded with capital put up by Liverpool and London merchants. They were still supplying credit to the planters on the strength of their crops but this was being done on the spot. Although this was good business in times of expansion and rising prices, it was ruinous in the 1840s because of falling prices. The collapse of the West Indian banks in 1849 was further complicated by the Sugar Equalisation Act of 1846.

Yet another problem was the fall in sugar prices because of world expansion in production. Foreign countries reduced their production costs so much that they could still undercut the British West Indian price of 22/6d per cwt in 1848. For example, Cuba could put raw sugar free on board at Havana at 12/- per cwt, and Louisiana could put raw sugar free on board at New Orleans at 15/- per cwt.

In the British West Indies, particularly in Guiana, the acreage under sugar was increased after the Napoleonic Wars. This increased the supply of sugar which, in turn, depressed the price. The planters were aware of the effect of limiting acreage to maintain prices, but in the early nineteenth century each territory was competing against the other to maximise its revenue from sugar.

With falling prices, the planters should have tried to reduce their production costs by modernisation and mechanisation, thus reducing dependence on labour. But mechanisation needed capital and the merchant-owned banks were not interested in financing developments in an industry which seemed to be facing terrible difficulties.

Another problem faced by West Indian planters was that they had to pay the 4½ per cent export duty on sugar, first imposed by the Plantation Duties Act of 1673. They protested repeatedly to the British government, but not until the extreme distress of 1838 was this duty removed. They also had to pay higher prices for their imports than in a free market, although in 1825 they were given some relief when manufactured goods from foreign countries were allowed to be imported directly to the colonies.

The Encumbered Estates Act 1854

In the 1830s many planters either sold their estates at a fraction of their former value or abandoned them to bush, unable to make a profit but unwilling to sell them. This process was most apparent in

Derelict sugar plantation

Jamaica where sugar production dropped by two-thirds in the twenty years after 1833.

The price of estate land was about one-fifth of its 1815 level throughout the British West Indies. In Jamaica it fell even lower and some planters even accepted one-twentieth of their estates' former value. By the mid-nineteenth century, about 500 estates had been sold or abandoned in Jamaica.

Even British Guiana, which had been increasing its sugar output before emancipation, temporarily suffered the same problems in the 1830s, although on a minor scale compared with Jamaica. About twenty estates were sold in the ten years after emancipation in British Guiana, due to labour problems rather than other difficulties.

Many estates were abandoned because they were mortgaged and so heavily in debt that no buyer could be found. By law, the buyer of such an estate had to take over the mortgage and the debts.

St Lucia, in 1833, was the first island to pass a law which allowed the government to seize abandoned estates and sell them without 'encumbrances'. This appealed to the British government as a cheap and easy way of bringing sugar estates into production again. In 1854 they passed the Encumbered Estates Act, but left it to each colony to decide whether to apply the Act. The only colonies which did not do so in the 1850s were Barbados, British Guiana and Trinidad.

The Act was a very short-sighted measure with disastrous long-term effects. It gave the merchant creditors (*merchants consignées*) first claim on the estate to recover their debts ahead of mortgages and other claims. Thus the estates passed into the hands of the Liverpool and London merchants. In charge of them were put attorneys, concerned not with the good running of the estate, but with the quickest possible sale of the sugar crop.

If the estate passed into the hands of another owner, the *consignée* had first claim on the crop and could buy it in London at the lowest price and sell it at a profit. The new owner had to send his crop in the *consignée's* ships and on his terms. All this made it very hard for the new owner to make a profit. Moreover the merchants only wanted to deal in sugar, and this discouraged experimentation and diversification in the islands.

However, the most serious effect of the 1854 Act was that it discouraged investment in the sugar industry. Nobody was willing to invest in plantations when the industry was declining and there was no hope of recovering debts.

The Royal Commission of 1882-83 recognised the ill effects of the Encumbered Estates Act and recommended its repeal. West Indian governments repealed their individual Acts in 1886, but by that time they had been in operation for thirty years and the damage had been done.

The Sugar Equalisation Act 1846

Free trade

In 1776 free trade ideas had been put forward by Adam Smith, an early British economist. These ideas were not widespread at first but the Industrial Revolution converted many people, especially merchants and industrialists, to free trade. They wanted cheap raw materials for their industries and saw the system of protective duties as an evil. Another economist, David Ricardo, wrote *Principles of Political Economy and Taxation* in 1817, supporting free trade, and this work dominated British economic thinking until the 1850s.

The Manchester School, led by Cobden and Bright, two radical politicians of the 1840s, also supported free trade. They were strongly against

David Ricardo

the West Indies and used the slogan, 'Jamaica to the bottom of the sea and the Antilles after it, rather than the interests of the people should be sacrificed'. It was calculated that the British people, because of the high cost of their sugar, were subsidising the British West Indian planters by £2,500,000 to £4,500,000 per year.

By the 1830s and 1840s there were large numbers of workers in the British towns, earning low wages and wanting cheap food. The politicians of the Manchester School convinced them that duties, especially those on North American corn, were keeping up the price of food. Eventually even the Tory government under Robert Peel, usually the party in favour of protection for English farmers and West Indian planters alike, was persuaded to adopt free trade policies. In 1846 the Corn Laws, allowing duties on foreign corn, were repealed to prevent further starvation, especially in Ireland. In the same year duties on foreign sugar were removed by the Sugar Equalisation Act. Finally, after 200 years, the Navigation Acts were repealed in 1849 and the British empire entered an era of free trade which lasted well into the twentieth century. Many planters regarded this act as the final straw and prophesied the end of the sugar industry. The period 1846 to 1854 was a critical one for sugar, but it survived.

There was some opposition to the Act in England by humanitarians who argued that slave-grown sugar should be kept out of England by continued duties. In particular this would have affected Cuba, the lowest cost producer of the time. However, the demand for cheap raw materials overrode humanitarian considerations and any sugar, free or slave-grown, was allowed to enter freely.

The Sugar Equalisation Act did not remove all the protective duties. The British West Indies were given time in which to adjust to foreign competition by lowering their costs. Initially this period was for five years, but the West Indian governments protested so strongly that it was put off until 1854.

Results of the 1846 Act

1 The inevitable fall in sugar prices led to more plantations going out of business. Some planters could not produce sugar below the London price, which in 1848 was 22/6d per cwt. Sugar from Cuba and Brazil could easily sell for 2/- per cwt below that. British Guiana, Jamaica and Trinidad all com-

plained that they could not produce sugar below the market price and wanted duties on foreign sugar brought back.

2 The only way most British planters could reduce costs was to reduce wages, and workers in the Eastern Caribbean were forced to accept wage cuts of up to 50 per cent. Sometimes planters faced strikes and riots, as in British Guiana, while in Jamaica many workers gave up plantation work because of lower wages. Generally, however, wage reductions of about one-third were accepted. This gives support to the belief that wages for plantation labour had been set too high.

3 In a few cases, chiefly in the larger colonies of Trinidad, British Guiana and Jamaica, new tools were introduced to economise on labour and reduce production costs. Planters could not afford large-scale mechanisation, but ploughs and harrows appeared. In British Guiana and Trinidad steam engines and vacuum pans were introduced, and these two territories became the most progressive in the British West Indies.

4 Between 1847 and 1848 there was a financial crisis in Britain which spread to the West Indies. Several Liverpool and London merchants who supplied credit to West Indian planters went bankrupt and the Planters Bank and the West India Bank called in loans, but repayment was not forthcoming. Thirteen firms of merchants in the British West Indies went bankrupt during this period.

5 There was a revival of the old clashes between Governor and Assembly. The worst trouble was in Jamaica, where the Assembly demanded the restoration of duties in 1849 and 1853. Sir Henry Barkly, who had dealt with similar problems in British Guiana, came to Jamaica to try to win them over. In 1849 and 1853 they refused to vote any taxes and the Governor was so short of money that he had to give unconditional pardons to 100 prisoners for whom he had no food. The British government offered a loan of £500,000 to the West Indies to help them over the crisis. The Jamaican Assembly was worried about accepting its share of this loan because it did not think it would be able to repay it when the sugar industry was declining so fast. At one time the Assembly even talked of asking for annexation by the United States.

There was trouble, too, in British Guiana in 1848 when the Combined Court, in protest against the Sugar Equalisation Act, insisted on a 25 per cent reduction in salaries on the Civil List. A settlement was reached when the British government promised a loan of over £200,000 to assist with immigration schemes.

6   There was a mistaken belief that the British West Indies would rise to the challenge of foreign, slave-grown sugar and produce free-grown sugar more cheaply. But free-grown sugar could never compete with the slave-grown sugar of Cuba and Louisiana.

Surviving the crisis

The British government refused to bow to pressure from the West Indian assemblies to restore duties and, therefore, the colonies were forced to compete. By the late 1850s sugar prices began to rise, reaching 37/5d per cwt in 1857. By the 1860s, conditions in the sugar industry had improved although this improvement was only temporary.

The loans offered by the British government in 1848 and 1853 were accepted by British Guiana and Trinidad, who put them towards the financing of immigration schemes which helped their sugar industry to survive. Barbados put its share into estate improvement, thus helping to maintain its relatively low cost of production. By the 1860s, the sugar industry had survived except in Jamaica where it continued to decline. Antigua, Barbados, British Guiana, St Kitts and Trinidad all survived the equalisation crisis.

British Guiana's production figures provide the best example of this.

1846   23,000 tonnes
1851   38,000 tonnes
1861   62,000 tonnes (just passing the pre-
            emancipation level)
1871   93,000 tonnes

Jamaica's figures show a sugar industry which failed to survive.

1832   71,000 tonnes
1852   25,000 tonnes
1888   13,000 tonnes

Foreign competition

Foreign producers were quick to take advantage of equal terms on the London market. Cuba, Louisiana and Brazil all produced slave-grown sugar very cheaply. Cuba's production was especially cheap and could undercut Antigua and Barbados which produced sugar at about 17/- per cwt, the lowest British price. Moreover, after equalisation, beet sugar became an even more dangerous competitor.

Cuba

The importation of 10,000 slaves into Cuba by the British in 1762 began the expansion of their sugar industry. Thereafter, it was stimulated by the Spanish government which allowed foreigners to import slaves freely into Cuba. The Haitian Revolution also helped, because French planters fled to Cuba with their slaves. The Napoleonic Wars enabled Cuba to trade freely with foreign countries when the demand for sugar was high.

In 1762 sugar was equal with tobacco and hides as Cuba's leading export, although even by 1815 it only reached about half of Jamaica's production. By 1828 sugar production equalled that of Jamaica, and by 1848 equalled the output of the British West Indies. By 1894 Cuba had become the first country in the world to pass the million tonne mark in sugar production. Before the Sugar Equalisation Act, Cuba had sold only about 10,000 tonnes of sugar in Britain, but by 1864 she was selling just under 150,000 tonnes.

Cuba possessed many natural advantages over the British West Indies in sugar production.

1   *Size* Cuba was ten times larger than Jamaica and could expand her sugar production easily just by putting more hectares under sugar. Sugar could be grown in every province, although the heaviest concentration was in the Camagüey-Maniabon region.

2   *Virgin Land* There were wide plains of virgin land in Cuba whose fertility gave a very high yield compared with that of the British West Indies.

3   *Water Power* Fast-flowing streams from the central mountains of Cuba provided a readily available source of power for the ingenios.

She also possessed many man-made advantages.

1   *Slave Labour* Cuba had slave labour until 1886, fifty years after the British West Indies had emancipated their slaves. This was no cheaper than the immigrant labour in British Guiana and Trinidad, but it provided a regular permanent labour force. In 1850 the slave population of Cuba was about 350,000, a little more than the slave population of Jamaica had been at emancipation (312,000). The Cuban sugar industry was labour-intensive but the

output per slave, at between three and six tonnes per slave compared with just over one tonne per slave in the British West Indies, was far higher.

2 *Immigrant Labour* Cuba expanded her industry between 1852 and 1874, relying on Chinese immigrant labour. They worked very long hours on eight-year contracts and were well suited to the more mechanised industry of Cuba. In this period 124,000 Chinese immigrants entered Cuba.

3 *Mechanisation* The great revolution in the Cuban sugar industry did not occur until the 1880s, but even before the Ten Years War, she was more mechanised than the British West Indies. The first steam mills were in operation from 1819. French sugar experts from Haiti had introduced the more efficient enclosed furnaces. Early in the nineteenth century. Cuba had vacuum pans in which the juice could be boiled at a lower temperature. The same heat that supplied the steam engine could be used for the vacuum pans. In the 1840s, the best machinery from France, made by Derosne, was imported into Cuba. Steam engines for the mills were imported from the United States, together with American expertise in machinery.

4 *Economies of Scale* In Cuba, unlike the Eastern Caribbean, there was enough land for sugar to be grown while tobacco was still a major industry. Therefore, the sugar industry avoided the 'teething problems' of the British West Indies. Sugar planters

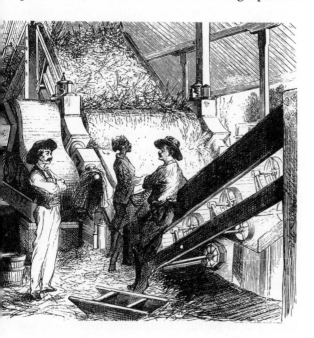
Grinding cane in Cuba

bought land cheaply from the old cattle grants of the sixteenth and seventeenth centuries which had never been taken up. Estates were, therefore, large and could achieve economies of scale, thus making them more efficient. They could support large mills run at full capacity and could afford to introduce new machines.

5 *Refined Sugar* As early as the Napoleonic Wars, sugar refineries had been developed in Cuba, and in 1864 Cuba put over 3,000 tonnes of refined sugar on the British market.

6 *Markets* Cuba's sugar industry was closely tied up with its American trade. She imported North American foodstuffs to feed her slaves and, in return sold sugar to North America, especially when the crop in Louisiana was not successful. Even if the Louisiana crop was good and little Cuban sugar could be sold in America, it could be sold in Europe although the profit was less due to protective duties and competition from beet sugar.

The sugar revolution in Cuba

The Ten Years War 1868-1878, in which the Cubans sought freedom from Spain, caused much destruction, but in the long run made possible the changes known as the 'Cuban Sugar Revolution'. During the war, pressure from inside and outside Cuba made the government stop Chinese immigration, and in 1880 slavery was abolished. Cuban sugar output could only continue at its high level if it switched from labour-intensive to capital-intensive methods or, in other words, to mechanisation. In the 1880s and 1890s world sugar prices were falling and Cuba, as a sugar economy, was forced to reorganise her sugar production in order to compete successfully.

Smaller producers went out of production and the 'Latifundia' were created. These were monster estates able to take advantage of economies of scale. The 'colono' system survived, but its nature changed. Whereas before, small growers had cultivated their canes on their own land and brought them to a central mill, in the 1880s they still grew cane in the outlying areas but the land was owned by the centrals which developed an increasingly strong hold over them. The centrals grew even larger, serving many plantations all linked by railways. Their capacity was immense, one central producing 20,000 tonnes of sugar in 1890 which was more than Jamaica's total sugar crop of 1888. Between 1880 and 1900, the number of sugar

A Cuban plantation

factories in Cuba fell by two-thirds. At the same time her sugar production roughly doubled, indicating that the capacity of each factory must have increased fivefold.

Most of the estates were still Cuban owned, even if much of the capital came from American banks. American ownership of over 60 per cent of the estates came after May 1920, in the period which Cubans refer to as 'The Dance of the Millions'. Between 1918 and 1920 the price of sugar rocketed. It had been fixed at 5½ cents per lb by the United States Sugar Equalisation Board, but after accusations of excessive profiteering from the sale of the 1919 crop inside the United States, the 1920 crop was put on the world market where it realised 23 cents per lb. Immediately the investors and distributers of sugar in the United States wanted to secure their source of supply in Cuba, so they poured millions of dollars into Cuba and bought land at inflated prices.

The Cubans also discovered that a large perma-nent labour force was not necessary on a sugar estate. The work was seasonal, and most of the labour was needed at crop time. Therefore Cuba changed to gang labour which moved about from estate to estate to harvest the crop. This cut costs for the planters considerably and helped Cuba to continue as a cheap producer.

By the end of the nineteenth century she had become a one-crop economy, totally dependent on the world price of sugar. This was shown in 1895 when the price of sugar fell to two cents per lb, and again in 1921 when the price of sugar fell so low that sugar producers could not pay their debts. More estates fell into American hands, and most of Havana's banks went bankrupt.

Louisiana and Brazil

Two other American sugar competitors were Louisiana in North America and Brazil in South America. Their climatic conditions were similar to the West Indies and their maturing time for cane roughly the same, about seven to nine months. However, they also possessed advantages over the British West Indies. Louisiana had the flat, fertile lands of the Mississippi Delta, and Brazil had almost unlimited fertile lands in the Bahia and Pernambuço regions. The production costs of Louisiana and Brazil were below even those of Barbados. Both countries had the advantage of slave labour, Louisiana until 1865, and Brazil until 1888.

Louisiana's cane sugar production was about half that of the British West Indies in 1844, but it was produced more cheaply and more efficiently, coming as it did from about 750 mills and only 100,000 slaves. Steam engines had been introduced as early as 1822. Undoubtedly Louisiana, and the United States, could have expanded sugar production many times over, but with the availability of cheap Cuban sugar they did not bother. In the nineteenth century, the United States protected Louisiana and Cuba from competition from beet sugar by protective duties, but these were abandoned in 1900. When the United States started its own beet sugar industry, the Louisiana planters protested in vain and, by that time, Cuba was a foreign country at the mercy of the United States importers.

Competition from Brazilian sugar in the mid-nineteenth century was partly the result of British investment. In the 1830s Brazil was producing under half the total British West Indian output. When duties were removed Brazil's sugar production expanded threefold, from 1833 to 1882, and it survived emancipation in 1888 because the industry was relatively modernised, with large-scale production on big estates in the north-east. The sugar industry was subsidised by the government who guaranteed a fixed return of not less than seven per cent on investment in order to encourage the building of large factories. By the end of the century Brazil's output was well over a quarter of a million tonnes, larger than the total output of the British West Indies.

European beet sugar

In 1747 Andreas Marggraf, a German chemist, extracted sugar crystals from some kinds of beet root, but his discovery was not exploited commercially until 1786. Then Franz Karl Achard planted beets on his Caulsdorf estate near Berlin. Frederick William III, King of Prussia, was interested and financed the world's first beet sugar factory in 1802 in Silesia. By 1810 it was clear that a beet sugar industry could be successful.

Slaves working in a Brazilian mill

Other European countries started beet sugar industries because:

1 It would make them independent of imported sugar.
2 It would provide employment
3 It would suit the rotation of crops then practised in Europe.

Napoleon encouraged the development of beet sugar in France during the Napoleonic Wars when cane sugar from Guadeloupe and Martinique was cut off. Soon Austria, Belgium, Holland and Russia were producing beet sugar as well as Germany and France.

Beet sugar was expensive to produce, about 24/- per cwt, and could not have competed with Caribbean sugar in a free market. However, because of the advantages of having their own sugar industry, European countries subsidised their beet sugar industries.

This competition was felt most keenly in the last two decades of the nineteenth century. Barbados saw the threat from beet sugar as early as 1876. The Ten Years' War in Cuba had helped the export of British West Indian sugar, but then came the impact of subsidised European beet sugar and prices fell. Cuba was the only Caribbean sugar producer to compete successfully. Britain, following her policy of free trade, imported more and more European beet sugar. By 1902 she was taking only 2½ per cent of her sugar from the British West Indies.

When considering the hardships of the British West Indies in 1896, the Norman Commission had pointed to 'competition of beet sugar produced under a system of bounties'. Between 1882 and 1892, British imports of European beet sugar had increased from 400,000 to 1,000,000 tonnes. The situation was equally serious for the French islands. By 1902, the price of cane sugar from Guadeloupe and Martinique had fallen to 16 francs per kilo (from over 80 francs two years previously).

Therefore, in 1903, European beet sugar-producing countries agreed to a conference—the Brussels Convention—at which they promised 'to suppress the direct and indirect bounties by which the production and exportation of sugar may profit'. However, European beet sugar continued to compete with Caribbean sugar on the world market.

In the 1914-18 War, European beet sugar collapsed. Sugar prices rose and continued to rise until 1920. Cuba expanded her production to over 4,000,000 tonnes per year and stockpiled sugar, thinking that the European beet production would take a long time to recover and prices would remain high. She was wrong. European sugar production recovered completely and in the 1920s the European sugar market was glutted. By 1929 the price of sugar had dropped to 8/- per cwt.

The backwardness of the British West Indian sugar industry

Causes

The industry was using seventeenth-century methods in the nineteenth century. The labour-intensive methods which slavery had encouraged continued, whereas other countries had adopted new methods to reduce labour and production costs.

1 Typical labour-intensive methods were the use of hoes instead of ploughs, and the carrying of heavy loads on their heads by gangs of men. Antigua was renowned for its backwardness, and there was not a pitchfork or a wheelbarrow in the island in 1846.

Until very modern times there was no labour saving method for topping and cutting the canes in croptime. It was not until after 1846 that attempts were made to cut labour costs by using the system of 'task gangs', in which large gangs of labourers moved from plantation to plantation in crop time, and then only in Antigua and St Kitts.

2 British West Indian plantations were not large enough to make economical use of the new machinery, such as the vacuum pan, the centrifugal drier or the steam mill, except possibly in Trinidad and British Guiana. The 'central' factory was the answer to this problem but it was not acceptable in the British West Indies.

3 Planters were held back by lack of capital. The new machinery, the huge centrals and ultimately a railway system, required large amounts of capital which were not available to the British planter who depended for his finance on his *merchant consignée*. The sugar industry in the British Indies did not attract British capital as did those of Cuba and Brazil. Even the French islands had capital available for the sugar industry through *La Société de Crédit Colonial* founded in 1860. All these foreign territories developed centrals or usines before the British islands. Two usines were built in Martinique

in 1862 and many plantations stopped crushing their own cane and took it to the usine.

The first centrals in the British West Indies were the *Usine Sainte Madeleine* in Trinidad in 1871 and the *Grand Cul de Sac Usine* is St Lucia in 1874. For the most part, centrals were a twentieth-century development in the British West Indies. Even then they were not universal because to work really well they required a system of 'feeder' railways. Most of the British islands are not large enough for this.

4   Planters were very conservative, for example many would not change to steam power because they did not want to cut down their timber for fuel. They refused to share factories or machinery because they feared loss of independence. Nowhere was this more apparent than in Barbados, where sugar estates had been in the same families since the middle of the seventeenth century and 400 factories were being used to produce the same amount of sugar that came out of twenty Cuban factories.

5   British planters knew that refined sugar would sell more easily in Europe and at a far higher price, but they were unable to produce it because of the opposition of merchants and industrialists in Britain. However, they must be blamed for not obtaining more sucrose from the cane. British mills only used a single crushing process, obtaining only 75 per cent of the juice from the cane. Cuban mills were regularly using triple crushing with dilution in the process and obtaining over 90 per cent of juice from the cane.

Trinidad and British Guiana were exceptions to most of these failings. Their plantations were larger than those of the other islands and could support up-to-date machinery. Their planters were not usually conservative as they had only acquired their plantations in the nineteenth century. Finally, due to their special labour problems they adopted labour-saving methods early in the century.

The Royal Commissions of 1882 and 1896

Towards the end of the century, the sugar industry was in such a distressed state that two Royal Commissions were appointed to investigate it and make recommendations for improvement.

The immediate reason for appointing the 1882-83 Commission was that most of the British West Indian islands could not repay the loans they had contracted between 1848 and 1853. The Commission was to enquire into the revenues and expenditures of the colonies, but it also concerned itself with the state of the sugar industry. Its report concluded that sugar was still the principal source of income, but,

> except in St Lucia where exports have trebled in value in the last thirty years, it is generally carried on under all the disadvantages of old-fashioned and faulty systems of cultivation and manufacture.

The Report encouraged small farmers in these words:

> It is said that thirty days labour on an acre of good soil in Jamaica will, in addition to providing a family with necessary food for a year, yield a surplus saleable in the market for from £10 to £30. It is to the possession of provision grounds that the industrious Negro turns with the greatest liking, and there exists in Jamaica a substantial and happily numerous population of the peasant proprietor class, which easily obtains a livelihood by the growth of minor tropical products of fruit and spices, cocoa and coffee, and so contributes to the general prosperity.

This was very over-optimistic about the fertility of the land, but basically the Report was recommending the diversification of crops to the small farmer because sugar was in decline. Already Jamaica was exporting bananas which was a favourite smallholder crop. Apart from suggesting a few improvements in cultivation and marketing, the Commission took the view that competition from beet sugar was too strong.

The Norman Commission of 1896 was sent out firstly because the price of sugar had fallen from 21/- per cwt in 1881 to 11/- per cwt in 1896, and secondly, because Joseph Chamberlain, Secretary of State for the Colonies, believed in the development of the colonies for the mutual benefit of themselves and the mother country. He believed that the British West Indies could be improved by science and technology and that marketing of their products could be helped by Imperial Preference.

The Norman Commission was very pessimistic about the sugar industry in the British West Indies. It recommended that only in Antigua, Barbados and St Kitts should sugar remain the staple crop. The other islands should diversify.

Its more specific recommendations were as follows:

1 The encouragement of small farming, suggesting a land settlement scheme and the creation of banks to help with finances.
2 Government loans to help modernise the sugar industry, especially by building central factories.
3 Agricultural departments in the islands to help with scientific cultivation and agricultural education in schools.
4 Diversification of crops, especially fruit.
5 Improvement of communications, in particular, the steamer service to New York.

The members of the Commission disagreed among themselves about whether beet sugar was the principal cause of the distress of the British West Indies. However, it did recommend the abolition of bounties for beet sugar paid by European governments.

The Norman Commission is an example of one Royal Commission whose advice and recommendations were acted upon.

Revival of sugar

After the Report of the Norman Commission, an Imperial Department of Agriculture for the West Indies was set up in Barbados in 1898. This was a real step forward. Its function was to encourage more scientific methods of cultivation, and to promote the diversification of crops. It was to co-ordinate the work of the Botanical Gardens which existed in each island and, through them, distribute better varieties of seeds to the planters and farmers. Finally, lecturers and demonstrators would be sent through the islands to demonstrate the new methods of cultivation.

The Imperial Department became the headquarters for research into the best varieties of sugar cane. The cane diseases of the 1890s showed the need for this. Unfortunately, the results of their work were not put into practice on a wide scale until 1920.

Cultivation

The most important development was that of selective cane-breeding. In 1888 J.B.Garrison and J.R.Rovell in Barbados succeeded in growing cane from seed (another scientist, working independently in Java made the same discovery). This led to new varieties of cane by selective breeding. Java was the first country to grow the new seedling

varieties commercially. They could be made stronger, more resistant to disease, or higher sucrose-yielding, or a combination of all three qualities.

The old 'noble' strains of cane in the British West Indies were commonly the transparent white and the Bourbon canes which were high yielding. These were crossed with wild canes to make them immune from disease.

Fertilisers and irrigation were more widely used. Fertilisers were still 'natural' not chemical, for example, guano from Peru was used widely in the British West Indies. Irrigation was important in Trinidad which has 1,270 millimetres of rain for seven months of the year and only 250 millimetres in the remaining five months. Floodwater damaged the canes in the old system, so they adopted the 'ridge-planting' method of sowing the canes, but maintained irrigation to the soil.

Manufacturing

The biggest reductions in production costs came as a result of improved manufacturing. The central factory system was responsible for this. However, central factories were only feasible if large supplies of cane were available. This meant that either plantations would have to increase in size, or several plantations would have to amalgamate to feed one factory.

Since emancipation, the planters in Trinidad and British Guiana had turned their estates into companies, either individually or together with other plantations. In Antigua and Jamaica, planters had also amalgamated to lower production costs. In Barbados they were reluctant to do so. By the turn of the century, British Guiana had fewer than 150 sugar estates. Barbados still had over 400.

The most important aspect of amalgamation was sharing the cost of the central factory. With costs shared, it was possible to develop steam mills. Trinidad and British Guiana found the fuel expensive, especially coal, but the manufacturing process was so much more efficient that costs were reduced. The quality of the sugar was improved as a double or triple crushing process could be used with little extra cost.

In the small islands, one or two centrals could serve the whole island. In 1904 there were two in Antigua, one with a capacity for 8,000 tonnes of sugar per year. There was one in St Kitts with a capacity of 10,000 tonnes per year. Rationalisation

The central in St Kitts

of the sugar industry was gradually taking place even in the oldest colonies.

Marketing

Improved marketing certainly helped the sugar industry. From 1875 to 1898, sugar from the British West Indies, especially from British Guiana, found a market in the United States. After the Spanish-American war of 1898 the United States had closer ties with Cuba, Puerto Rico and the Philippines and took more and more sugar from them.

With the decline of the United States market, the Canadian market developed. Starting in 1898, Canada offered increasingly favourable terms to sugar from the British West Indies and by 1909 was taking 133,000 tonnes of sugar. By the Ottawa Empire Trades Agreements of 1912, Canada gave preference to British West Indian sugar. During the First World War and for ten years after it, the British West Indies sold most of their sugar to Canada. This continued until 1932 when, once again, Britain became their biggest market.

Prices had been high during, and immediately after, the First World War because European beet sugar production had stopped. The British West Indies enjoyed a sugar boom. Britain had found difficulty in obtaining sugar and had had to pay a high price for it. There was pressure to end free trade and introduce Imperial Preference by which British West Indian sugar would be able to enter Britain protected from foreign competition. In 1919 Britain offered a preferential duty which resulted in increased sales of sugar to Britain. At the Ottawa Conference of 1924-5 Britain adopted a policy of Imperial Preference with much lower duties on colonial produce. This helped the British West Indies through the depression of the late 1920s and 1930s by guaranteeing a market at a higher price than the prevailing world prices. In 1926 Britain had set up the Empire Marketing Board to help British and colonial trade.

With the approach of the Second World War, Britain wanted to secure her supplies of sugar. In 1939 she undertook to buy all the output of the British West Indies sugar industry at a price which would cover the costs of production. This arrangement was repeated in 1944 and 1948. New arrangements were made by the Commonwealth Sugar Agreement in 1951, and in 1953 the British West Indies entered the International Sugar Agreement. Basically these agreements give a fixed price quota, that is, a guaranteed price for a fixed amount of sugar, to the British West Indies. It can exceed its quota in production, but the surplus has to be sold in a free world market where the price could be below the cost of production.

At times during this century the British West Indian sugar industry has enjoyed periods of relative prosperity. Between 1913 and 1924 its production doubled, and it doubled again between 1928 and 1938. From 1939 to 1953 the industry was prosperous, but in more recent times quotas and competition together with Britain's entry into the European Common Market have again threatened the industry.

Sir Henry Norman

11

Alternatives to Sugar after 1850

The need for alternative crops

Before the Norman Commission

Most of the crops which provided alternatives to sugar after 1850 were not new to the West Indies. Some were indigenous and had been used by the Arawaks, while others had been export crops from the earliest colonial times. In some islands they had even pre-dated sugar as commercial crops.

Wild cotton of very good quality with a long staple was exported from Barbados from its earliest days. On a visit in 1631, Sir Henry Colt remarked that cotton was the hope of the people. It was placed on the list of enumerated goods in the 1660 Navigation Act. By 1724 Antigua, Montserrat, Nevis and St Kitts, as well as Barbados, were all recording exports of cotton. Apart from the early twentieth century, the period 1784-1802 was the most prosperous for the cotton industry. It was of the utmost importance to Barbados when sugar declined in 1787. A stimulus to cotton-growing came from the American Loyalists who had settled in the Bahamas, and the Turks and Caicos Islands.

At one time during the Napoleonic Wars, 70 per cent of the cotton imported into Britain came from the West Indies. However when production in the southern states of North America began to expand after the invention of Eli Whitney's saw-gin in 1793, production in the British West Indies declined sharply. It revived again briefly during the American Civil War of 1861-5, and was an obvious

115

choice as an export crop in the early twentieth century when the sugar industry was struggling.

Coffee had been introduced into the West Indies by the Spanish and has been grown continuously in Jamaica from the sixteenth century to the present day. In 1791 the Jamaican Assembly mentioned coffee as an alternative export crop and it became important as a second crop during the French Wars. In Dominica, St Vincent, Grenada and St Lucia, coffee was cultivated as an alternative export crop in the late eighteenth century, because sugar prices were low. Consequently, these islands were always more diversified in their crops than Barbados and the Leewards. When the British took over Trinidad in 1797, they found 130 coffee plantations in production there.

The cacao plant was native to South America and was introduced into the West Indies by the Spaniards. It was always a minor export crop, especially in the eighteenth century. When the sugar industry declined, in the 1830s and 1840s, cacao was one of the products given priority by local agricultural societies.

The British West Indies, particularly Barbados, suffered from sugar monoculture, but cacao, coffee, cotton, arrowroot, ginger, indigo, pimento and tobacco were all known as possible alternative exports before 1896. Jamaica had the most diversified economy of the British islands. By 1870 other crops including coffee, pimento, ginger, logwood and cinchona trees made up 55 per cent of her exports.

Small farming and alternative crops

Emancipation provided a reason for turning to alternative crops. The best the ex-slaves could hope for was a smallholding. They had to grow subsistence crops to keep themselves alive, but for cash crops they wanted something that would give a high yield from a small acreage. The ideal crops were spices, although competition from the East and Zanzibar was very fierce. Spices, chiefly nutmegs, were tried in Grenada. Ginger and pimento became relatively important in Jamaica. Arrowroot became very important in St Vincent where the government divided up unused estates into small lots of between two and four hectares to encourage small farming. This policy was also followed in Trinidad in the 1860s to persuade the immigrants to stay. Cacao, which had always been grown by the Spanish and later the French, became an important crop there. In Dominica, the ex-slaves went into the hilly interior and grew coffee on their smallholdings. Limes were introduced in about 1850 by Dr John Imray, and were ideally suited to small farming. Montserrat also adopted limes in 1852.

The importance of the Norman Commission

One of the most important recommendations of the Norman Commission was diversification. Because of this, the Imperial Department of Agriculture for the West Indies tried to discover which crops were best suited to which islands. It aimed at introducing 'new' crops in areas where sugar was not the best crop. Most of them had been tried before, but there were some new suggestions for export crops, for example, oranges, rice, sisal, pineapples, and rubber.

The Department in Barbados was to co-ordinate the work of the Experimental Stations in Trinidad and Jamaica, and the Botanical Gardens in most of the islands. By 1908, separate Departments of Agriculture had been set up in Jamaica, Trinidad

Growing arrowroot in St Vincent

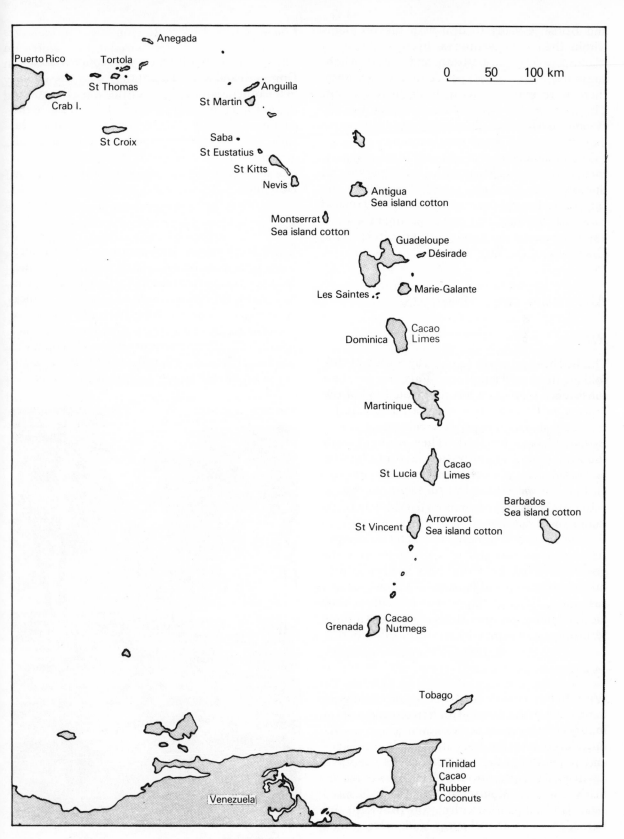

Map 6   Eastern Caribbean islands showing alternative crops

and British Guiana to deal with the problems within their own territories. Even in the small islands like Antigua, Barbados and St Kitts where sugar made up over 90 per cent of the exports, there were experiments with alternative crops. The Department was particularly hopeful in the Windward Islands which had a history of alternative export crops and active small farming.

The Imperial Government paid for the Department in Barbados and subsidised the Experimental Stations and Botanical Gardens. In 1922, the Imperial College of Tropical Agriculture in Trinidad took over the work of the Department and, in 1960, it became the Faculty of Agriculture in the University of the West Indies.

Alternative crops 1896-1925

Rice

This had been grown in Trinidad by runaway black soldiers from the Napoleonic Wars, but only as a subsistence crop. As it was the staple food of the Indians and Chinese, its production increased after their arrival. The Indians were cultivating rice in British Guiana by 1865. They brought with them their skill in cultivation, and production increased throughout the nineteenth century, although it was still only a subsistence crop.

In 1899 British Guiana imported nearly 9,000,000 kilograms of rice, but by the end of the First World War she was exporting nearly 11,000,000 kilograms. Its cultivation was still in small units, but the government had built rice mills to expand production. Trinidad and Jamaica also grew rice as a cash crop, although export was difficult as they faced competition from British Guiana. All three territories faced competition from North America.

Cotton

West Indian cotton is of fine quality. Consequently there was a demand for it from producers of luxury cotton garments. Sea-island cotton was re-introduced into the Leeward Islands, Barbados and St Vincent at the beginning of the twentieth century. The cotton from St Vincent was particularly good. In Montserrat, and Nevis, disused estate land was planted with cotton. In St Kitts and Barbados, the marginal sugar lands were turned over to cotton.

Limes

The production of limes was concentrated in Dominica and St Lucia, but they were also grown in the other islands. They were used as a flavouring in food and drink and also had a limited use in the chemical industry. Production expanded in the early twentieth century and while they were still grown with other crops in smallholdings, plantations exclusively for limes were developed in Dominica.

Coconuts

These were grown throughout the West Indies. They were put to commercial use in the manufacture of copra from the milky flesh of the nut, as well as by exporting whole nuts to non-tropical countries for food. Coconut fibre also has a commercial use in mat-making. Coconuts were not usually turned into coconut oil, but the copra was used as cattle feed and fertiliser. In the 1914-18 war copra prices rose rapidly and production doubled.

Coconut palms

Dancing cocoa

Prices remained high between 1918 and 1921 and Trinidad increased its coconut production to meet the high demand.

Coconut palms could be grown easily from shoots obtained from the whole nut. Consequently they are attractive to the small farmer who had previously not considered them of commercial value. Each coconut palm could yield between 50 and 100 nuts, so they were very high yielding on land which would probably be too sandy and low-lying for other crops. In Trinidad, especially, many coconut plantations were established between 1914 and 1921.

Rubber

There were native 'rubber' trees in British Guiana and Trinidad. In British Guiana some trees produced a milky juice which was turned into gutta percha. This could be used for insulating cables and for the early type of golf balls. In the second half of the

nineteenth century when rubber tyres came into use, Britain looked for new areas in which to grow rubber. Imported rubber trees were planted in Trinidad in 1864, and the high prices for rubber early in the twentieth century encouraged British Guiana and Trinidad to expand rubber production. Rubber trees were grown in plantations and needed relatively large areas of land.

Cacao

This was widely grown in the West Indies but, in the period 1896 to 1925, it was particularly associated with Trinidad, Grenada, St Lucia, and Dominica, as an alternative crop. Trinidad, especially, concentrated on it because it could be grown on Indian immigrant smallholdings, and on banana plantations, growing under the canopy of the taller banana palms. Cacao production did well in the early twentieth century and at one time cacao became Trinidad's chief export.

119

Spices

Arrowroot production in St Vincent was expanded at the beginning of the century. Grenada adopted nutmegs as an alternative crop and grew other spices experimentally. Ginger was also tried in the Eastern Caribbean, but Jamaica was the only island in which commercial production was successful. The demand for spices, however, was fickle and it was unwise for a small island to rely on them.

Bananas

Banana growing was a fairly well developed industry before the Norman Commission. The Spanish had introduced bananas into Hispaniola in 1516 and they were grown in Jamaica soon afterwards. However, the variety which became such a successful export crop was brought into Jamaica by a French botanist from Martinique and grown on his Bel Air plantation in St Andrews. It was the 'Gros Michel' variety, a large plant and fruit which became popular with the peasants in the north - east of the island.

An American sea captain, picking up bananas from Cuba, decided to try a small cargo of Jamaican bananas as an experiment, having heard that they were superior in quality. In 1866 he picked up the fruit at Port Antonio and took it to Boston. Its popularity was instant. As long as sailing ships could complete the 3,200 kilometres to Boston in between two to three weeks, the bananas would arrive in good condition. In 1868 another American captain, Lorenzo Dow Baker, returning from New York to Central America, called at Port Antonio for another cargo of Jamaican bananas for which he paid 1/- per bunch.

By 1880, trade had increased to such an extent that Captain Baker founded the Boston Fruit Company to export bananas to the United States. In 1882 his company established their own plantations; Bog near Port Antonio and the Bowden Estates near Port Morant. Most of the bananas were, however, still produced by smallholders.

Collecting and counting bananas

120

The Royal Commission of 1882 acknowledged the great contribution which bananas were making to Jamaica's economy.

In 1899 the Boston Fruit Company merged with the company of another American, Minor Keith, who had constructed a railway and begun to grow bananas in Costa Rica. Baker wanted increased supplies of bananas and Keith wanted the established markets of North America.

The new company—the United Fruit Company—dominated the Jamaican and Caribbean banana industry for thirty years. It had a monopoly of Jamaica's banana output, and this worried the small producers who felt that they were being forced to accept whatever price the company offered. The Empire Marketing Board encouraged the small producers to break this monopoly. In 1929, the Jamaica Banana Producers' Association was set up. It paid about 2/6d per bunch which was 5d more than the United Fruit Company. This development ensured that the banana industry in Jamaica was controlled by the small producer.

In 1912, fruit (bananas and citrus) made up over 50 per cent of Jamaica's exports, reaching its peak in 1920. During the depression, banana production remained high and in 1937 Jamaica was exporting 27,000,000 stems of bananas, constituting 60 per cent of her exports. During the Second World War, there was no market for bananas, but the British Government agreed to cover the cost of the crop. In the immediate postwar period, sugar regained its long-lost position as Jamaica's chief export, but since then fruit, chiefly bananas, has taken over again.

Disappointment with alternative crops

With the exception of bananas, the alternative crops developed after 1896 were not a great success. This was due partly to natural causes and partly to market forces.

Limes in St Lucia and Dominica were struck by root tip disease which gradually destroyed the plants. Witchbroom disease hit the cacao plants, and the cotton plants suffered from pink boll worm disease. On top of this, in 1912 Panama disease destroyed the banana crop and, since it affected the soil, made it useless for further production for some years. In 1942 another banana disease, leaf spot, attacked the crop.

Agricultural departments could fight these diseases, but the West Indies were helpless in the face of adverse market forces. The rubber industry collapsed suddenly between 1913 and 1914, when Malayan rubber reached the European market. Limes did not sell when synthetic citrus flavouring was discovered, although now the West Indies has switched to the production of lime oil. During the depression, few people could afford sea-island cotton and the industry collapsed in the late 1920s. Since the Second World War, sea-island cotton has regained its popularity. The cacao industry could not compete with the Gold Coast's (Ghana) production which soon dominated the world market.

Unfortunately natural disasters, loss of markets, world depression and the ending of emigration opportunities all came together in the 1930s. This combination of disasters produced great hardship in the British West Indies.

Minerals

Alternative lasting sources of wealth were the petroleum products of Trinidad and the bauxite of British Guiana. (Jamaica's bauxite industry was developed at a much later period.)

Petroleum products in Trinidad

Trinidad has two petroleum products, asphalt and oil, which helped her survive the decline of sugar and quickly became her chief exports.

At La Brea in Trinidad in 1595, Sir Walter Raleigh saw a pitch lake which, he reported, was large enough to fill all the ships of the world. It was first used to caulk ships.

Geologists, examining the lake later, thought it was a stage in the breakdown of organic marine deposits into petroleum. However, as the pitch lake continues to be supplied with fresh crude oil from an underground source, it is now thought to be the cone of a sedimentary volcano. It contains an estimated ten million tonnes of asphalt.

In 1886, the Trinidad Government allowed an American, A.L. Barber, to take asphalt from the lake for twenty-one years, in return for royalties and duties, giving the government a revenue of over £10,000 per year. This was renewed in 1907, but in 1925, wanting increased revenue, the government transferred the concession to the Trinidad Lake Asphalt Company which agreed to pay £24,000 per year.

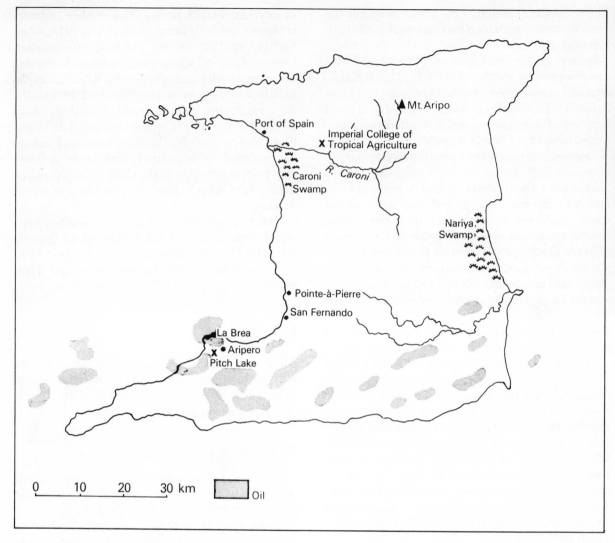

Map 7   Trinidad: minerals and ports

The asphalt from La Brea was put into wagons and taken to the port of La Brea (now to a new port, Brighton) and loaded on ships. It was used for road surfacing, lining canals and reservoirs, facing dams and for waterproofing of all kinds.

In 1866 oil was found at Aripero, but it was not exploited because there was little demand for mineral oil. Indeed in North America it was called 'black water' and regarded simply as a hazard for cattle. Prospecting for oil resumed in 1905. In 1910, the Trinidad Oilfields Company was formed and began exporting oil to the United States.

Oil exports could not keep up with increasing demand, although the industry expanded rapidly throughout the First World War. By 1936, Trinidad's petroleum products were worth about £4,000,000 and made up over half her exports. They have remained Trinidad's leading export and provide over 80 per cent of her export earnings.

Prospecting continued and an oil-bearing belt was discovered, running across the south of the island from the north-west to the south-east. More recently it was found to extend under the sea off the west coast and this is now being exploited. Trinidad has become a major oil-refining centre with crude oil coming in from Columbia, Venezuela and even Saudi Arabia.

Undoubtedly oil provided by far the greatest alternative source of wealth in the British West Indies. It has made Trinidad the most prosperous of all the large islands. (Grand Cayman has a higher per capita income.)

Digging pitch in southern Trinidad

Bauxite in British Guiana

Bauxite occurs in most tropical countries of the world, but its composition varies and most of it is not worth exploiting. However, the bauxite in British Guiana and Jamaica consists of trihydrate ores and is of great commercial value. One drawback to bauxite mining is that it scars the country, so its exploitation is only worthwhile if the land is not needed for other purposes.

Geological surveys in 1868 and 1873 recorded bauxite along the Demerara River. Later, extensive deposits were discovered between the Demerara and Berbice Rivers. In 1910, Sir John Hamilton, the Government Geologist, determined the composition of the deposits but still nothing was done to exploit them.

In 1915 an American, George Mackenzie, bought land along the Demerara River supposedly to grow oranges. His true intentions were revealed in 1916 when he founded the Demerara Bauxite Company. The first exports of bauxite ore came out of the Three Friends field in 1917. Ocean-going ships can now sail up the Demerara River to Linden (formerly named Mackenzie after the man who founded the industry), where they land the bauxite.

The industry started too late to catch the high demand of the First World War and suffered badly from lack of demand in the Depression. However, the Second World War created a high level of

Drilling for oil in Trinidad

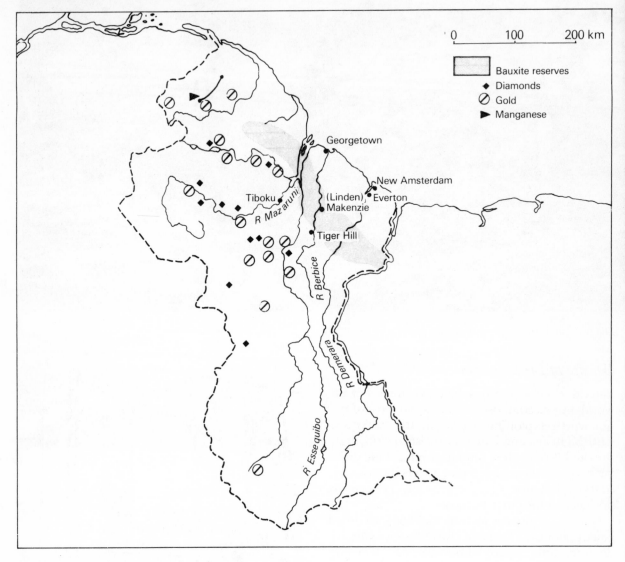

Map 8   British Guiana: minerals and ports

demand which has been maintained. Bauxite now makes up just under 40 per cent of Guyana's exports, making her the fifth largest producer in the world.

The Demerara Bauxite Company was brought out by the Aluminium Company of Canada (ALCAN), but in 1970 Guyana nationalised the bauxite industry. Although founded in the early twentieth century, the industry's great contribution to the Guyanese economy came after 1939.

Bauxite in Jamaica

This is another example of an industry which bolstered the economy when sugar declined.

The presence of alumina in the interior was determined in 1869, but not until 1942 when scientists were investigating the low fertility of the soil was it 'rediscovered'. Because of the Second World War, there was a high demand for aluminium products and, as the reserves were conservatively estimated at 5,000,000 tonnes, mining companies immediately began investigating it. (Recent surveys have put Jamaica's reserves of bauxite at between five to six hundred million tonnes). In 1942 there were three mining companies involved, one Canadian and two American. In the 1960s this had increased to five.

The bauxite yielding area is about 2,600 square kilometres in the centre of Jamaica. As it was

Bauxite mine near Linden

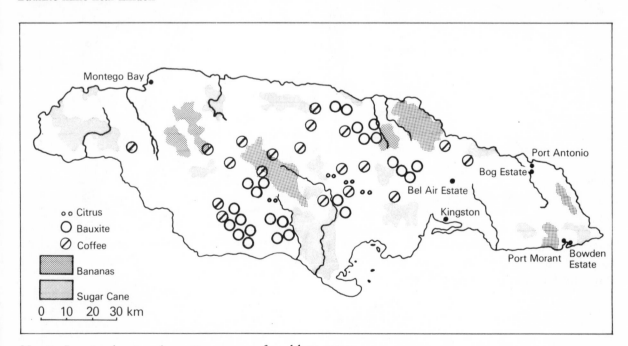

Map 9 Jamaica showing alternative sources of wealth to sugar

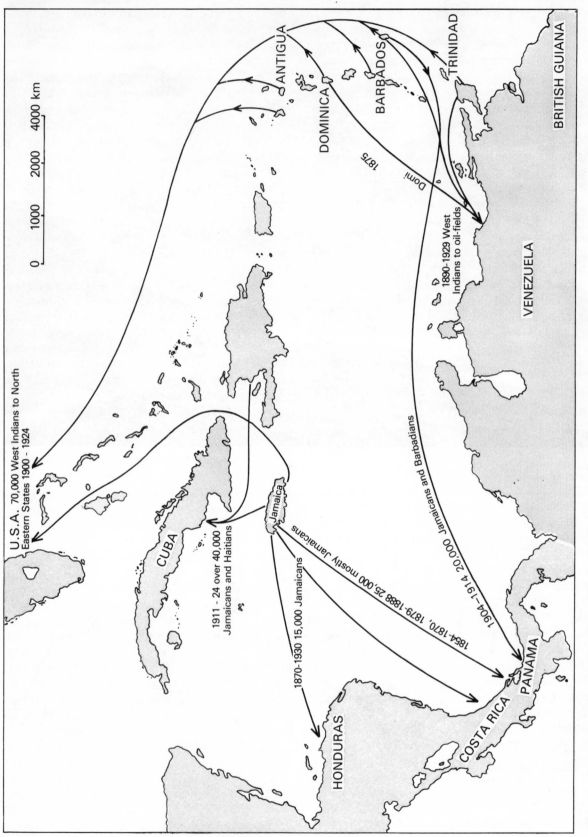

Text labels within the map image:

U.S.A. 70,000 West Indians to North Eastern States 1900 - 1924

ANTIGUA

DOMINICA

BARBADOS

TRINIDAD

BRITISH GUIANA

Domi 1875

1890-1929 West Indians to oil-fields

VENEZUELA

CUBA

Jamaica

1911 - 24 over 40,000 Jamaicans and Haitians

1870-1930 15,000 Jamaicans

1904-1914 20,000 Jamaicans and Barbadians

1854-1870, 1879-1888 25,000 mostly Jamaicans

HONDURAS

COSTA RICA

PANAMA

Map 10   Emigration from the British Caribbean islands, 1854 to 1925

126

suitable grazing land for cattle, the government required the mining companies to preserve it for this purpose. With open-cast mining this is difficult to do, but the companies tried in order to retain the goodwill of the local population. The Industrial Development Corporation, founded in 1952, kept a check on the companies and planned the growth of the industry. This was rapid, due to demand from the United States.

By the late 1950s, Jamaica was producing 5,000,000 tonnes per year and was the largest bauxite producer in the world. Between 1960 and 1964 her exports to the United States rose by over 60 per cent and by 1970 bauxite derivatives made up half her total exports. The 1970 production of nearly 12,000,000 tonnes earned about £100,000,000. Jamaica now produces over 20 per cent of the world's bauxite. Although Jamaica benefits from royalties and duties, investment in the industry has nearly all come from Canada and the United States. A National Bauxite Commission was set up in 1972 to ensure that Jamaica benefits from her most valuable asset.

Emigration, 1854-1925

Background to emigration

Movement of settlers between the British islands had always been common for a variety of reasons. For example:

1   In 1657, Luke Stokes with 1,600 men, women and children and all their slaves, emigrated from Nevis because of scarcity of land and the danger of Carib raids. He went to Jamaica where there was abundant land and freedom from taxation.

2   In 1664, Thomas Modyford and 800 settlers with all their slaves emigrated from Barbados to Jamaica, after considering settling in Carolina and St Lucia.

After emancipation, emigration became even more common. Often ex-slaves had little or nothing to tie them to their island. Many of them wanted to get as far away from their 'roots' as possible, and from the lack of available land, the low wages and the unemployment. The commonest emigrations were from the small islands of the eastern Caribbean, like Barbados, to Trinidad, or British Guiana where there was a chance of acquiring their own land or earning high wages. This only involved the men. Any women and

children were left behind. It was confined to the British islands because there was still slavery in the foreign colonies. Later, emigration became more diverse and more distant.

The period of these emigrations, 1854-1925, coincided with the first generation of freedom, with the difficulties and decline of the sugar industry and the search for smallholdings and alternative crops to grow on them. It was a period of great change and great challenge for the blacks. Some of them met this challenge by emigrating. There are two ways of looking at emigration: one is that the individual is meeting an opportunity with courage and a spirit of adventure; the other, that he is not facing up to the struggle with adversity and is deserting his home.

In most of the British islands there was little work apart from the hated drudgery of the plantations. Wages were low and there was little land available. The blacks met with economic, social and political injustices and racial prejudice. Most people had to stay and suffer these hardships, and invariably the women and children. For some men, at certain times in the nineteenth century, there was the opportunity to emigrate.

Panama

There were three waves of emigration to Panama before 1925.

1   In 1854 an American company began the construction of a railway across the Isthmus of Panama and 2,000 West Indians, mostly Jamaicans, emigrated to work on it. This railway provided employment for many other emigrants throughout the 1860s.

2   In 1879 Ferdinand de Lesseps, builder of the Suez Canal, formed a company to build a canal across the Isthmus of Panama. Work began in 1882 and labour was imported from Europe, China and the West Indies. West Indians stood up to yellow fever better than the others, but so many died that the scheme was abandoned in 1888. About 25,000 West Indians were employed in this period. As with the railway, most of them were Jamaicans.

3   By the Hay-Pauncefort Treaty of 1901, the United States bought out de Lesseps. In 1903, when Panama seceded from Colombia, she allowed the United States a strip of land sixteen kilometres wide across the Isthmus on which to build the canal. Scientists had traced yellow fever to the *aedes*

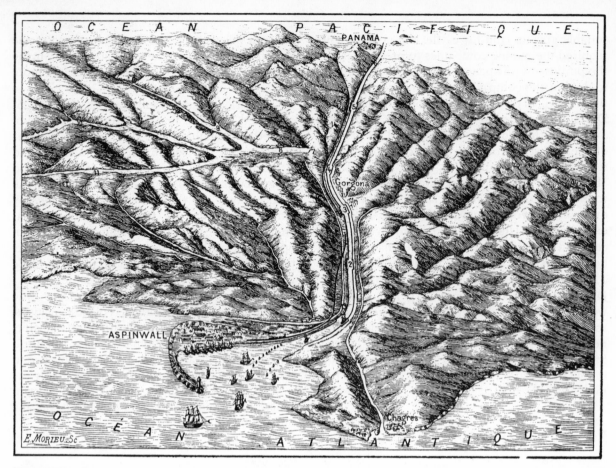

Panama Canal

mosquito and this had been eliminated from the Isthmus when work began in 1904.

Between 1904 and 1914 over 20,000 West Indians, mostly Jamaicans but with a large contingent of Barbadians, went to work on the canal. When it was finished, there was still work in the Canal Zone until 1920. On the canal construction, West Indians were paid about four shillings per day. Much of this was repatriated. It is estimated that Barbadian labourers repatriated £500,000 in this period. Jamaicans coined the phrase 'Panama money' and they even had a popular song, 'Colon man a-come', which referred to the migrants who returned to Jamaica relatively rich.

Today there are said to be 60,000 people of West Indian descent in the Canal Zone, chiefly living in the towns of Colon and Cristobal.

Costa Rica and Honduras

When American companies started producing bananas in Costa Rica and Honduras in the 1880s,

the demand for labour there was high. Again it was mainly Jamaicans who emigrated. Some of them settled along the coastline, especially in the great banana port of Limon, using their savings to buy land or open shops. Others stayed temporarily, repatriating their money. During the Depression of the 1930s, the government stopped immigration except for clerical and skilled workers.

Cuba

After the abolition of slavery in 1886, thousands of West Indians, mostly Haitians and Jamaicans, went to Cuba to work on the sugar plantations. Emigration was particularly popular between 1911 and 1921, when conditions in Jamaica were very bad and the Cuban sugar plantations were expanding. During the First World War, Cuba had such a sugar boom that labourers from Barbados joined the Haitians and Jamaicans emigrating to Cuba. Well over one hundred thousand British West Indians had emigrated to Cuba before the

Construction of Panama Canal

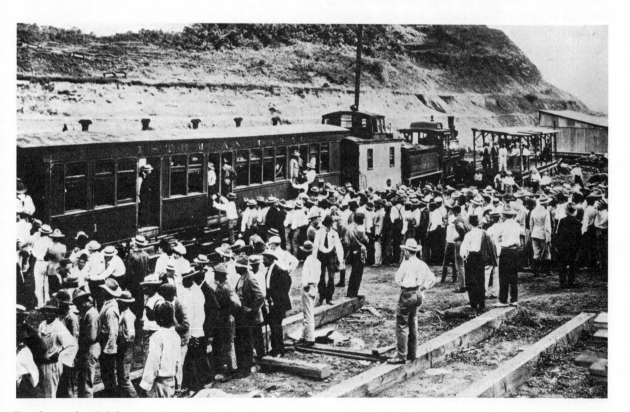

Pay-day in the Culebra Cut Zone

ban. In 1924 immigrants were deported from Cuba and this added greatly to the unemployment and hardship in their home islands.

United States

Emigration started as a trickle before 1900 and rose to nearly 11,000 in 1924. It was unrestricted until 1925 and no passports or even work contracts were needed. At first the West Indians went to Boston, the original banana port, but later they went to the industrial cities of the north-east, Baltimore, Philadelphia and especially to New York.

In 1925 unrestricted immigration ended. This caused considerable hardship in the British West Indies, partly because the repatriation of large sums in United States dollars dried up and partly because yet another area of employment was closed.

Venezuela

In 1875 labourers from Dominica went to work in the Venezuelan gold-fields. The development of the oil industry there in the 1920s attracted labour from all over the West Indies, but this stopped abruptly in 1929 when the Venezuelan government banned black immigration.

Conclusion

It is difficult to know to what extent emigration benefited the British West Indies. On the debit side, was the loss of thousands of young, able-bodied and often talented men, leaving behind a largely unproductive and dependent population, mainly women and children. It is estimated that in the 1920s, 40 to 45 per cent of the population was under fifteen.

On the credit side, the emigrants repatriated money and often contributed far more to the family home than if they had stayed behind. Often it was used to buy a smallholding when the emigrant returned home, another benefit to the family and the island. An emigrant to the United States could expect to earn as much in an hour as he could in a day in the West Indies.

Emigration was a 'safety-valve'. Without it, there would have been more hardships, and more economic and civil strife, with no hope of relief. When opportunities for emigration came to an end in the 1920s, tensions built up which culminated in riots and strikes ten years later. The ending of emigration did not cause this unrest, but it was a contributory factor, as there was no longer a means of releasing tension.

Codrington College, Barbados

12

Social Welfare 1838-1914

As a result of slavery, labourers in the West Indies were accustomed to being dependent on their masters for all their needs. After emancipation, they were forced to rely on themselves, and on what little help was available from the colonial legislatures.

The latter, like most nineteenth century governments, followed a policy of *laissez-faire* with regard to social welfare. What little provision they made for poor relief, help to the old and sick, education and health was carried out with the help of the various churches and voluntary organisations like the Salvation Army.

As the century progressed, the government played an increasing part in the provision of social welfare. There were two main reasons for this. Firstly, the extension of Crown Colony government meant that financial aid as well as technical advice and assistance was available from Britain. Secondly, the introduction of large scale East Indian immigration to the West Indies necessitated the provision of medical and other social services which were later extended to the population in general.

Advances in social welfare, particularly education, had been made by the end of the century but these were limited by *laissez-faire*, by lack of money due to the depression, the high rate of population growth and the lack of interest of the wealthy in the welfare of the poor. Such facilities as there were tended to be limited to the towns, and little was done for the isolated rural areas.

131

Education

Very little education of any kind had been available in the West Indies before 1834. Children of wealthy parents were educated privately and the boys were often sent to Britain or America to complete their education. Children of poorer parents had virtually no formal education.

The planters opposed any kind of education for slaves in the eighteenth century because they felt it would unsettle them and give them 'ideas beyond their station in life'.

Charity schools

Barbados was the pioneer in education. In 1686 a charity school for poor whites, possibly the first in the West Indies, was started in St George's Parish, Barbados, from a gift of land and £1,000 from two planters, John Elliot and Rowland Bulkeley. Jamaica also had early charity schools. In 1694 Raines Waite bequeathed money which led to the foundation of Alley School and Manchester High School. A more famous school was Wolmer's, arising from the bequest of John Wolmer, a Kingston jeweller, in 1728.

There were many other charity foundations in the first half of the eighteenth century, but they were all for poor whites with the exception of Codrington College, Barbados. Christopher Codrington, who died in 1710, left money to found a school for slave children. Building began in 1716, but when it was opened as Codrington Grammar School in 1743, the first pupils were white. There were protests that the will had been broken, but the first intake of coloured and black pupils was not made until the next century.

The first schools maintained by public subscription were also in Barbados. These schools catered for coloured children and sometimes slave children. In 1818 a school was started by public subscription and £100 from the Church Missionary Society in Bridgetown. The Colonial Charity School, enrolling 89 pupils, including 32 slave children, was also opened in 1818 in Barbados. Combermere, a famous Barbadian school, was originally the Boys' Central School in Bridgetown in 1819. Barbados also claimed the first girls' school; the Girls' Central School was founded in 1827.

These schools had very few pupils by modern standards and served only a very small proportion of the population. The level of education was primary, or perhaps little higher, except in the case of Codrington College which had grammar school status. Barbados was not typical of the islands. Dominica was very backward in education. Visitors to the West Indies in the early nineteenth century commented on the poor education of all classes of society, the lack of education amongst the whites being especially surpising to them.

Mission schools

In Britain the first grant of public money for education was made in 1833. In 1835 the British Government decided to make a similar grant to education in the British West Indies. A grant of £25,000 a year was made which was raised to £30,000 a year until 1846. The Negro Education Grant was divided amongst the colonies roughly in proportion to their numbers of freed slaves. For example, Jamaica received £7,000 per year and Barbados £3,000.

It gave a great impetus to education in the British West Indies. The number of schools in Jamaica increased from 36 in 1833 to 307 in 1836. It matched the enthusiasm with which the freed slaves embraced education. The government divided the grant between the missions, because they were most deeply involved in education. Unfortunately this arrangement favoured the 'Protestant' islands, and 'Catholic' islands like Trinidad and St Lucia were neglected. The British government were unwilling to grant money to Catholic missions.

Mandeville School, Jamaica

132

The Negro Education Grant could be used only for the provision of buildings and furniture. The running costs of the schools, such as teachers' salaries and books, had to be met by the missions and subscriptions. Thus many of the new schools soon collapsed because of the very great burden of running them.

The supply of teachers was always a problem. In the early days qualified teachers could not be found on the islands and they had to be brought out from Britain at great expense. A bequest of £1,000 by Lady Mico in 1670 for ransoming Christian slaves captured by Barbary pirates had never been used for that purpose, and in 1827 Thomas Fowell Buxton proposed to the Court of Chancery that it should be used for the education of freed slaves. By then, the bequest had increased to £127,000. Some was used to send out teachers from Britain, but soon two teacher training colleges were set up in the West Indies; one in Antigua, the other in Jamaica. They were known as 'Mico Colleges'. The Jamaica college trained about ten teachers per year, but with the expansion of schools in 1836 the supply of teachers was still totally inadequate. Most schools were staffed by unqualified teachers whose attendance was sometimes irregular. Other schools had to close through lack of teachers. The Mico bequest was also useful in filling the gap in education left by the Negro Education Grant in the Catholic islands of Trinidad and St Lucia. Here it was applied to founding ordinary primary schools.

The attendance of pupils was very irregular. After the initial thirst for education, people became less enthusiastic. An average satisfactory attendance at school in the West Indies was set as low as 100 days per year (nowadays pupils are always expected to attend for over 250 days). Very few pupils, except at the leading schools, achieved even this low attendance.
The reasons were
a) when fees were charged many parents could not meet them;
b) black parents became disillusioned with education when they saw it was not freeing their sons from the soil;
c) child labour in gangs was a popular way of supplementing the family income;
d) children were kept away from school for such tasks as picking coffee;
e) with so many broken homes, parental guidance and compulsion for attendance were lacking.

When the Negro Education Grant lapsed in 1846 the rate of increase in the number of schools fell dramatically. From 307 schools in Jamaica in 1836 the number had risen to only 379 in 1867. Because the Negro Education Grant had neglected Trinidad, the number of schools there was always low in the nineteenth century; in 1846 there were forty schools, and in 1880 there were still only ninety-six.

The dual system

The Church and the State continued to be partners in education after 1846, but local governments made a much smaller contribution than the British government had done, except in the case of Barbados. For example, between 1835 and 1845 Jamaica had received £7,000 per year. In 1846 the Jamaican Assembly voted only £3,000 for that year. The planter-dominated assemblies refused to vote money for the education of blacks because they believed it would make them independent of the estates.

However, some people in the colonies saw the necessity for developing a proper education system instead of leaving it to the missions and the benevolence of individuals such as Bishop Coleridge in Barbados. Government departments, variously called 'Education Committees' or 'Boards of Education', were established to control education. For example, under the influence of Richard Rawle, 'Schoolmaster-General' of Barbados from 1842 to 1864, an Education Committee was established in 1850. In Trinidad a Board of Education was set up in 1851 on the initiative of Lord Harris. In British Guiana the Board of Education dates from 1862.

There was much controversy over the linking of education with religion and proposals that the State should take over responsibility for education. Quite naturally this feeling was strongest in Trinidad, where most of the schools were Catholic and the language of instruction French or Spanish. Lord Harris, who became governor in 1846, abolished denominational education in 1851 and made the Board of Education entirely responsible for the schools. No school fees were to be charged and the schools would be funded from local rates. The Board would also licence teachers. Religious instruction was removed from the curriculum, but one day a week was free for the pupils to attend their churches.

However, most colonies were not so radical. They saw the need for more state control, but compromised with the churches. In Trinidad, by the Keenan Report of 1869, the churches had to apply to the Board of Education for permission to run a school. If the school was to receive government funds certain other conditions had to be met: it would have to be opened for 200 days per year, and take pupils of whatever class, colour or creed. The churches would have control over the buildings, staffing and curriculum. An inspectorate was established to ensure that the school was maintaining approved standards. These arrangements were typical of those followed in the other colonies.

State aid to church schools enabled governments to provide education for a greater number of pupils at less expense to public funds. It also pleased the churches. It was an expedient in the nineteenth century when colonial governments were short of funds. The Education Commissions of 1848 and 1851 in British Guiana had suggested complete state control, but the churches protested so strongly that a compromise was reached and state control was exercised by an Inspector of Schools who was in complete control over education when the Board of Education was not in existence. In Barbados, because the Church of England was by far the strongest religious body in the island, the system was more uniform. The Society for the Propagation of the Gospel, the London Missionary Society, and the Church Missionary Society were all under the wing of the Bishop of Barbados. Inspectors from the Education Committee maintained standards approved by the government.

Education under Crown Colony government

After the establishment of Crown Colony government in all the colonies except Barbados, education remained one of the most pressing problems. Jamaica provided the best example of the way in which the education was expanded. The number of schools more than doubled by the end of the century, from under 400 in 1867 to about 900 in 1896. The number of pupils attending schools in the British islands multiplied about five times during this period. However, education was still very limited in extent and quality at the end of the century. Most colonies were spending only about 5 per cent of their revenue on education; only about half the children of primary age were attending any

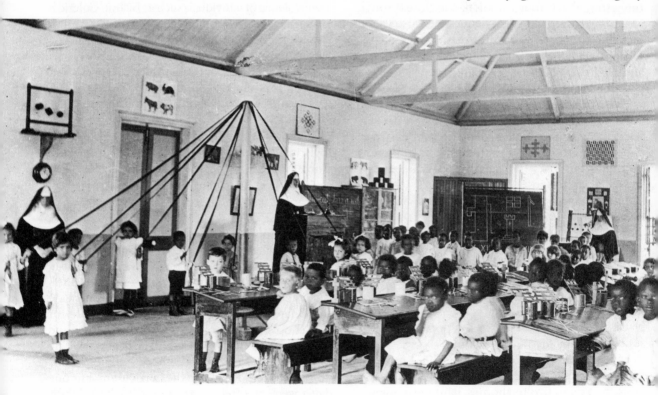

An infant's school in Jamaica

school at all; only about 10 per cent of the population over five years old could read and write; and less than 5 per cent of pupils in any island received any kind of secondary education.

In 1870 elementary education was made compulsory in Britain. West Indian governments tried to introduce compulsory education, but conditions prevented its practical enforcement. For example, the 1876 Education Ordinance in British Guiana made education compulsory up to the age of eleven, but there was no chance of implementing it as even some people in authority thought that it was much better for the young to be working in the fields. In any case there were not enough schools in the British West Indies to make compulsory education work, and there was not the money to build more.

Secondary education

To free the lower classes from their bondage to the soil, much more than primary education was needed. The blacks soon realised this, but the fee-paying, charity schools were well beyond their means and they were excluded by the colour bar. Lord Harris in Trinidad had seen the need for secondary education open to all, and in 1859 Queen's Collegiate School was founded and financed by £3,000 per year out of public funds . Yet in 1859 only one-fifth of the pupils were coloured and none was black. By 1880 there were three secondary schools in Trinidad, but under 20 per cent of the 350 pupils attending them were coloured.

The situation in Barbados was better in that there were more secondary schools. The leading ones were the Lodge School (Codrington Grammar School), Harrison's Free School in Bridgetown and Queen's College for Girls (Girls' Central School). However, there was still discrimination on the grounds of colour. There were only a few coloured pupils at the Lodge School in spite of the fact that Codrington's original endowment had been for black children. John Mitchinson, the Bishop of Barbados, condemned the racial discrimination he found in his Education Commission in 1873. In Jamaica the famous secondary schools like Wolmer's, Munro, Ruseas, Titchfield and Mannings were still for the sons of whites.

Special mention must be made of Barbados. Under Mitchinson's influence, Codrington College became affiliated with the University of Durham, England, and could award degrees. So in Barbados it was possible to have education from primary to university level without leaving the island.

Curriculum

The curriculum in mission schools had been based on religious instruction. After emancipation, reading and writing were introduced, chiefly to aid religious instruction. This type of curriculum was irrelevant to the social needs of the blacks, and it seemed to have been influenced by the planter-governments of the time to inculcate obedience and duty.

In the 1850s, the curriculum in most islands expanded. Under Richard Rawle's influence the Barbados Education Act of 1858 introduced arithmetic and even grammar, geography, history and music. This was more in line with a British curriculum, but still irrelevant for the needs of most pupils in the islands. Technical subjects like agriculture, carpentry and mechanics were much more suited to agricultural communities. When a subject like history appeared on the curriculum, it was British history, enforcing colonial ideas on West Indian pupils and giving them no sense of independence and pride in their own countries. Trinidad was following the syllabi of the Irish National Board in the 1860s. It was a good curriculum for Ireland, and the books were praised by Keenan's Commission of 1869, but it was not suited to Trinidad. The need for scientific and practical training in schools was realised , but little could be done about it. Teachers and instructors could not be found for these subjects. Therefore, well into the twentieth century, the curriculum in most cases remained literary and academic.

Social results of education by 1914

Education had achieved very little in welding together an integrated society by 1914. In theory the schools were open to all classes, colours and creeds, but in practice education, especially at the higher levels, was the preserve of the upper classes. Education still created barriers to social advancement and preserved divisions in West Indian society.

In spite of these criticisms, the basis of an education system for all had been established by 1914. Between 1865 and 1914 a small educated coloured and black middle class of teachers, civil servants, lawyers, church leaders, doctors and newspaper editors, emerged. Among them were leaders of society such as George William Gordon, Sir Conrad Reeves, Edward Jordan and Charles O'Neale.

Public health and medical services

These had been provided by the plantation owners before abolition, but afterwards the majority of people could neither afford nor get medical treatment. There were very few hospitals and those that existed were badly staffed and equipped.

There was great need for public health and medical services because of the large number of endemic diseases in the West Indies, such as cholera, dysentery, malaria, smallpox, typhoid, typhus and yellow fever which led to a high mortality rate. In the 1850s there were several epidemics of cholera, ranging from the Jamaica outbreak in 1851, in which 32,000 people died, to the British Guiana outbreak in 1853. Barbados and the Bahamas were also affected. The unhealthiness of British Guiana was recognised by the setting up of a Board of Health, employing a number of British doctors in 1832, but this was an exception.

Infant mortality was particularly high in the West Indies. In the days of slavery it accounted for about 50 per cent of slave children. In Jamaica in the 1890s, 43 per cent of all deaths were infants. Undernourished children had little resistance to disease, and there was little hope of recovery because of the lack of medical services. The sick received no proper treatment. If they had no family to care for them, they frequently ended up in prison as vagrants. This was the situation George William Gordon encountered in the prisons of St Thomas in 1863. In Port of Spain, the lepers found in the streets ended up in prison.

As disease does not respect social class, the whites were concerned about the situation, especially after the cholera epidemics of the 1850s. Public health legislation in the British West Indies dates from this time. The lead had come from Britain where the state had assumed responsibility for public health in 1848. After the findings of the Sanitary Commissions in the West Indies, Boards of Health were set up. Hospitals were established in the cities and the dispensary system in rural districts. As a result of the reforms of Sir John Peter Grant between 1866 and 1874, a Medical

Early hospital in St Vincent

Department and a government medical service were begun in Jamaica. Free medical treatment and medicines were given. In 1878 a Public Health Ordinance was passed in British Guiana which established a Central Board of Health for the whole colony, and separate health authorities for the towns of Georgetown and New Amsterdam. From 1850, there had been Boards of Health to deal with the health of immigrants because they were the responsibility of the Government.

Throughout the West Indies, hospitals were confined to the large towns. For example, the Government Colonial Hospital was sited in Port of Spain in 1840. This was only partly financed from public funds and served mainly white patients. The General Hospital of Port of Spain was opened in 1858 to serve the whole community. Health services were considerably better in the towns. In spite of the dispensaries, the bulk of the rural population had no medical services before 1914.

Public works

In many cases public works complement public health. Refuse-collecting, mains water, sewerage and drainage are all public works which improve sanitation and promote the health of the people. Unfortunately the towns in the British West Indies were built before the importance of public works was realised. Some cities in the British African colonies, built in the twentieth century, had mains water and an underground sewerage system from the start, for example, Nairobi and Kampala in

Trinidad in 1894

East Africa. Introducing public works after most of the city has already been built causes considerable upheaval, and often is not carried out satisfactorily. This caused increased administrative problems for West Indian governments in the nineteenth century.

Public works were carried out under Crown Colony government mainly in the 1870s. Under Sir John Peter Grant's governorship a scheme for public works was begun in Jamaica. In 1872 the capital was moved from Spanish Town to Kingston; a mains water supply was begun; a gasworks was built; and a new, more hygienic market, the Victoria Market, was opened. All these were put under a Public Works Department. General sanitation in Kingston was improved, but drainage and sewerage remained the chief problem.

Trinidad had always been under Crown Colony government and so it began its public works earlier than the other colonies. In 1847 Dr Verteuil began to improve sanitation in Port of Spain, and refuse collection began. In 1861 an underground sewerage system was built, and a public baths and wash-house were supplied with mains water. All this caused much digging - up of roads which was locally called 'trenching', but it was the price of progress. It was made worse because the main streets had been macadamised in 1860.

In 1883 Sir Henry Irving set up a Public Works Department in British Guiana, well financed and with considerable power because the problem of public works in British Guiana was much greater than in the other territories. Drainage was, perhaps, the chief problem, but the difficulties of bridge-building were such that British Guiana did without roads. Steam pumps were very expensive, up to $20,000, and they had to be continually maintained. The sea-defences, essential if the coastal belt was to remain productive, were also continually causing problems.

Gradually the towns were cleaned up and modernised but, as with medical services, the rural areas were neglected and it was still left to individuals to carry out their own improvements in drainage, irrigation and water supplies.

Communications

In most of the colonies, settlements were cut off from each other and the easiest links were by sea. For example, in Jamaica the estates were linked to the sea by tracks. Travel round the island was accomplished by hopping from one port to another: from Port Antonio, to Port Maria, Falmouth and Montego Bay. 'Roads' were rough tracks, often impassable in the wet seasons. In British Guiana the natural method of communication was by water. Towns were sited on the coast or up the river mouths. East/west travel was accomplished by going downriver to the coast, by sea to another river and upriver to the destination. Communication difficulties caused the failure of many of the free villages in British Guiana. Only those near Georgetown and New Amsterdam had easy access to markets. For a long time there were only two recognised roads in British Guiana, the East Coast Road and the East Bank Road (of the Demerara River), both leading out of Stabroek (Georgetown). The law required each estate to be fronted by a road in case of slave revolts, and linked to the nearest river. In 1900 the roads were still confined to the coast, but in 1913 the Bartica/Potaro Road became the first inland highway.

Public roads were built in Jamaica after 1866 and came under the Public Works Department. Ease of transport and travel still depended very much on the weather. All-weather, tarmac roads came much later in the century and were at first confined to the towns. Trinidad had tarmac roads in Port of Spain in 1860, but Trinidad had the advantage of the Pitch Lake.

All-weather roads enabled better transport to be introduced. In the 1860s hansom cabs were being used in Kingston and Port of Spain. By 1870 streetcars, running on steel rails and drawn by mules, were seen in Kingston. A tramway began in

'Four Roads' tram in St Vincent

Port of Spain in 1883. Electrification of this tramway came in 1895. Finally the first motor car was seen in Trinidad in 1900.

The British West Indies were behind Cuba in railways. The Havana to Guïnes Line in 1838 was the first railway in the West Indies. Indeed, outside North America, Cuba was the leading railway builder in the Americas. The British West Indian sugar estates would have benefited from railways just as the Cuban ones did, but they were developed later and were private enterprises to begin with. For example, the East Coast Railway in British Guiana was under the Demerara Railway Company. It was begun in 1848 and reached its terminus at Mahaica in 1864. When the Government wanted extensions, it subsidised the Company. In Jamaica railways were begun in the 1870s, the first linking the new developments in St Catherine's Valley to Kingston. Before the end of the century railways had also been constructed in Trinidad and Barbados.

Other means of travel and transport were by sea. In the days of sail, west to east voyages in the Caribbean had been very difficult. Steamships altered this. They were arriving regularly in the West Indies in the 1840s from Britain. They brought the islands closer together and helped to establish new routes.

The first aeroplanes appeared in the British West Indies just before the beginning of the First World War. When one flew into British Guiana in 1913 the people did not realise how important air services would be to modern Guyana.

Personal communication by post was slow, governed by the state of the roads and the sea routes. There had been private postal services in the British West Indies from the end of the eighteenth century and postage stamps dated in the 1790s still exist. The postal services became public in the middle of the nineteenth century. In Trinidad they formed one of the functions of the police.

When the transatlantic cable reached Kingston in 1870 telegraph communication with Britain was opened. The era of the telephone was dawning. In the early 1880s the first telephones appeared in Kingston and Port of Spain.

The improvement in communication did much to change life in the West Indies. Not only was communication between individual islands easier but for the first time they were constantly in touch with world affairs by transport and wireless.

Revision questions

Chapter 1

*1 What did 'no peace beyond the line' mean? When and how did it apply to Spain and her enemies in the seventeenth century?
2 Who were the buccaneers?
3 Show how and why England dominated the Caribbean up to 1763. Why did this domination come to an end?
4 What were the effects of the War of American Independence on the British West Indies?
5 Refer to the picture on page 3 and answer the following questions:
   a) How did this man typify the attitude and behaviour of buccaneers?
   b) How is the word 'buccaneer' derived?
   c) Name FIVE famous buccaneers.
   d) How were they employed to fight for European governments?
   e) When and how were they suppressed in Jamaica?

Chapter 2

*1 What part did the mulattoes play in bringing about revolution in St Domingue?
2 Give an account of the career of Toussaint L'Ouverture.
3 Refer to the picture on page 17 and answer the following questions:
   a) What great event in history began with this meeting?

b) How did the government of France change in the next five years?
c) What ideas spread from France to her empire in this period?
d) What different classes of people can you identify in this picture?
e) Who was the King of France at this time?

Chapter 3

1 How did the French colony of St Domingue become the independent country of Haiti?
*2 What difficulties did Haiti experience on independence?
3 Copy the outline of Haiti from page 19 and mark in:
   a) the city which became Cap Haitien after independence;
   b) the area of the slave rising of 1791;
   c) the place where the British troops landed in 1793;
   d) the area flooded in 1800;
   e) the part ruled by Pétion.

Chapter 4

*1 Consider the attitude of the planters in the British islands to
   a) slave marriage
   b) slave education
   c) Christianity for slaves
   d) manumission. Compare and contrast these attitudes with those of the French planters.

*2 Give an account of the Spanish slave laws and show how they were more humane than the English.

3 Refer to the picture on page 35 and answer the following questions:
a) Why are the slaves in the picture happy?
b) What are the slaves buying and selling?
c) Suggest what a slave might do with the money he obtains.
d) Why did planters allow this activity to take place?
e) Why did the missionaries criticise this activity?

Chapter 5

1 Who were the Maroons? How did the Jamaican Maroons harass the government in the eighteenth century?

2 Give an account of any ONE slave revolt (*not* the St Domingue Revolt) in the West Indies.

3 Refer to the picture on page 49 and answer the following questions:
a) In which parish was this town situated?
b) What is the name of the pot-holed limestone area nearby?
c) How much land was allotted around this town by the agreement of 1739?
d) Name three other such towns in Jamaica.
e) How did the government know what was going on in this town in the eighteenth century?

Chapter 6

*1 What was the part played in the British anti-slavery movement by
a) the Quakers;
b) the Clapham Sect;
c) the Nonconformists?
How did the West Indian interest oppose them?

2 What part was played in the British anti-slavery movement by each of the following:
Granville Sharp; Thomas Clarkson; Thomas Fowell Buxton?

3 Why did the transatlantic slave trade go on after 1807?

4 Refer to the picture on page 65 and answer the following questions:
a) Where was this settlement?
b) What was the purpose of this settlement?
c) Who encouraged its foundation? When was it founded?

d) What was the name of the fleet of ships based there?
e) What did these ships do?

Chapter 7

*1 How did the British government try to bring about amelioration in the British islands between 1807 and 1833?

2 What difficulties were nonconformist missionaries faced with in the British islands before 1833?

3 Why was the apprenticeship system introduced? How did it work? Why was it abandoned in 1838?

4 Refer to the photograph on page 69 and answer the following questions:
a) What was this man's occupation in Britain?
b) Who did he take over this work from?
c) How did he influence the abolition movement in Britain?
d) What resolution did he introduce in 1823?
e) What was the result of his work?

Chapter 8

1 Contrast the position of the ex-slaves in Barbados with those in Jamaica in the decade immediately after emancipation. (In your answer you may like to consider attitudes, opportunities, exisiting conditions and wage levels).

2 Why is the distinction between large and small territories so important in dealing with the labour problem after emancipation?

3 Give an account of the 'Free Village Movement' in Jamaica after emancipation.

4 Do a detailed project on 'Free Villages' in Jamaica, Guiana or any other island of your choice.

Chapter 9

1 Why did the British West Indian colonies turn to immigrant labour schemes after emancipation?

2 Give an account of the immigrant labour schemes between 1834 and 1876, and comment on their success.

3 Describe East Indian immigration into the British West Indies between 1838 and 1917. What were the effects of East Indian immigration on

a) the sugar industry;

b) the social life of the British West Indian Colonies?

4 Describe the immigrant labour schemes in the non-British territories of the Caribbean area in the nineteenth century.

5 Study the map of the Far East on page 91 and answer the following questions:

a) Why was Indian labour cheaper than Chinese?

b) Why were labourers recruited from Agra /Oudh and Behar rather than from other areas?

c) Compare the recruitment from Maçao and Canton with that from Kwangtung and Fukien.

d) How was the recruiting of Indians conducted?

e) Name the principal places for Indonesian recruitment. Where did they go to in the Caribbean area?

Chapter 10

1 Why were there so many abandoned estates in Jamaica between 1800 and 1850?

2 Why did some British islands pass Encumbered Estates Acts? What effects did these acts have in the British West Indies and why were they repealed in 1886?

3 What were the reasons for and the effects of the Sugar Equalisation Act, 1846?

4 Account for the backwardness of sugar production in the British West Indies, and the superiority of Cuban production in the second half of the nineteenth century.

5 How did the British West Indies attempt to put new life into their sugar industries in the late nineteenth and early twentieth centuries?

6 Refer to the picture of a sugar beet plant on page 80 and answer the following questions:

a) How was the extraction of sugar from this plant developed?

b) Why did certain European countries develop their own beet sugar industries?

c) How was this expensively-produced sugar able to compete with the cheaper sugar from the West Indies in the nineteenth century?

d) What happened with regard to European beet sugar in 1903?

e) What effects did European beet sugar have on the world market between 1903 and 1929?

Chapter 11

1 Why was the Norman Commission sent to the West Indies? What did it report? What were effects of its report?

2 Give an account of the alternative crops to sugar which were tried in the Eastern Caribbean Islands between 1897 and 1925, with reasons for their successes and failures.

3 Describe the development of the Jamaican banana industry between 1866 and 1939.

4 Show how minerals were developed as alternative sources of wealth to sugar in British Guiana and Trinidad between 1900 and 1925.

5 Why was there so much emigration from the British Islands between 1900 and 1925?

6 Refer to the picture of the construction of the Panama Canal on page 127 and answer the following questions:

a) What were the chief obstacles to be overcome in the construction?

b) When do you think this picture was taken? Give reasons for your date.

c) What earlier construction had taken place in this area?

d) What political steps had been taken so that the United States could construct this canal?

e) What special links do the people of the British West Indies have with this area and when and how were they developed?

Chapter 12

1 Why was 1870 the turning point in the history of social welfare in the British West Indies?

2 Give an account of the development of education in Barbados up to 1900.

3 What were the obstacles facing education in the British West Indies in the nineteenth century, and how far were they overcome?

4 What were the main developments in

a) Public Health,

b) Public Works,

in the British West Indies before 1914?

5 Refer to the picture on page 138 and answer the following questions:

a) When do you think this photograph was taken? Give reasons for your answer.

b) Can you describe how a tram works?

c) What other form of transport is shown here?

d) What other forms of transport were available in St Vincent when this photograph was taken?

Further reading

General Texts

Augier, Gordon, Hall and Reckord, *The Making of the West Indies,* Longman, 1960

Edward Brathwaite, *The People Who Came,* Books 1-3, Longman

Sir Alan Burns, *History of the British West Indies*, George Allen and Unwin, 1954

E.H. Carter, G.W. Digby. R.N. Murray, *History of the West Indian Peoples*, Nelson

Isaac Dookhan, *A Pre-emancipation History of the West Indies*, Collins, 1971

Isaac Dookhan, *A Post-emancipation History of the West Indies*, Collins, 1975

Sheila Duncker, *A Visual History of the West Indies*, Evans, 1965

A. Garcia, *History of the West Indies*, Harrap, 1965

R.N. Murray, *Nelson's West Indian History*, Nelson, 1971

J.H. Parry and P.M. Sherlock, *A Short History of the West Indies*, Macmillan 3rd edition, 1971

P.M. Sherlock, *West Indian Nations*, Macmillan, 1973

Eric Williams, *From Columbus to Castro*, Andre Deutsch, 1970

Island Histories

Paul Albury, *The Story of the Bahamas*, Macmillan, 1975

Michael Anthony, *Profile Trinidad,* Macmillan, 1975

C. V. Black, *History of Jamaica,* Collins, 1965

C. V. Black, *A New History of Jamaica,* Collins-Sangster, 1973

Vere T. Daly, *The Making of Guyana,* Macmillan, 1974

Vere T. Daly, *A Short History of the Guyanese People,* Macmillan, 1975

Narda Dobson, *A History of Belize*, Longman, 1973

F.A. Hoyos, *Barbados–A History from the Amerindians to Independence*, Macmillan, 1978

C. Ottley, *The Story of Port of Spain*, Longman, 1970

Eric Williams, *History of the People of Trinidad and Tobago*, Andre Deutsch, 1974

W.S. Zuill, *The Story of Bermuda and her People*, Macmillan, 1973

Special Texts

Buccaneers
C.H. Haring, *The Buccaneers in the West Indies in the Seventeenth Century*

Wars
Sir Alan Burns, *History of the British West Indies*, Chapters 14-17
Parry and Sherlock, *A Short History of the West Indies*, Chapters 8-9

Haitian Revolution
C.L.R. James, *Black Jacobins*
Eric Williams, *From Columbus to Castro*, Chapter 15

Slavery
Eric Williams, *Capitalism and Slavery,* Chapel Hill, North Carolina

E. Goveia, *Slave Society in the British Leeward Islands,*
New Haven, 1965

Slave Resistance
Vere T. Daly, *A Short History of the Guyanese People,*
Chapter 15
C. V. Black, *A New History of Jamaica,* Chapters 8, 11
and 13

Abolition
Sir Alan Burns, *History of the British West Indies,*
Chapters 19-20
Augier, Gordon, Hall and Record, *The Making of the
West Indies,* Chapters 12-14

Immigrant Labour
Eric Williams, *History of the People of Trinidad and
Tobago,* Chapters 8 and 9
Vere T. Daly, *A Short History of the Guyanese People,*
Chapters 18 and 21
Tara Chard, *A Short History of the Indian People,*
Macmillan

Sugar in the nineteenth century
Augier, Gordon, Hall and Record, *The Making of
the West Indies,* Chapters 18, 22
Eric Williams, *From Columbus to Castro,* Chapters
20-21
Parry and Sherlock, *A Short History of the West Indies,*
Chapter 13
W.R. Aykroyd, *Sweet Malefactor,* Heinemann, 1967

Alternatives to Sugar
Augier, Gordon, Hall and Record, *The Making of
the West Indies,* Chapter 22
C.V. Black, *A New History of Jamaica,* Chapter 18

Social Welfare
D. Lowenthal, *West Indian Societies,* Oxford, 1972

Education
S.C. Gordon, *A Century of West Indian Education,*
Longman, 1963

Religion
A. Caldecott, *The Church in the West Indies,* Frank
Cass, 1970

Index

Abercromby, General Sir Ralph, 28
Abolition Act (1807), 60, 65-6
Achard, Franz Karl, 109
Adams, President John, 22, 27
Aeroplanes, 139
Ainslie, George Robert, 47
Aix-la-Chappelle, Peace of (1748). 11
Akara, slave leader, 52
Aluminium Company of Canada (ALCAN), 124
American Civil War, 79, 115
Amiens, Treaty of (1808), 29
Amis des Noirs, Société des, 17,20
Antigua, 7, 9, 12, 14, 70, 71, 73, 74, 80-2, 84-5, 89, 118; slaves, 33, 35, 36, 45; labour problems, 83, 84; immigrants, 92; sugar, 106-12; cotton 115
Anti-slavery movement, 61-6; 'Monthly Reporter', 68; and emancipation, 68, 72-4
Apodoca, Admiral, 29
Apprenticeship system, 73-7
Arawaks, the, 46, 155
Arrowroot, 81, 116, 120
Ashanti slaves, 42, 45
Asiento, the, 10, 11
Asphalt, 121-2
Atta, slave leader, 52

Bahamas, 9, 34, 115
Baker, Captain Lorenzo Dow, 120, 121
Baker, Moses, 70

Balcarres, Lord, 50
Baltimore, emigrants to, 130
Bananas, 81, 111, 120-1; diseases, 121
Baptist missionaries, 37, 53, 70-2; the 'Baptist War', 53-4, 72, 73; and free villages, 86-7
Barbados, 7, 9, 12-14, 52, 66, 68, 71, 72, 80, 82, 85, 88-90, 100, 103, 104, 118, 127, 139; buccaneers, 3; slaves, 31-4, 36-8, 45, 52-3, 67, 69, 74; labour problems, 83, 84; sugar 106, 109-12; cotton 115, 118; and education 132-5
Barber, A.L. 121
Barkly, Sir Henry, 105
Basle, Treaty of (1795), 22
Bathurst, Lord, 61, 69
Battle of the Saints, 14
Bauxite, 121, 123-4, 127
Baymen, British, the, 11, 29, 46
Beaumont, Joseph, 96, 97
Beet sugar, 27, 109-10
Belize, 29, 32-3, 46
Benbow, Admiral John, 10
Berbice, 14, 28, 29, 45, 47, slave revolt (1763), 46, 50-2
Berlin Decres (1806), 30
Bermuda, 13, 73; slaves, 34, 37, 56, 74
Berry, Admiral Sir John, 7
Biassou, black leader, 21
Blake, Admiral Robert, 7
Bleby, Methodist missionary, 54
Bligh, Captain William, 81
Boards of Health, 136

Bolivar, Simon, 27
Bore, Etienne de, 27
Bossuet, Jacques, 56
Boston, emigrants to, 130
Boston Fruit Company, 120,121
Botanic Gardens, 112, 116
Boukman, slave leader, 19, 20, 41
Boyer, Jean-Pierre, 24-6
Brazil: slaves, 32; Maroons, 47; sugar 105, 108-10
Breda, Treaty of (1667), 7
Bright, John, 104
Britain: and the Revolutionary Wars, 21, 25 28-9; and Haiti 26, 27; war with U.S.A. (1812-14), 30; the West India interest, 60-1, 64-5, 69, 90; West India Committee, 73
British Guiana, 74, 81, 90, 95, 104, 118, 127, 136-9: labour problems, 83, 84, 89; sugar, 85, 104-6, 110-13; free villages, 86, 87; immigrants, 90, 92-7, 99, 106; rice, 118; rubber, 119; bauxite, 123-4; and education, 133-5; cholera, 136; roads, 138; railways, 139
Brougham, Henry, 62, 65
Brussels Convention (1903), 110
Buccaneers, 2-7; French, 3, 6-7; Bases, 4; English buccaneers of Port Royal, 4-7; suppression, 6
Bulkeley, Rowland, 132

147

Les Saintes, 12, 28
Lesseps. Ferdinand de, 127
Letters about Mexico
    (Schoelcher), 77
Letters of marque, 4, 6
Le Vasseur, Governor of
    Tortuga, 4, 6
Limes, 116, 118, 121
Lisle, George, 70
Locke, John, 56
Lodge School, Barbados, 135
London Missionary Society,
    53, 134
London, Treaty of (1604), 2
Long, Edward, 57
Louis XIV, 2, 6, 7, 10, 56
Louis XVI, 19, 21
Louis XVIII, 26
Louisiana, 23, 25; sugar, 27,
    103, 107-9
Lubolo, Juan (Juan de Bolas), 47
Lynch, Sir Thomas, 6

Macas, immigrants from,
    93, 95, 97, 99
Macaulay, Zachary, 62, 65
Mackenzie, George, 123
Madeiran immigrants, 90, 92
Madrid, Treaty of (1670), 2, 5
Magistrates, special or
    stipendiary, 75-6
Maltese immigrants,92
Manchester School, the, 104-5
Mansfield, Earl of, 63
Mansfield (Mansvelt), Edward
    4-5
Manumission, 32, 36, 40
Marggraf, Andreas, 109
Marie Galante, 9, 12
Marronage and the Maroons,
    21, 27, 44, 46-50, 86, 92;
    First Maroon War, 48-9; Second
    Maroon War, 21, 29, 50
Martinique, 6, 9, 12, 14, 17, 21,
    28, 29, 45, 120; slaves, 43, 77;
    immigrants, 94, 98; sugar, 110
Maurepas, Haitian leader, 24
Mauritius, 73, 102
Métayage, 85
Methodist missionaries, 37,
    53, 54, 70, 71
Mico, Lady and the 'Mico
    Colleges', 133
Mills, Alice, 36
Minerals, 121-7
Missionaries, 37, 53, 70-2, 86,
    87, 100; persecution, 37, 71-2;

mission schools, 132-3
Mitchinson, Bishop John, 135
Modyford, Sir Thomas, 4, 5, 7,127
Molasses Act, 12, 13
Mole St. Nicolas, Saint
    Domingue, 20, 22, 25
Molesworth, Colonel, Governor
    of Jamaica, 6
Monk, George, 7
Montego Bay, Jamaica, 50, 53, 54
Montserrat, 7, 9, 10, 14, 116;
    coffee, 115;cotton, 118
Moravian (United Brethren)
    missionaries, 37, 54, 70
Morgan, Sir Henry, 5, 6
Moskito Indians, 48
Moslem immigrants, 100, 101
Motor cars, 139
Mulattoes, 17-21, 25, 32, 39, 79
Munster, Treaty of (1648), 2
Murray, General, Governor
    of Demerara, 36, 69

Napoleon I, 26, 29, 30, and
    Toussaint, 23-4; plans for
    North American empire, 23-4
    re-institutes slavery, 24, 77
    and beet sugar, 110
Napoleonic Wars, 10, 15, 29-30,
    71, 102, 103, 106, 107, 110, 115,
    118; effects of, 30
Navigation Acts, 7, 115; repealed
    (1849), 105
Negro Education Grant,
    132, 133
Nelson, Admiral Lord, 29
Netherlands, the, and the
    Dutch colonies, 1, 2;
    Dutch Wars, 4, 7; and
    American War of Independence,
    13, 14; and Revolutionary Wars,
    28; and Napoleonic Wars, 29;
    slaves, 31, 47; abolition of slave
    trade, 66; immigrants, 97, 98;
    beet sugar, 110
'Neutral Islands', the, 11-13
Nevis, 3, 4, 7, 9, 10, 14, 45, 127;
    immigrants, 92; cotton,
    115, 118
New Orleans, 103
New York, 7, 112; emigrants
    to, 130
Nijmegen, Peace of (1678), 6, 9
Norman Commission (1896),
    110-12, 116, 120
North, Lord, 60
Nutmegs, 116, 120

Ogé, James, 19, 25
Oil, 121, 122
O'Neale, Charles, 136
Ottawa: Empire Trade
    Agreement (1912), 114
    Conference (1924-5), 114

Packer, Joseph, 44
Palmares Republic, 47
Palmerston, Lord, 79
Panama, captured by
    Morgan, 5-6; Canal and
    Canal Zone, 127-8; Isthmus,
    46, 127-8
Paris, Treaty of, (1814), 29
Peel, Sir Robert, 105
Pétion, mulatto general,
    24-6
Petits blancs, 18, 20
Petroleum products, 121-2
Philadelphia, emigrants to, 130
Phillippo, James, 86, 87
Pimento, 116
Pineapples, 81, 116
Pitt, William (Earl of Chatham),
    11-12, 21
Pitt William, the Younger,
    21, 27, 65; and the slave
    trade, 64, 65
Plantation Duties Act (1673),
    103
Planters' Bank, Jamaica,
    75, 103, 105
Pondicherry, immigrants from,
    97, 98
Port-au-Prince, 20, 21, 24, 26
Port-of-Spain, Trinidad, 81,
    86, 87, 136-9; hospitals, 136
Port Royal, Jamaica:
    buccaneers, 3, 7; naval base, 9
Porto Bello, 4, 11
Portuguese, the 31, 32, 47, 93,
    95, 97, 99
Postal services, 139
Prince Regent (George IV), 53
Providence Island, 3-5, 45
Prussian sugar beet
    industry, 27, 109-10
Public health and public
    works, 136-7
Puerto Rico, 20, 28, 29, 39,
    46, 66; slaves, 43, 78;
    sugar, 113

Quakers, the: missionaries,
    37; and slavery, 56, 61, 62
Quamina, slave leader, 45